British Social Attitudes

Attitudes

The 27th
REPORT

Exploring Labour's Legacy

The **National Centre for Social Research** (NatCen) is an independent, non-profit social research organisation. It has a large professional staff together with its own interviewing and coding resources. Some of NatCen's work – such as the survey reported in this book – is initiated by NatCen itself and grant-funded by research councils or charitable foundations. Other work is initiated by government departments or quasi-government organisations to provide information on aspects of social or economic policy. NatCen also works frequently with other institutes and academics. Founded in 1969 and now Britain's largest social research organisation, NatCen has a high reputation for the standard of its work in both qualitative and quantitative research.

The contributors

John Appleby
Chief Economist at the King's Fund

John Bartle
Senior lecturer in the Department of Government at the University of Essex

Alex Bryson
Senior Research Fellow at the National Institute of Economic and Social Research (NIESR)

Caroline Bryson
Partner of Bryson Purdon Social Research (BPSR)

Elizabeth Clery
Research Director at NatCen and Co-Director of the *British Social Attitudes* survey series

John Curtice
Research Consultant at the *Scottish Centre for Social Research*, part of NatCen, and Professor of Politics at Strathclyde University

Nan Dirk de Graaf
Official Fellow at Nuffield College, Oxford University

Rory Fitzgerald
Deputy Director of the Centre for Comparative Social Surveys, City University London

John Forth
Research Fellow at the National Institute of Economic and Social Research (NIESR)

Eric Harrison
Senior Research Fellow at the Centre for Comparative Social Surveys, City University London

Anthony Heath
Professorial Fellow and University Professor of Sociology at Nuffield College, Oxford University

Yaojun Li
Professor of Sociology at the University of Manchester

Natalie Low
Research Director at NatCen

Rachel Ormston
Research Director at the *Scottish Centre for Social Research* and Co-Director of the *Scottish Social Attitudes* survey

Michael Orton
Senior Research Fellow at the Institute for Employment Research, University of Warwick

Alison Park
Research Group Director at NatCen and Co-Director of the *British Social Attitudes* survey series

Ruth Robertson
Research Officer at the King's Fund

Karen Rowlingson
Professor of Social Policy and Director of Research at the Institute of Applied Social Studies, University of Birmingham

Frank Steinmaier
Visiting Research Fellow at City University London during the summer of 2010

James A. Stimson
Raymond Dawson Professor of Political Science at the University of North Carolina at Chapel Hill

Eleanor Taylor
Researcher at NatCen and Co-Director of the *British Social Attitudes* survey series

Los Angeles | London | New Delhi
Singapore | Washington DC

British
Social
Attitudes

work
Schools NHS exams
Devolution NHS
CONSTITUTION
TRUST WAGES
INSECURITY Expenses WELFARE
EDUCATION NHS
Schools Constitution
Banking WORK Devolution
social mobility EXPENSES exams
Schools IDENTITY
DEVOLUTION HEALTH Ageism
EXAMS WAGES Social mobility
CONSTITUTION
BANKING NHS Schools
WORK TRUST
Expenses
SOCIAL MOBILITY TRUST Redistribution class
INSECURITY Expenses Devolution
Constitution EXAMS
INEQUALITY Schools
Welfare CLASS
devolution identity NHS
TRUST Expenses
WELFARE AGEISM
Health education TRUST
CONSTITUTION BANKING HEALTH EXAMS
Schools NHS Trust Social mobility Welfare
devolution Constitution
education HEALTH IDENTITY Banking Trust
TRUST REDISTRIBUTION Inequality Education
Expenses WELFARE ageism SOCIAL MOBILITY Schools Class
NHS Exams Expenses nhs DEVOLUTION
Devolution
Schools BANKING Class Expenses EXAMS
IDENTITY WAGES Welfare Constitution
NHS Banking AGEISM SCHOOLS NHS
Devolution work
Constitution WAGES
exams

British Social Attitudes

The 27th
REPORT

Attitudes

Exploring Labour's Legacy

Editors
Alison Park, John Curtice, Elizabeth Clery
and Catherine Bryson

SAGE Publications Ltd
1 Oliver's Yard
55 City Road
London EC1Y 1SP

SAGE Publications Inc.
2455 Teller Road
Thousand Oaks, California 91320

SAGE Publications India Pvt Ltd
B 1/I 1 Mohan Cooperative Industrial Area
Mathura Road
New Delhi 110 044

SAGE Publications Asia-Pacific Pte Ltd
33 Pekin Street #02-01
Far East Square
Singapore 048763

Library of Congress Control Number:

British Library Cataloguing in Publication data

A catalogue record for this book is available from the British Library

ISBN 978-0-85702-572-2

Printed by MPG Books Group, Bodmin, Cornwall
Printed on paper from sustainable resources

Contents

6   A tale of two crises: banks, MPs' expenses and public opinion

John Curtice and Alison Park   **131**

7   Resentment or contentment? Attitudes towards the Union 10 years on

Rachel Ormston and John Curtice   **155**

8   Age identity and conflict: myths and realities

Rory Fitzgerald, Eric Harrison and Frank Steinmaier   **179**

9   Post-war British public opinion: is there a political centre?

Appendix I: Technical details of the survey   225

List of tables and figures

Chapter 3

Chapter 4

Chapter 7

Chapter 8

Table conventions

1. Figures in the tables are from the 2008 *British Social Attitudes* survey unless otherwise indicated.
2. Tables are percentaged as indicated by the percentage signs.
3. In tables, '*' indicates less than 0.5 per cent but greater than zero, and '–' indicates zero.
4. When findings based on the responses of fewer than 100 respondents are reported in the text, reference is made to the small base size.
5. Percentages equal to or greater than 0.5 have been rounded up (e.g. 0.5 per cent = one per cent; 36.5 per cent = 37 per cent).
6. In many tables the proportions of respondents answering "Don't know" or not giving an answer are not shown. This, together with the effects of rounding and weighting, means that percentages will not always add to 100 per cent.
7. The self-completion questionnaire was not completed by all respondents to the main questionnaire (see Appendix I). Percentage responses to the self-completion questionnaire are based on all those who completed it.
8. The bases shown in the tables (the number of respondents who answered the question) are printed in small italics. The bases are unweighted, unless otherwise stated.

Introduction

The first *British Social Attitudes* survey took place in 1983 and, since then, nearly 80,000 people have taken part in what has become an annual study. Their generosity has helped make *British Social Attitudes* the authoritative guide to public opinion in modern Britain, and to the ways in which our attitudes and values are shifting over time. Our aim is that these robust and impartial survey findings give a voice to the general public, and paint a picture of what Britain *really* thinks and feels, in all its richness and diversity.

This report continues this theme but focuses in particular on exploring whether and how Britain's attitudes and values have reacted to the Labour party's period in office. We begin with two chapters about inequality. In Chapter 1, we consider attitudes towards income inequality and redistributive policies, while Chapter 2 examines trends in people's perceptions of social mobility and their views about actual and ideal pay levels.

Chapters 3, 4 and 5 focus on change and reform in three key policy areas. Chapter 3 considers education, focusing particularly on how attitudes towards state education have changed over the last ten years. Chapter 4 looks at health, examining trends in satisfaction with the NHS and how these have been affected by Labour's key policies in this area. And in Chapter 5, we examine how shifts in the labour market over the last 25 years have affected views on working in Britain.

Chapter 6 examines the impact of the two events which dominated Labour's final term in office; the global recession and the political scandal surrounding MP's expenses. Chapter 7 looks at another key political development, this time from the early days of the Labour administration; Scottish devolution. It explores attitudes north and south of the border towards the devolution of power in Scotland and examines how these have changed over the decade since devolution began.

Chapter 8 uses data from the *European Social Survey* to consider the nature of age identity in Britain and the extent to which it might form the basis of future conflict or collective action. Finally, Chapter 9 considers Britain's political centre, and assesses whether and how the political centre has shifted over the last thirty years.

Most of the tables in the report are based on *British Social Attitudes* data from 2009 and earlier years. Conventions for reading the tables can be found at the start of the report. Full details of all the questions included in the 2009 survey can be found at www.natcen.ac.uk/bsaquestionnaires.

A number of chapters make use of data from other surveys than *British Social Attitudes*. Three are worthy of particular mention; *Scottish Social Attitudes* (results from which are discussed in Chapter 7), the *International Social Survey Programme* (Chapter 2) and the *European Social Survey* (Chapter 8).

Our thanks

British Social Attitudes could not take place without its many generous funders. The Gatsby Charitable Foundation (one of the Sainsbury Family Charitable Trusts) has provided core funding on a continuous basis since the survey's inception and in doing so has ensured the survey's security and independence. A number of government departments have regularly funded modules of interest to them, while respecting the independence of the study. In 2009 we gratefully acknowledge the support of the Departments of Health, Work and Pensions and Education (previously Department for Children, Schools and Families). We also thank the Department for Business, Innovation and Skills, and the Economic and Social Research Council (ESRC).

The Economic and Social Research Council (ESRC) continued to support the participation of Britain in the *International Social Survey Programme* (ISSP), a collaboration whereby surveys in over 40 countries administer an identical module of questions in order to facilitate comparative research. Some of the results are described in Chapter 2.

We are also grateful to Professor Richard Topf of London Metropolitan University for all his work in creating and maintaining access to an easy to use website that provides a fully searchable database of all the questions that have ever been carried on a *British Social Attitudes* survey, together with details of the pattern of responses to every question. This site provides an invaluable resource for those who want to know more than can be found in this report. It is located at www.britsocat.com.

The *British Social Attitudes* survey is a team effort. The research group that designs, directs and reports on the study is supported by complementary teams who implement the survey's sampling strategy and carry out data processing. The researchers in turn depend on fieldwork controllers, area managers and field interviewers who are responsible for all the interviewing, and without whose efforts the survey would not happen at all. The survey is heavily dependent too on staff who organise and monitor fieldwork and compile and distribute the survey's extensive documentation, for which we would pay particular thanks to Pauline Burge and her colleagues in NatCen's administrative office in Brentwood. We are also grateful to Sandra Beeson in our computing department who expertly translates our questions into a computer assisted questionnaire, and to Roger Stafford who has the unenviable task of editing, checking and documenting the data. Meanwhile the raw data have to be transformed into a workable SPSS system file – a task that has for many years been performed with great care and efficiency by Ann Mair at the Social Statistics Laboratory at the University of Strathclyde.

Many thanks are due to David Mainwaring and Imogen Roome at our publishers, Sage.

Finally, we must praise the people who anonymously gave up their time to take part in our 2009 survey. They are the cornerstone of this enterprise. We hope that some of them might come across this volume and read about themselves and the story they tell of modern Britain with interest.

The Editors

1 Do we still care about inequality?

Karen Rowlingson, Michael Orton and Eleanor Taylor[*]

Income inequality in the UK rose dramatically after 1979 and now stands at historically high levels (Joyce *et al.*, 2010). It is the subject of increasing attention (e.g. see Hills, 2004; Lister, 2007; Ridge and Wright 2008; Dorling 2010; Hills *et al.*, 2010) and there is growing evidence that inequality has negative effects on health (e.g. Wilkinson and Pickett, 2009), crime (Neumayer, 2005), happiness (Layard, 2005), social mobility (e.g. Blanden *et al.*, 2005), and social cohesion (e.g. Galbraith, 1977). Some argue that inequality damages the social fabric and quality of life for everyone, not just those at the bottom of the income distribution (Wilkinson and Pickett, 2009). But not everyone takes this view, including the Vice-Chair of Goldman Sachs who argued that the general public should "tolerate inequality as a way to achieve greater prosperity for all" (quoted in the *Daily Telegraph,* 21st October 2009).

Labour governments from 1997 to 2010 chose not to focus their policies on inequality, but rather on poverty. Tony Blair explained that:

> [It's] not that I don't care about the gap [between high and low incomes]; so much as I don't care if there are people who earn a lot of money. They're not my concern. I do care about people who are without opportunity, disadvantaged and poor (Blair, 2005).

It is noteworthy that the Labour government presided over a period both of increasing income inequality and of growing evidence of its detrimental effects, and yet still did not see its role as trying to reduce income inequality directly.

---

[*] Karen Rowlingson is Professor of Social Policy and Director of Research at the Institute of Applied Social Studies at the University of Birmingham. Michael Orton is Senior Research Fellow at the Institute for Employment Research at the University of Warwick. Eleanor Taylor is a Researcher at the *National Centre for Social Research* and is Co-Director of the *British Social Attitudes* survey series.

At the General Election in May 2010, there was a swing in public support from Labour to Conservative, suggesting that public support for redistributive policies was declining (Curtice, 2010). The resulting coalition government that came to power has stated an intention to tackle issues around inequality, declaring that "addressing poverty and inequality in Britain is at the heart of our agenda for government" (HM Government, 2010:1). However, the precise nature and effect of their policies on poverty and inequality are yet to be seen, though measures being taken to reduce the budget deficit look set to increase inequality still further.

Understanding the public's attitudes to inequality and redistribution, and how they may alter over the coming 'period of austerity' is important for policy makers and commentators alike. Of course, that is not to say that politicians will seek to take account of public opinion, or indeed to challenge it (as did Margaret Thatcher, as a 'conviction politician'). However, understanding how people feel about inequality and redistribution and how that altered during the previous administration, will be a sound starting point for monitoring how they may change in coming years.

So what does the British public think about inequality and redistribution? Recent analysis of *British Social Attitudes* data found that while a majority of the British public saw the gap between high and low incomes as too large, only a minority directly supported redistribution (Orton and Rowlingson, 2007).[1] This appears to be a puzzle: if people see income inequality as too great, why do many not support policies to directly reduce inequality? *British Social Attitudes* includes a number of questions on people's attitudes towards income inequality and redistribution which allow us to go some way to solve this puzzle. Some of these questions have been asked periodically since 1987. Others are part of a new set of questions asked in 2009, which were designed to understand in more depth how the public perceives income inequality. The 2009 survey, on which most of this chapter is based, captures people's views a year into recession and in the final year of the Labour government.

Using these data, we explore three possible explanations for the apparent mismatch between concern over inequality and support for redistribution. The first potential explanation is that some people reject redistribution for reasons of self-interest; for example, if they are on high incomes and would have to pay higher taxes. The second possible explanation is that people have underlying beliefs about inequality which affect their support for redistribution. For example, some people may see inequality as due to individual laziness on the one hand and hard work on the other, and so see the solution at an individual level rather than at a national policy level. Some may see inequality as a 'necessary evil' in order to maintain Britain's prosperity. And some may consider inequality to be an inevitable part of modern life which it is not possible to change through policy levers. The third possible explanation is that people may support other ways of reducing inequality rather than direct redistribution.

Before attempting to address these three explanations, the first part of this chapter investigates the nature of public attitudes to income inequality and redistribution in greater depth than has been undertaken previously, and reports on how the relationship between the two is changing over time. Subsequent sections seek to address each of the three explanations for the inequality:redistribution puzzle, the evidence from which we draw upon in our concluding section.

Attitudes to income inequality and redistribution

Income inequality

So, how concerned is the British public about income inequality? How has this changed over time? Are people concerned about the gap between the bottom and the top of the income distribution, or with discrepancies within the distribution? And how far are people's views associated with the position they perceive themselves to be on the income ladder?

Three questions in *British Social Attitudes* which measure people's attitudes towards income inequality all show high levels of public concern. To measure people's attitudes to this issue, we asked the following question:

Thinking of income levels generally in Britain today, would you say that the gap between those with high incomes and those with low incomes is ...

> *... too large*
>
> *... about right*
>
> *... or, too small*

We also asked respondents to indicate how much they agreed or disagreed with the following two statements:

Differences in income in Britain are too large

Ordinary working people do not get their fair share of the nation's wealth

As shown in Table 1.1, 78 per cent of people say that the gap between those with high incomes and those with low incomes is "too large"; 73 per cent agree that "differences in income in Britain are too large"; and 60 per cent agree that "ordinary working people do not get their fair share of the nation's wealth".[2]

Table 1.1 Attitudes towards income inequality in Britain

	All
The gap between those with high incomes and those with low incomes is ...	%
... too large	78
... about right	16
... too small	2
Base	*2267*
Differences in income in Britain are too large	%
Agree	73
Neither agree nor disagree	17
Disagree	8
Base	*1925*
Ordinary working people do not get their fair share of the nation's wealth	%
Agree	60
Neither agree nor disagree	24
Disagree	14
Base	*2942*

Table 1.2 shows how levels of concern about income inequality have changed over the past 20 years or so. It shows a steady increase in concern about income inequality from 2004 to 2009, coinciding with a period in which poverty and inequality increased.

Table 1.2 Concern about income inequality, 1987–2009[3]

	1987	1991	1995	1999	2002	2004	2006	2009
% saying the income gap is too large	79	79	87	81	82	73	76	78
% agree differences in income are too large	74	79	n/a	80	n/a	63	n/a	73
% agree working people do not get their fair share of the nation's wealth	64	67	66	60	63	53	55	60

n/a = not asked

None of these questions capture people's views about where on the income ladder they feel there are the worst inequalities. Based on findings from their deliberative[4] research, Bamfield and Horton (2009:12) argue that:

> ... the gap that immediately comes to mind for most people is not so much the gap between top and bottom, but rather the gap between those in the middle and those at the very top – that is, 'the super-rich' rather than just 'the rich'.

This would also make sense given that the growth of inequality in the last 20 or so years has been fuelled particularly by increasing income and wealth at the very top (among the top one per cent particularly; see Hills, 2004). How people think about income inequality across different groups is likely to affect their views on redistribution, particularly if, as Bamfield and Horton report, people's immediate thoughts are to the gap between the middle and the very top. In this case, people may not support redistribution from the top to the bottom, because they are concerned about the middle rather than those on the lowest incomes.

Another question in *British Social Attitudes* allows us to explore this further. We asked what people saw as the main income gap problem in Britain:

> *Thinking about the gap in income between those on high incomes and those on low incomes, which do you think is the biggest problem facing Britain today?*

> *Is it the gap in income between people ...*

> *... at the very top and near the top,*

> *... the top and in the middle,*

> *... the middle and at the bottom,*

> *... or, is it the overall gap in income between people at the top and people at the bottom*

People's responses to this question do not support Bamfield and Horton's suggestion that people are thinking about the 'super-rich' (see Table 1.3). Most people (64 per cent) think that the main problem is the overall gap in income between people at the top and people at the bottom. Some (19 per cent) think the main problem lies in the gap between the middle and the bottom. Very few people see the main problem as between those at the very top and near the top or between those at the top and in the middle. So it is the overall gap that is the main concern.[5]

Table 1.3 Perceptions of the biggest problem with the income gap facing Britain today

The biggest problem facing Britain today is the gap in income between people ...	All
	%
... at the very top and near the top	4
... at the top and in the middle	7
... in the middle and at the bottom	19
... overall gap in income	64
Base	2267

Two questions come to mind when looking at these findings. The first is what people have in mind as "high incomes" and "low incomes" when responding to this question. The second, and, perhaps, more important, is where they view themselves along the high, middle and low income continuum. That is, to what extent are people's views influenced by their own income level? These are pertinent questions when it comes to understanding people's views on redistribution – namely whether they feel they would be one of those benefiting or losing out.

The first point can be addressed by looking at a question which asks people what they see as a "high income" and a "low income":

> *A lot of people talk about incomes being high or low. Thinking about a person living on their own, how large would their income have to be before you would say they had a high income?*

> *And again, thinking about a person living on their own, how small would their income have to be before you would say they had a low income?*

The average (mean) figure for a "large income" is close to £44,000. In terms of "low income", the average figure is nearer to £13,000 (for an examination of how respondents' earnings estimates relate to actual earnings for a range of job types see the chapter by Heath *et al.* in this report).

Not surprisingly, perhaps, what people view as a high or a low income is linked to their own household income (Table 1.4[6, 7]). Broadly, the higher the person's household income, the higher the figure they are likely to cite for both small and large incomes. However, note that there is far less variation across the income groups about what is viewed as a "low income" – with around £3,500 between the average figure given by those in the lowest income quartile and those in the highest income quartile. The greatest variation comes in what is viewed as a "high income" – with nearly £16,000 difference between those in the highest and lowest income quartiles.

Those on household incomes of less than £15,000 per year think that a small income for an individual is about £11,000 and they think that a large individual income is over £32,000 per year. Those on household incomes of over £44,000 think a small individual income is closer to £15,000 and a high individual income over £48,000 per year. In monetary terms, it seems that those on higher incomes view the gap between rich and poor as larger than those on lower incomes.

Table 1.4 Average (mean) levels of income considered to be small and large, by household income

	What is a small income per year?	What is a large income per year?	Base
Household income	Mean (£)	Mean (£)	
All	12,681	40,774	3421
Less than £14,999	11,395	32,427	733
£15,000–£25,999	11,152	34,079	834
£26,000–£43,999	13,314	39,672	650
£44,000 or more	14,836	48,249	690

This finding also suggests that very few people consider themselves to be on a high income, and this is confirmed by another question which asks people directly if they consider themselves to be on a high, middle or low income:

Among which group would you place yourself ...

... high income

... middle income

... or, low income?

Table 1.5 shows that those in the lowest quartile are very likely to view themselves as on a low income (84 per cent do so). And as we look up the income quartiles, a greater proportion of people put themselves into the "middle" rather than "low income" group. What is striking is that virtually no one, even those in the highest income quartile, considers themselves to be on a high income. Only nine per cent of those in the highest income quartile view themselves as being on a "high income".

Table 1.5 Respondents' self-perceived income, by household income

	Household income				All
	Less than £15,000	£15,000– £25,999	£26,000– £43,999	£44,000 plus	
Respondent considers themselves to be on a ...	%	%	%	%	%
... low income	84	59	31	9	44
... middle income	16	40	68	78	52
... high income	*	*	1	9	4
Base	*480*	*556*	*421*	*459*	*2267*

This analysis supports previous research (e.g. Evans and Kelley, 2004) which has found that people have a strong tendency to place themselves in the middle of the income distribution, and suggests ignorance of the actual distribution. This is very likely to affect attitudes to inequality and redistribution. If few people view themselves as being in the 'high income' group, then the problems of inequality, and need for the redistribution of income away from the top, is an issue for others and not themselves.

Redistribution

Having clarified that the majority of the British public are concerned about levels of income inequality, we turn now to how this relates to people's views on the role of government in redistributing income. So, do people think it is the government's responsibility to redistribute income from those who are better-off to those who are worse-off? Have people's views changed over time? And how do people's views on redistribution relate to their views on income inequality?

  British Social Attitudes includes four questions on public views on the role of government in redistributing income, as shown in Table 1.6. We asked respondents to indicate whether they agreed or disagreed with each of the following statements:

> *It is the responsibility of the government to reduce the differences in income between people with high incomes and those with low incomes*

> *The government should provide a decent standard of living for the unemployed*

> *Government should redistribute income from the better off to those who are less well off*

> *The government should spend more on welfare benefits for the poor, even if it leads to higher taxes*

Table 1.6 Attitudes to government redistribution of income

	Govt responsibility to reduce income differences	Govt should provide a decent standard of living	Govt should redistribute income	Govt should spend more on benefits for the poor
	%	%	%	%
Agree	57	51	36	27
Neither agree nor disagree	21	26	27	55
Disagree	19	20	34	43
Base	1925	1925	2942	963

Table 1.6 suggests that people's support for redistributive policies is greater than their support for the concept of 'redistribution' or government help for 'the poor'. This is apparent in people's reactions to the questions, which vary substantially depending on the precise terms used. For instance, while 57 per cent of the public agree that "it is the responsibility of the government to reduce the differences in income between people with high incomes and those with low incomes" only 36 per cent agree that "government should redistribute income from the better off to those who are less well off". This suggests quite strong support for the idea that the government should reduce the income gap between those on high and low incomes but support drops dramatically when redistribution is explicitly mentioned and even further when support for 'the poor' through the benefits system is mentioned (27 per cent agree that "the government should spend more on welfare benefits for the poor even if it leads to higher taxes").

However, while only a minority explicitly support redistribution (when it is directly referred to in the question), this does not mean that the majority *oppose* it. In actual fact there are broadly equal numbers of people who support and oppose redistribution, with nearly three people in ten sitting on the fence.

Perhaps the negative reaction to the 'r word' is a legacy of New Labours reticence about appearing to be an Old Labour tax and spend party. In office, Labour never made any proud claims about redistribution but, if anything, pursued redistribution by stealth. The negative reaction to the 'p' word (poverty, or poor) is also reflected in other research which shows great scepticism about the existence of poverty in Britain and lack of sympathy for people out of work, but great concern for people working for very low wages (Castell and Thompson 2007; Bamfield and Horton 2009; Hanley 2009).

Table 1.7 shows the proportion of people agreeing with each of the four *British Social Attitudes* questions on redistribution, alongside people's views on three measures of income inequality reported earlier in Table 1.2. As well as showing findings from the 2009 survey, it shows how attitudes have changed over the past 20 or so years. The findings from 2009 in the far right-hand column corroborate previous findings that levels of public support for redistribution are substantially lower than levels of concern about income inequality (Orton and Rowlingson, 2007).

It also shows an overall increase in support for redistribution from 2004 to 2009, looking at two of the redistribution measures in the table ("the government is responsible for reducing inequality", and "the government should redistribute income"); the increase in support on the first measure is substantial, whereas on the second it is only slight. This sits alongside an increase in concern about income inequality, which, as mentioned earlier, coincides with a period in which poverty and inequality increased. But the trend is rather different when it comes to views that "the government should spend more on welfare benefits for the poor, even if it leads to higher taxes". Support for this statement has declined dramatically each time it has been asked since 1991.

Perhaps the key point here is that, although there is an apparent relationship between attitudes to inequality and attitudes to redistribution, with attitudes to inequality rising and falling roughly in parallel with attitudes to redistribution, in recent years the gap between the two has widened even further. In 1987, there was a 34 percentage point gap between those who thought inequality was too high and those who wanted the government to redistribute income. By 2009, the gap has widened to 43 per cent.

Table 1.7 Attitudes to inequality and redistribution, 1987–2009[8]

	1987	1991	1995	1999	2002	2004	2006	2009
% saying the income gap is too large	79	79	87	81	82	73	76	78
% agree differences in income are too large	74	79	n/a	80	n/a	63	n/a	73
% agree ordinary working people don't get fair share of wealth	64	67	66	60	63	53	55	60
% agree govt responsible for reducing inequality	n/a	64	n/a	65	n/a	43	n/a	57
% agree govt should provide decent standard of living	n/a	n/a	n/a	n/a	n/a	n/a	n/a	51
% agree govt should redistribute income	45	48	47	36	39	32	34	36
% agree govt should spend more on benefits	55	58	50	40	44	36	35	27

n/a = not asked

So, we are left with the puzzle of why support for redistribution is not as strong as we might expect given concern about inequality. Here we return to the three explanations posed earlier in the chapter, starting with the idea that self-interest reduces support for redistribution.

Explaining differences in concern about income inequality and support for redistribution

Self-interest

Previous research has suggested that one of the drivers of attitudes to redistribution is self-interest (Sefton, 2005). If people are motivated by self-interest they will oppose redistribution if they are on high incomes because they are likely to lose out from redistributive policies. But if they are on low incomes they are likely to gain and so support redistribution. Do *British Social Attitudes* data support this hypothesis?

As we are interested in people's explicit support for redistribution, here we use the question which asks whether government should 'redistribute' income from the better off to those who are less well off. We look at levels of support for redistribution across people in different income groups. The answer is, yes, *to some extent*, the data support the idea that people are motivated by self-interest. Table 1.8 shows that there is a strong link between income and attitudes to redistribution. Just about half (48 per cent) of those in the lowest quartile support redistribution but this drops to just 28 per cent for those in the highest quartile. Those on higher incomes may well be concerned that redistribution will involve them in paying higher taxes. That said, nearly three in ten of them do support redistribution, suggesting a fair degree of altruism rather than self-interest in the higher income population. Moreover, there are many in the lowest income quartile (those likely to benefit the most from redistribution) who do not support the idea.

However, we saw earlier that most of those on high incomes actually perceive themselves to be on 'middle' incomes. So perhaps they do not see themselves at risk of losing out from redistributive policies? Looking at people's *perception* of the level of their income, 28 per cent of those who perceived themselves to be on a high income still support redistribution (though due to the small sample size we should exercise caution in drawing firm conclusions from these data). So self-interest cannot be the only driver of people's attitudes here.

Table 1.8 Support for redistribution, by actual and perceived income

	% agreeing that "government should redistribute income"	Base
Household income		
Less than £14,999	48	626
£15,000–£25,999	39	756
£26,000–£43,999	33	570
£44,000+	28	629
Perception of own income		
Low	44	853
Middle	30	983
High	28	80

A further question allows us to explore the issue of self-interest beyond simply looking at the views of people in different income groups. We asked how people view themselves in relation to self-interest:

> *Some people think it is important to put yourself first while other people think it is more important to think about others. Which of the statements on this card comes closest to your view?*
>
> *Put yourself first and leave others to do the same*
> *Put yourself first but also consider other peoples needs and interests*
> *Consider everyone's needs and interests equally, including your own*
> *Put other peoples needs and interests above your own*

Table 1.9 shows that very few people put themselves at either end of the spectrum. Four per cent say that they put themselves first and leave others to do the same, but nearly a third (32 per cent) say that they put themselves first but also consider other people's needs. More than half (53 per cent) say that they consider everyone's needs equally and one in ten (11 per cent) say that they put other people's needs above their own.

Table 1.9 Perceptions of own levels of self interest and consideration of others

	All
	%
Put yourself first and leave others to do the same	4
Put yourself first but also consider other people's needs	32
Consider everyone's needs and interests equally, including your own	53
Put other people's needs and interests above your own	11
Base	2942

Of course, the way people answer this question may not perfectly reflect their actual behaviour as people may not wish to say they are self-interested even if they are. However, the variation in how people answered this question means we can see whether attitudes to redistribution are affected by perceptions of self-interestedness. Table 1.10 takes those in the lowest and highest income quartiles and then divides each of these groups in terms of their answers to the question above on self-interest. Among those in the lowest quartile, there is very little difference in their views about redistribution, whether they are someone who says they put themselves above other people's needs or someone who considers everyone's needs equally. But among those in the highest quartile, those who say they put themselves first are somewhat less likely to support redistribution compared with those who say they are more altruistic. This therefore provides some further evidence of the role of self-interest in affecting attitudes to redistribution. However, once again, it shows that self-interest provides only part of the explanation, as a quarter of those on high incomes who say they put themselves first, nevertheless support redistribution.

Table 1.10 Concern about inequality and support for redistribution, by demographic factors

	% agreeing that "government should redistribute income"	Base
Income in lowest quartile	48	626
Put yourself first but also consider other people's needs	50	111
Consider everyone's needs and interests equally, including your own	49	201
Income in highest quartile	28	629
Put yourself first but also consider other people's needs	24	147
Consider everyone's needs and interests equally, including your own	31	223

Underlying beliefs about inequality

If self-interest cannot entirely explain attitudes to redistribution, another possible explanation relates to peoples underlying beliefs about inequality. Previous studies have certainly found some links between underlying attitudes, beliefs and values. In *British Social Attitudes: the 1985 Report*, Young (1985: 30) argued that people's views about inequality:

> … are based more on philosophy than income or social class ... public attitudes to inequality seem to be infused with symbolic overtones.

More recently, Castell and Thompson (2007) have argued that attitudes to poverty are strongly influenced by whether or not people hold collectivist or individualist world views, that is, whether they believe in doing things for the good of society or community, or believe in the independence of individuals. And this certainly fits with Sefton's clustering of people into Samaritans, Club Members and Robinson Crusoes (2005). In his analysis, the Samaritans held the most collectivist world views and were the most supportive of redistribution. The Robinson Crusoes were the most individualist and were the least supportive.

Underlying beliefs about inequality are therefore likely to be important in relation to support for redistribution. For example, people may be concerned about inequality, but if they think it is due to individual laziness on the one hand and individual hard work on the other, they may see the solution at an individual level rather than at a national policy level. Alternatively, if they consider inequality to be an inevitable part of modern life they may not think it is possible to change this through policy levers. And, finally, some people may be concerned about inequality but see it as a 'necessary evil' in order to maintain Britain's prosperity.

We asked the following two questions:

Why do you think there are people who live in need?
Because they have been unlucky
Because of laziness or lack of willpower
Because of injustice in our society
It's an inevitable part of modern life

Why do you think that some people have higher incomes than others?
Because they have been lucky
Because they work hard
Because of injustice in our society
It's an inevitable part of modern life

The most common answer (given by 38 per cent) to the first question about need is that it is simply an inevitable part of modern life. The next most common answer is that people in need are lazy (26 per cent). Almost one in five (19 per cent) explain people living in need by injustice in society and 12 per cent say they were simply unlucky. With regards to why some people have higher incomes than others, the most common answer is that they work hard (given by 46 per cent) followed by inevitability (27 per cent) and then injustice (13 per cent) and good luck (nine per cent) (Table 1.11).

Table 1.11 Perceptions of why some people live in need and why some people have higher incomes than others

	Live in need	Have higher incomes
	%	%
Bad/good luck	12	9
Laziness/hard work	26	47
Injustice in society	19	13
Inevitable part of modern life	38	27
None of these/don't know	5	4
Base	*2267*	*2267*

As we might expect, there is a correlation between these two variables. For example, half of those who explain higher income in terms of injustice also explain need by injustice. Combining people's answers to these two questions, we divided people into five groups. The groupings show people's combined explanations for living in need/having a higher income, as presented in Table 1.12.

Table 1.12 Combined explanations for why people live in need/have higher incomes than others

	All
Reasons why people live in need/have higher incomes than others	%
Fickle fate (bad/good luck)	3
Fixed fate (inevitability)	17
Individual agency (laziness/hard work)	18
Structural constraints (injustice)	7
Other (mixed responses)	54
Base	2267

So about one in five of the public explain inequality in relation to fate whether that is fickle fate (good or bad luck) or some kind of fixed fate (inevitability). Another one in five explains inequality in relation to individual agency (the view that people work hard to achieve higher incomes while others live in need because they are lazy). Less than one in ten of the population give structural explanations (social injustice) for inequality at both the top and the bottom. Over half of the respondents (54 per cent) gave mixed responses. Many of these mixed responses mention inevitability for poverty and hard work for high incomes. This shows that about half the public do not hold consistent views on this with more positive views about those on high earnings than about those in poverty. This reflects similar findings in previous research (Dean and Melrose, 1999; Bamfield and Horton, 2009).

There is certainly a link between support for these different explanations and people's attitudes towards redistribution. Table 1.13 shows that there is much lower support for redistribution among those who use individualistic explanations (laziness/hard work) for need/high incomes than those who use more structural explanations (injustice). For example, among those who explain high incomes in terms of hard work only 30 per cent support redistribution compared with 56 per cent of those who explain high incomes in terms of injustice.

Table 1.13 Explanations for individuals living in need or having a high income, by levels of support for redistribution

	% agreeing that "government should redistribute income"	Base
Reasons why people live in need		
Bad luck	45	214
Laziness/lack of willpower	32	466
Injustice in society	50	370
Inevitability in modern life	30	762
Reasons why people have high incomes		
Good luck	44	171
Hard work	30	872
Injustice in society	56	254
Inevitability in modern life	34	554

We also used these questions to investigate whether any link between income and attitudes to inequality/redistribution could be in terms of empathy and socio-cultural difference (Bowles *et al.*, 2001; Shapiro, 2002; Alesina and Glaeser, 2004). Those who are closest to poverty and low income may have more understanding and empathy towards others in a similar position whereas those on higher incomes may have much less understanding and empathy.

Table 1.14 shows some link between income and explanations of poverty/high incomes but not that much. Those in the highest income quartile are actually no more likely to say that people live in need due to laziness/lack of willpower than any other income group. In fact, they are slightly more likely to mention injustice. They are, however, more likely than other income groups to say that people have high incomes due to hard work and they are less likely to put high incomes down to good luck. Those in the third quartile for household income (£26,000–43,999 per year) are the least likely, compared with other income groups, to say that people on high incomes are in this position because they have worked hard. They are more likely than other income groups to say that high earnings are due to inevitability or injustice. Perhaps this group see other people earning a bit more than they do and feel that it is not deserved. This links in to theories of 'relative deprivation' where people, sometimes on high incomes, can feel deprived if they see others around them (their 'reference group') earning more than them, undeservedly (Runciman 1972; Shapiro 2002; Rose 2006).

Table 1.14 Explanations for people living in need or having high incomes, by income quartiles

	Income quartiles				All
	Less than £15,000	£15,000– £25,999	£26,000– £43,999	£44,000 plus	
People live in need because of ...	%	%	%	%	%
... bad luck	14	13	11	10	12
... laziness/lack of willpower	26	27	24	26	26
... injustice in society	16	19	19	20	19
... inevitability in modern life	39	35	42	39	38
People have high incomes because of ...	%	%	%	%	%
... good luck	9	12	8	4	9
... hard work	46	45	41	53	47
... injustice in society	13	15	15	12	13
... inevitability in modern life	28	25	32	28	27
Base	*480*	*556*	*421*	*459*	*2267*

Another underlying belief that might affect attitudes to redistribution is a belief about whether or not inequality causes general or specific social problems (e.g. crime, ill health, etc.), and/or is a moral issue. We asked various questions to explore the nature of people's views about inequality:

> *Please say how much you agree or disagree with the following statements.*
> *Large differences in people's incomes ...*
> *... are necessary for Britain's prosperity*
> *... are inevitable whether we like them or not*
> *... are unfair*
> *... give people an incentive to work hard*
> *... are morally wrong*
> *... contribute to social problems like crime*

Table 1.15 shows, again, that there is a strong streak of fatalism around inequality with 76 per cent of people agreeing that large differences in peoples incomes are inevitable whether we like them or not. The table also shows that most people think that inequality contributes to social problems like crime (63 per cent) and is unfair (52 per cent) but another majority of the population (61 per cent) see inequality more positively as giving people an incentive to work hard. By contrast, 36 per cent see inequality as morally wrong. Only 27 per cent see inequality as necessary for Britain's prosperity.

Table 1.15 Views about large differences in people's incomes

	All
% agreeing that large differences in people's incomes ...	
... are inevitable whether we like them or not	76
... contribute to social problems like crime	63
... give people an incentive to work hard	61
... are unfair	52
... are morally wrong	36
... are necessary for Britain's prosperity	27
Base	*2267*

These views about inequality are very closely linked to support for redistribution (see Table 1.16). For example, among those who agree that inequality is morally wrong, 52 per cent support redistribution. Those who see inequality as necessary for prosperity are much less likely to support redistribution (29 per cent). It is therefore clear from this analysis that peoples underlying views of inequality are strongly related to whether or not they support redistribution.

Table 1.16 Support for redistribution, by attitudes about large differences in people's incomes

	% agreeing that "government should redistribute income"	*Base*
Large differences in people's incomes ...		
... are morally wrong	52	*709*
... are unfair	48	*1001*
... contribute to social problems like crime	42	*1236*
... are inevitable whether we like them or not	32	*1492*
... give people an incentive to work hard	31	*1150*
... are necessary for Britain's prosperity	29	*533*

So far, we have seen evidence that both self-interest and underlying beliefs about inequality affect attitudes to redistribution. But which of these is the key driver of attitudes here? We ran a logistic regression model (see Table A.1 in the chapter appendix; further information on regression can be found in Appendix I of this report) to measure the independent effect of self-interest (in the form of household income) and underlying beliefs.[9] We also included some standard demographic variables which have been included in previous analysis of attitudes to redistribution (e.g. Sefton, 2005). The variables which have a statistically significant independent effect on attitudes to redistribution, after controlling for other factors are: household income; housing tenure; the explanations people give for why some people live in need and why others have high incomes; and whether or not people see income inequality as morally wrong. The other variables in the model (age, education, economic activity, social class) do not have a statistically significant, independent effect.

As far as income goes, those on lower incomes are more likely, after controlling for other factors, to support redistribution. This supports the view that self-interest is a key driver of attitudes here. As far as tenure goes, those in social rented housing are more likely to support redistribution compared with both owner-occupiers and those in private rented accommodation.

Those who think that people live in need because they are lazy are less likely to support redistribution, after controlling for other factors. And those who think that people on high incomes have got them through hard work are also less likely to support redistribution. So, underlying beliefs are also important drivers, independent of income or other factors. In fact, one of the most powerful independent drivers of attitudes to redistribution is whether or not people think that inequality is morally wrong. If they do, they are much more likely than others to support redistribution.

Support for other forms of government intervention

So far in this chapter we have seen that both self-interest and underlying beliefs are associated with people's attitudes to redistribution. But a third explanation for the discrepancy between concern for income inequality and levels of support for redistribution is that the public may support *other* forms of government intervention to reduce income inequality. Presenting people with a range of options, we asked (see first column in Table 1.17):

> *Thinking overall about the gap in income between those on high incomes and those on low incomes, what if anything do you think should be done to reduce this gap?*

People are also asked to pick the *one* priority that they thought would be the best way to reduce the income gap (see second column in Table 1.17).

Table 1.17 shows a propensity for people to be concerned more about equal *opportunities* than necessarily equal *outcomes*, and, as such, support policies aimed at facilitating this. The most popular answer (given by 62 per cent of people) is to provide better education and training opportunities. Twenty-five per cent of people support the creation of jobs. There is also support for helping those in low-paid work, not only by reducing taxes on low incomes (which is discussed below) but by increasing the minimum wage (said by 54 per cent).

We saw, above, that around half (51 per cent) support providing a decent standard of living for the unemployed but when *benefits* for the poor or those on low incomes are mentioned, the public seems to back away. Concern for people at the bottom is mainly directed at those in work, as there was very little support for benefits to be raised for people on low incomes (17 per cent).

Although we saw above that only 36 per cent of people support redistribution explicitly, people's responses to this question show that there is a fair amount of support for redistributive policies, when posed in more specific terms. Forty per cent (in Table 1.17) support an increase in taxes for those on high incomes and 56 per cent support a reduction in taxes for those on low incomes. So there does seem to be more implicit support for redistribution than explicit support. This reinforces previous research which found that although people were unwilling to support openly redistributive policies, they did support the general principle of spending on those who needed it and raising the money from those who could afford it (Hedges, 2005). Sefton's work using *British Social Attitudes* data (Sefton, 2005) also found differences in support for 'explicit' and 'implicit' redistribution (the latter was measured by describing packages of taxation and spending which were redistributive in their impact).

Table 1.17 Public views about the best ways to reduce the income gap

	All	One priority
What government should do to reduce the income gap	%	%
Better education or training opportunities should be provided to enable people to get better jobs	62	30
Taxes for those on low incomes should be reduced	56	21
The minimum wage should be increased	54	18
Taxes for those on high incomes should be increased	40	12
There should be an upper limit on very high incomes	25	7
The government should create jobs for those that need them	25	6
Benefits for those on low incomes should be increased	17	4
Other	2	*
Nothing should be done	2	*
Base	*2267*	*1775*

Multiple answers were allowed, therefore the first column sums to more than 100

We explored the issue of taxation further by looking at a question which asked people what they thought about the level of taxes for people on high and low incomes. For each group respondents were asked:

Generally, how would you describe taxes in Britain today?

Table 1.18 shows that people think that those on low incomes pay too much tax and there is certainly no appetite for taxes to be raised on middle incomes. Views about taxes for those on high incomes are more mixed but with more people saying they are too low than saying they are too high.

Table 1.18 Public views about levels of taxation for different income groups

Views about levels of taxation	For those on low incomes	For those on middle incomes	For those on high incomes
	%	%	%
Much too high	21	6	7
Too high	51	36	18
About right	21	48	37
Too low	2	4	28
Much too low	*	*	4
Can't choose/not answered	5	6	5
Base	*967*	*967*	*967*

As we might expect, these views vary depending on whether or not people consider themselves to be on a low, middle or high income. Whereas 33 per cent of the population as a whole say that taxes for those on high incomes are either too low or much too low, only 12 per cent of those who consider themselves to be on high incomes say that taxes on high incomes are too low (though we pointed out earlier that only four per cent of the population consider themselves to be on a high income, so this is a small minority of people).

In our discussion above, we raised the fact that a key driver behind people's concern about inequality is concern about lack of equal opportunities, although concern about inequality of outcomes is also an issue for many. We asked respondents how much they agreed or disagreed with the following statements:

Children from better-off families have many more opportunities than children from less well-off families

Some people have higher incomes than others because they are born to rich parents and have advantages from the start

There can never be equal opportunities in a society where some people have higher incomes than others

People in Britain today have similar opportunities regardless of their income

It is clear from their answers that most people do not think that there *is* equal opportunity in Britain. Eighty per cent of people agree that children from better-off families have greater opportunities than those from less well-off families and 68 per cent agree that some people have higher incomes than others because they were born to rich parents and had advantages from the start (see Table 1.19). Having said that, people also acknowledge that the relationship between equal opportunities and equal outcomes is not simple; with 62 per cent of the public thinking that it is not possible to have equal opportunities in a society where there are unequal outcomes.

Table 1.19 Views about equal opportunities

	All
% agreeing that …	
… children from better-off families have many more opportunities than children from less well-off families	80
… some people have higher incomes than others because they are born to rich parents and have advantages from the start	68
… there can never be equal opportunities in a society where some people have higher incomes than others	62
… people in Britain today have similar opportunities regardless of their income	27
Base	*1925*

Conclusions

In this chapter we set out to investigate why it is that the majority of the British public thinks the gap between those on high and low incomes is too large, but far fewer support government redistribution of income from the better off to the worse off. The first point to make here, however, is that while levels of support for redistribution are not particularly high, nor are levels of opposition. A substantial minority (28 per cent) sit on the fence, neither supporting nor opposing redistribution. Furthermore, part of the issue seems to be with the term 'redistribution', as more people answer favourably about redistribution when the general principle is put forward without the explicit term. As suggested earlier, this could be due to the reluctance of parties on the left to talk positively about redistribution, which has become synonymous with an 'Old Labour' 'tax and spend' approach. Whatever, overall, our findings suggest that political leaders and lobby groups could play a role in influencing public opinion here.

Having said all this, explicit support for redistribution still seems low in comparison with levels of concern about income inequality. We came up with three possible explanations which might explain this apparent puzzle. Each seems to play a part, with no one single explanation solving the puzzle.

One explanation for lower levels of public support for redistribution – in comparison to levels of concern about income inequality – is self-interest. Those on higher incomes, who might lose out from redistribution, are less likely to support redistribution than those on lower incomes. But self-interest cannot explain views about redistribution entirely, given that a quarter of those on higher incomes, who say when asked that they put themselves first over others, still support redistribution. Perhaps some of these see it in their own best interests to reduce inequality (for reasons of social cohesion or economic performance). Moreover, support for redistribution is by no means universal among those on lower incomes, who are the likely beneficiaries.

Another part of the puzzle can be solved by understanding people's underlying beliefs about inequality. Those who see inequality as caused by factors outside people's control (e.g. social injustice or bad luck) are much more likely to support redistribution than those who see it as due to laziness on the part of 'the poor' and hard work on the part of 'the rich'. Likewise, those who see inequality as morally wrong are much more likely to support redistribution than other groups. There is not a strong relationship between people's income levels and their underlying beliefs (that is, people's underlying views do not simply reflect their own self-interest) and it is clear that both income and underlying beliefs are independently important in affecting attitudes to redistribution.

The third explanation, namely that people may support other kinds of government intervention aimed at reducing income inequalities, provides further evidence for solving the puzzle. While some may not support 'redistribution' explicitly, many support policies which are implicitly redistributive. There is a strong concern about lack of equal *opportunities* for children and so strong support for policies which would promote more equality of opportunity. However, the public recognises that equal opportunities and equal outcomes are linked and that government action is needed on both fronts. In particular, people are concerned about those on the lowest incomes. There is strong support for a minimum standard of living for everyone and also strong support for lower taxes for those on low incomes.

At a time when the recession and resulting cuts in public expenditure look set to impact most on those at the bottom, it seems that the British public will be concerned about consequential increases in income inequality.

Notes

1. There is a body of research which has investigated attitudes to redistribution further (e.g. Hills, 2001; Taylor-Gooby and Hastie, 2002; Taylor-Gooby *et al.*, 2003; Hedges, 2005; Georgiadis and Manning 2007).
2. Sefton (2005) has argued that the wording of questions means that people may sometimes be thinking about the income gap between the very rich and the very poor, and at other times the difference between the 'not-so-rich' and 'not so-poor'.
3. Bases for Table 1.2 (and Table 1.7 rows 1 to 3).

	1987	1991	1995	1999	2002	2004	2006	2009
% saying the income gap is too large	2847	1445	1234	2091	1148	2146	2170	2267
% agree differences in income are too large	1212	1066	n/a	804	n/a	1737	n/a	1925
% agree ordinary working people don't get fair share of wealth	2493	2702	3135	2450	2900	2609	3748	2742

n/a = not asked

4. Deliberative research is a technique for exploring views on issues about which the public may have little or no knowledge or where it will be given information on which to reflect.
5. The difference between our findings and those of Bamfield and Horton could be due to the different methods used (their finding was based on a small sample of people involved in deliberative discussion groups covering a range of issues). It could also be due to the timing of the different pieces of research. Bamfield and Horton's fieldwork took place in the second half of 2008 whereas the *British Social Attitudes* survey took place in 2009, and it may be that publicity over bank bonuses and so on was more widespread in 2008 than 2009 when media coverage and public debate turned more towards the recession and impending government spending cuts.
6. This analysis doesn't take account of the number of people in a household, therefore some will appear to be on much larger incomes than others.
7. Five cases with outlying estimates of 'high' or 'low' income (less than £100 or higher than £5,000,000) were removed from the analysis.
8. Bases for Table 1.7 (rows 4 to 7).

	1987	1991	1995	1999	2002	2004	2006	2009
% agree govt responsible for reducing inequality	n/a	1066	n/a	804	n/a	1737	n/a	1925
% agree govt should provide decent standard of living	n/a	n/a	n/a	n/a	n/a	n/a	n/a	1925
% agree govt should redistribute	2493	2702	3135	2450	2900	2609	3748	2942
% agree govt should spend more on benefits	1281	2481	3135	2450	2900	2609	2822	967

n/a = not asked

9. Our model explains 20 per cent of the variation in answers to the question about redistribution.

References

Alesina, A. and Glaeser, E. (2004), *Fighting Poverty in the US and Europe: A World of Difference*, Oxford: Oxford University Press

Bamfield, L. and Horton, T. (2009), *Understanding attitudes to tackling economic inequality*, London: Fabian Society

Blair, T. (2005), 'We've got to carry this on', *Progress*, March, available at http://www.progressonline.org.uk/articles/article.asp?a=1066 (accessed 17th June 2010)

Blanden, J., Gregg, P. and Machin, S. (2005), *Intergenerational Mobility in Europe and North America*, London: Centre for Economic Performance

Bowles, S., Fong, C. and Gintis, H. (2001), 'Reciprocity and the welfare state', working paper, available at http://discuss.santafe.edu/files/developments/RECIPR1.pdf

Castell, S. and Thompson, J. (2007), *Understanding attitudes to poverty in the UK: getting the public's attention*, York: JRF

Curtice, J. (2010), A New Mood on Tax and Spend?, *Policy and Politics, Election Special*

Dean, H. and Melrose, M. (1999), *Poverty, Riches and Social Citizenship,* Basingstoke: Macmillan.

Dorling, D. (2010), *Injustice: why social inequality persists*, Bristol: The Policy Press

Evans, M. and Kelley, J. (2004), 'Subjective social location: data from 21 nations', *International Journal of Public Opinion Research*, **16(1)**: 3–38

Galbraith, J. (1977), *The Affluent Society* 2nd edition, London: Hamish Hamilton Ltd

Georgiadis, A. and Manning, A. (2007), *Spend It Like Beckham? Inequality and Redistribution in the UK, 1983–2004,* CEP Discussion Paper No. 816, London: Centre for Economic Performance, LSE

Hall, J. and Quinn, J. (2009) 'Goldman Sachs vice-chairman says: 'Learn to tolerate inequality'', The Daily Telegraph, available at http://www.telegraph.co.uk/finance/financetopics/recession/6392127/Goldman-Sachs-vice-chairman-says-Learn-to-tolerate-inequality.html

Hanley, T. (2009), *Engaging public support for eradicating UK poverty*, York: JRF

Hedges, A. (2005), *Perceptions of Redistribution: report on qualitative research*, CASE paper 96, London: London School of Economics

Hills, J. (2001), 'Poverty and social security: what rights? Whose responsibilities?', in Park, A., Curtice, J., Thomson, K., Jarvis, L. and Bromley, C. (eds.), *British Social Attitudes: the 18th Report*, London: Sage

Hills, J. (2004), *Inequality and the State*, Oxford: Oxford University Press

Hills, J., Brewer, M., Jenkins, S., Lister, R., Lupton, R., Machin, S., Mills, C., Modood, T., Reese, T. and Riddell S, (2010), *An anatomy of economic inequality in the UK: Report of the National Equality Panel*, London: Government Equalities Office

HM Government (2010), *State of the nation report: poverty, worklessness and welfare dependency in the UK,* London: Cabinet Office

Joyce, R., Muriel, A., Phillips, D. and Sibieta, L. (2010), *Poverty and Inequality in the UK: 2010*, London: IFS

Layard, R. (2005), *Happiness: lessons from a new science,* London: Allen Lane

Lister, R. (2007), 'The real egalitarianism? Social justice "after Blair"', in Hassan, G. (ed.), *After Blair*, London: Lawrence Wishart

Neumayer, E. (2005), 'Inequality and violent crime: evidence from data on robbery and violent theft', *Journal of Peace Research*, **42(1)**: 101–112

Orton, M. and Rowlingson, K. (2007), *Public Attitudes to Inequality*, York: Joseph Rowntree Foundation

Ridge, T. and Wright, S. (2008), *Understanding inequality, poverty and wealth*, Bristol: The Policy Press

Rose, D (2006), 'Social Comparisons and Social Order: Issues Relating to a Possible Re-study of WG Runciman's Relative Deprivation and Social Justice', ISER Working Paper 2006–48, Colchester; University of Essex

Runciman, W. (1972), R*elative Deprivation and Social Justice: A Study of Attitudes to Social Inequality in 10th century England*, Harmondsworth: Penguin

Sefton, T. (2005), 'Give and take: attitudes to redistribution', in Park, A., Curtice, J., Thomson, K., Bromley, C., Phillips, M. and Johnson, M. (eds.), *British Social Attitudes: the 22nd Report*, London: Sage

Shapiro, I. (2002), 'Why the poor don't soak the rich: Notes on democracy and distribution', *Daedalus*, **130(4)** (winter): 118–128

Taylor-Gooby, P. and Hastie, C. (2002), 'Support for state spending: has New Labour got it right?', in Park, A., Curtice, J., Thompson, K., Jarvis. L. and Bromley, C. (eds.), *British Social Attitudes: the 19th Report*, London: Sage

Taylor-Gooby, P., Hastie, C. and Bromley, C. (2003), 'Querulous citizens: welfare knowledge and the limits to welfare reform', *Social Policy and Administration*, **37(1)**: 1–20

Wilkinson, R. and Pickett, K. (2009), *The spirit level: why more equal societies almost always do better*, London: Allen Lane

Young, K. (1985), 'Shades of opinion', in Jowell, R. and Witherspoon, S. (eds.), *British Social Attitudes: the 1985 Report*, Aldershot: Gower

Acknowledgements

The authors would like to thank the Economic and Social Research Council (grant number RES-062–23–1671) for its support for our research which included a module of questions on the *British Social Attitudes* survey.

Appendix

The multivariate analysis technique used is OLS regression, about which more details can be found in Appendix I of the report. The dependent variable is agreement/disagreement with the statement "Government should redistribute income from the better off to those who are less well off" as measured on a 5 point scale. A positive coefficient indicates higher support for this statement whilst a negative coefficient indicates lower support for this statement. For categorical variables, the reference category is shown in brackets after the category heading.

Table A.1 Logistic regression on whether people agree that "government should redistribute income from the better off to those who are less well off"

	Coefficient	Standard error	p value
Age (18–34)			0.920
35–54	-0.109	0.163	0.504
55–64	-0.111	0.219	0.614
65+	-0.129	0.321	0.688
Household income quartile (less than £14,999)			0.005
Quartile 2 (£15,000–£25,999)	*-0.460	0.193	0.017
Quartile 3 (£26,000–£43,999)	*-0.551	0.231	0.017
Quartile 4 (£44,000+)	**-0.881	0.248	0.000
Education (degree)			0.521
Higher qualification below degree	-0.322	0.233	0.166
A level or equivalent	-0.130	0.224	0.561
O level or equivalent	0.026	0.221	0.907
CSE or equivalent	-0.237	0.287	0.408
No qualifications	0.056	0.261	0.831
Tenure (owned/being bought)			0.027
Rented (LA/HA)	*0.465	0.198	0.019
Rented other	-0.118	0.199	0.552
Economic activity (in paid work)			0.317
Unemployed/full-time education	0.459	0.261	0.079
Sick/disabled	0.323	0.322	0.317
Retired	-0.187	0.280	0.505
Looking after home	0.012	0.285	0.966
Social class (managerial and professional)			0.960
Intermediate occupations	-0.110	0.221	0.620
Own account workers	-0.010	0.242	0.969
Lower supervisory/technical occupation	-0.017	0.218	0.938
(semi-routine and routine occupations)	-0.124	0.197	0.527
Why people live in need? (inevitable)			0.018
Unlucky	*0.470	0.202	0.020
Lazy	0.159	0.168	0.346
Injustice	**0.482	0.176	0.006
Why some have higher incomes? (inevitable)			0.001
Lucky	0.105	0.237	0.657
Work hard	-0.275	0.154	0.073
Injustice	*0.504	0.201	0.012
Inequality morally wrong (agree)			0.000
Neither agree nor disagree	**-0.666	0.161	0.000
Disagree	**-1.078	0.152	0.000
Constant	0.453	0.325	0.163
R2 (adjusted)			

Base: 1334

* = significant at 95% level ** = significant at 99% level

2 How fair is the route to the top? Perceptions of social mobility

Anthony Heath, Nan Dirk de Graaf and Yaojun Li[*]

There has been considerable controversy among academics in recent years as to whether social mobility has been declining in Britain. Both social scientists and policy makers have been much exercised by the question of whether there has been any change in patterns of intergenerational mobility – that is, in the extent to which the occupations or economic positions of sons and daughters are higher, lower or the same as those of their fathers (or mothers). (See, for example, the report of the Cabinet Office, 2008.) High rates of intergenerational mobility are usually taken to be a sign of an 'open' dynamic society where there is equality of opportunity for people from different backgrounds, whereas a high degree of intergenerational stability suggests a more 'closed' society where privileged positions are passed on from one generation to another.

The actual trends over time have been a source of considerable academic dispute. One frequently quoted piece of research by the economists Blanden and Machin (2007) showed that intergenerational earnings mobility has declined over recent decades (see also Ermisch and Nicoletti, 2007). Sociological researchers, however, such as Goldthorpe and Mills (2008), have suggested that intergenerational occupational mobility has been fairly stable over the last 30 years. (The two different findings are not formally incompatible since there could well have been changing patterns of earnings within occupational classes; although see Erikson and Goldthorpe (2010) for a discussion of the divergent findings.[1]) All researchers, however, do agree that there is less intergenerational mobility in Britain than in many other highly developed societies (see, for example, Breen, 2004), and all main political parties have taken the issue seriously. As Harriet Harman argued in her introduction to the report of the National Equality Panel:

---

[*] Anthony Heath is Professorial Fellow and University Professor of Sociology at Nuffield College, Oxford University. Nan Dirk de Graaf is Official Fellow at Nuffield College, Oxford University. Yaojun Li is Professor of Sociology at the University of Manchester.

> [Equality matters] for individuals, who deserve to … have the opportunity to fulfil their potential … for the economy, because the economy that will succeed in the future [is], not one which is blinkered by prejudice and marred by discrimination; for the society, because an equal society is more cohesive … (Harman, 2010: v)

Our concern in this chapter, however, is not with resolving debates about actual levels of social mobility but to explore people's perceptions of their own occupational mobility, their perceptions of the routes to upward mobility and their perceptions of the inequalities between the positions in the occupational structure to which mobility gives access. Sociologists have often argued that it is people's perceptions that will determine how they respond to events. This is particularly likely to be the case with social mobility, as the statistical techniques that sociologists and economists use to measure mobility are likely to be completely opaque to most lay people, including most policy makers. Ordinary people will have no direct experience of the abstract concepts used by social scientists such as 'relative social mobility' or of the measures used, such as 'odds ratios'. But they may nonetheless have perceptions of whether or not they themselves have moved up the social ladder, compared with their mothers and fathers, whether there have been unfair obstacles to their attempts to climb the ladder, and whether the gaps between the rungs have become larger.

People's perceptions of unfair obstacles are likely to be of particular significance, both in terms of generating pressures for reform and in terms of the wider legitimacy of elite institutions. Perceptions that access to higher-level positions is unfairly blocked can also lead to a lack of effort – 'there's no point in trying' – and can in turn become a self-fulfilling prophecy.

Broadly speaking, Britain officially subscribes to an ethos of equal opportunities and meritocracy, where one's life chances should depend on one's own talents and effort. As the National Equality Panel (NEP) argued:

> … the crucial test of whether inequalities in outcomes are seen as fair or unfair will depend on whether they reflect choices made against a background where the opportunities open to people were equal …, or whether they stem from aspects of their lives over which they have manifestly little control. (NEP, 2010: 4)

The latest *British Social Attitudes* survey confirms that equality of opportunity is indeed an ideal to which the great majority of the public subscribe. As many as 95 per cent of people agree[2] with the statement *"In a fair society every person should have an equal opportunity to get ahead."*

One of the key questions that we will attempt to answer in this chapter is whether people in Britain feel that the opportunities to gain access to advantageous outcomes are indeed fair or whether they depend on prior privileges open only to the few. However, the NEP seems to assume that fair access and equal opportunities will be sufficient to justify inequality of outcomes. In contrast we would argue that fair access may indeed be a necessary condition for inequalities of outcome to be seen as fair, but it may well not be a sufficient condition. People may still object to the magnitude of the inequalities in pay and reward given nowadays to top jobs, even if the routes to these top jobs are seen to be entirely fair and open. In other words, as well as looking at rates of mobility and at the fairness of the mobility chances open to people, we also need to consider the perceived fairness of the outcomes to which mobility gives access.

As part of the *International Social Survey Programme* (ISSP; further information on the ISSP can be found in Appendix 1 of this report.), *British Social Attitudes* in 2009 carried a number of questions on perceptions of occupational mobility, of the factors perceived to be associated with 'getting ahead', and of the acceptability of the inequalities in outcomes for those who have got ahead. These questions replicated similar questions asked in previous rounds, with some of the questions going back to 1987.

In the first section of this chapter we look at trends in perceptions of occupational mobility. Are people now less likely to think than people 20 years ago that they have been upwardly mobile? And how do these perceptions relate to more 'objective' sociological measures of occupational mobility?

In the second section we then look at people's perceptions of what is needed in order to get ahead. To what extent do people perceive the factors involved to be ones that would normally be regarded as legitimate such as the 'meritocratic' factors of effort and educational achievement? Or are they rather less legitimate ones such as coming from a privileged background or who you know? How have these perceptions changed over time? Is there a growing groundswell of discontent about what it takes to get ahead? And is it the case that, as previous scholars have often argued, the successful are more likely to take a favourable view of the legitimacy of the processes involved, whereas the unsuccessful are more likely to view them as illegitimate?

In the third section we shift our attention from perceptions of processes of mobility to perceptions of the nature of the positions themselves, especially their level of reward. How acceptable do people find the current inequalities between occupational positions? And is it the case that people who think that the access routes to these positions are fair and open are also more likely to find the outcomes fair and legitimate?

Perceived social mobility

We begin, then, by looking at people's perception of their own mobility; that is, at their own occupational status relative to that of their fathers. In 2009, *British Social Attitudes* asked a question that was first asked in 1987, and which therefore allows us to chart trends in people's perceptions of their occupational mobility over the last 22 years. Unfortunately the original question asked only about mobility compared with one's father, although nowadays one would also want to ask about mobility compared with one's mother, too.

We asked:

> *Please think of your present job (or your last one if you don't have*
> *one now)*
>
> *If you compare this job with the job your father had when you were*
> *16, would you say that the level or status of your job is (or was)*
>
> *Much higher than your father's*
> *Higher*
> *About equal*
> *Lower*
> *Much lower than your father's*
> *I have never had a job*

Table 2.1 shows the trends over time.

Table 2.1 Perceived rates of intergenerational occupational mobility, 1987–2009

	1987	1992	1999	2009
Level/status of job is ...	%	%	%	%
... much higher than father's	16	18	14	12
... higher than father's	30	30	26	27
... about equal	26	27	27	28
... lower than father's	17	14	15	16
... much lower than father's	4	5	7	7
... never had a job	2	2	1	1
Base	*1212*	*1066*	*804*	*958*

Two features stand out from Table 2.1. The first concerns perceived 'long-range' mobility, that is, people thinking that they are in a *much* higher or much lower position than their fathers. In all four years, perceived long-range upwards or downwards mobility was relatively rare. Thus only around 20 per cent of people in each year thought that their position was much higher or much lower than that of their father. More detailed investigation shows that people who believed that they had experienced such long-range mobility were typically ones who had moved from semi- or unskilled manual origins to professional or managerial positions, or *vice versa*. And standard accounts of 'objective' occupational mobility also show that such long-range mobility is relatively rare (e.g. Goldthorpe, 1987).

   Second, again in all four years, there were more people who thought that they had been upwardly mobile than people who thought that they had experienced downwards mobility. Thus in the most recent survey, 39 per cent think that they are in a higher job than their fathers (combining both the responses "much higher" and "higher"), while only 23 per cent think they are lower. This perceived excess of upwards over downwards mobility accords well with the data from sociologists' 'objective' measures of mobility based on comparisons of fathers' and sons' (or daughters') occupational positions: over the last half-century, Britain has seen an expansion of higher-level managerial and professional occupations and a contraction of traditional working-class or manual jobs (see, for example, Li and Heath, 2010, Table 6.1). There has thus been greater 'room at the top' for sons as compared with their fathers, whose occupational careers were typically shaped some 20 to 25 years earlier.

So far, then, the results for subjective perceptions of mobility are in close accord with standard sociological accounts. When we turn to trends over time, however, the two stories diverge. Whereas sociologists have typically found no change over time in overall rates of occupational mobility, people's perceptions are more pessimistic. They give a story of a lower level of perceived upwards mobility in the most recent decade, while perceived downwards mobility has remained stable or if anything increased too. The changes are most noticeable in the case of 'long-range' upwards – which has declined from 16 per cent in 1987 to 12 per cent in 2009 – and of long-range downwards mobility – which has increased from four per cent to seven per cent in 2009. These are not especially large changes, but the direction of change seems clear enough (and the differences between 1987 and 2009 are statistically significant). So in this respect the public's reports tally with the analysis of the pessimists such as Blanden and Machin who have found declining earnings mobility in the more recent period.

It is naturally of considerable interest to check whether these perceived changes correspond at all closely to what might be (somewhat misleadingly) termed the 'objective' patterns of change in mobility as measured by sociologists from data on the occupations of fathers and sons (or daughters). We have used data from the General Household Survey for 1987, 1992 and 2005 (the most recent available) and from the British Household Panel Study for 1999 in order to estimate 'objective' measures of long-range upwards, short-range upwards, long-range downwards, short-range downwards and, of course, intergenerational stability broadly comparable to the structure of Table 2.1.

In estimating the percentages we have divided occupations into three broad classes. Our highest class is the 'salariat', which is composed of professional and managerial workers in relatively secure salaried positions with occupational pensions and the like. These would generally be regarded as the most desirable positions in the labour market, although we must remember that there will be very considerable variation within this class between those in senior posts and those in more junior posts. Our lowest class is composed of semi- and unskilled workers in manual or personal service occupations (described as 'routine' positions in official classifications). We can term this the class of 'routine' workers. In between these two classes comes what we can term the 'intermediate' class containing positions such as clerical, shopkeepers and trades people, foremen, technicians and skilled manual workers. (This classification corresponds broadly to those used by sociologists such as Goldthorpe, 1987; Goldthorpe and Mills, 2008[3]).

We then define long-range mobility as any intergenerational movement between the salariat and the routine class, while short-range mobility is defined as movements between these two classes and the intermediate class. It is important to recognise that the exact amount of mobility that we find will depend on how many classes we identify. Sociologists often use a seven-class schema developed by John Goldthorpe and his colleagues, and if we were to use this more elaborate scheme we would inevitably find more mobility and less stability. However, our concern here is not with the absolute level of mobility but with the trends over time. We would not expect the trends to differ much between our three-class classification and more elaborate ones.

The results are shown in Table 2.2.

Table 2.2 'Objective' rates of intergenerational occupational mobility, 1987–2009[4]

	1987	1992	1999	2009
Mobility between classes	%	%	%	%
Long-range upwards	4	4	5	7
Short-range upwards	24	26	28	27
Stable	47	46	46	43
Short-range downwards	24	21	18	21
Long-range downwards	2	3	3	3
Base	10,297	12,080	6,931	8,839

Sources: General Household Survey (1987, 1992, 2005); British Household Panel Survey (1999). All respondents aged 18 and over, with no upper age limit, classified according to present or last main job

Table 2.2 shows even less long-range mobility than people had perceived in Table 2.1. However, as we noted above, this is partly an artefact of how many classes we have distinguished and where we have drawn the boundaries between them. The more important difference between the two tables, however, is in the character of the trends. Whereas Table 2.1 had shown a decline in long-range upwards mobility (and something of a decline in short-range upwards mobility, too), Table 2.2 shows the reverse, with both long-range and short-range upwards mobility increasing over time. This is a striking disparity between the 'subjective' and 'objective' trends.

How are we to account for this discrepancy in the trends shown by Tables 2.1 and 2.2? One possibility is that people, when interpreting whether their own occupation is at a higher or lower level or status than that of their father, are taking into account their social standing relative to other people. Sociologists on the other hand tend to focus on access to certain types of occupation, which are assumed to have a fairly constant character over time.

One of the key points that sociologists make is that the size of the salariat has been growing – which is why there is increasing 'room at the top' and hence more upwards mobility. And this is indeed what we find in the data on which Table 2.2 is based: in 1987, 30 per cent of the population were in the salariat, whereas by 2005 this had increased to just over 40 per cent. However, someone who occupies a position at the bottom of the salariat would, in 2005, have 39 per cent of the population 'above' him, whereas someone in the same position in 1987 would have had only 29 per cent of people above him. His or her relative standing was thus lower in 2005 than it would have been 20 years before. So someone who is a junior manager today, and whose father was also a junior manager 20 years earlier, may feel that he has slipped down the occupational ranking since there will now be many more people above him in the ranking than there were in his father's time.

In other words, in answering our questions, people may be thinking about where they stand in the ranking, whereas sociologists typically consider the employment conditions of the job that they hold. This has interesting parallels with debates over educational measurement. Educationists make a distinction between 'norm-referenced' and 'criterion-referenced' measurement; a norm-referenced test measures whether the test-taker did better or worse than other people who took the test, whereas a criterion-referenced test measures whether the test-taker has reached a specified standard or criterion (such as being able to add two single-digit numbers together). In effect we believe that people may well be taking a norm-referenced approach to social standing, whereas sociologists typically take a criterion-referenced approach to the measurement of social mobility.

This may also explain why people's subjective reports are more in accord with the judgements of the economists about trends in social mobility. Economists typically look at movement between percentile categories, such as the top and bottom 10 per cent of earners, which is, in effect, a norm-referenced approach and essentially focuses on people's relative standing within the income hierarchy. It would seem, then, on this evidence, that the economists' findings may well be vindicated by the public's approach to understanding social mobility.

Perceptions of what is needed to get ahead

We turn next to consider whether this decline in perceived mobility is associated with any decline in the extent to which people think that access to elite occupations has become more slanted towards people from privileged backgrounds and less based on the kinds of principle, such as meritocracy, that are generally regarded as legitimate in a liberal democracy that espouses equality of opportunity.

Meritocracy was once famously defined by Michael Young, in his satire *The*

Rise of the Meritocracy (1958), as a situation where positions were allocated on the basis of 'IQ plus effort'. Nowadays, sociologists and policy makers would regard meritocracy as more a matter of whether people were allocated on the basis of their formal achievements (such as their educational qualifications) and effort as opposed to a society where allocation was governed by 'ascriptive' factors such as family background, race or gender. There have been heated debates about whether Britain is, in fact, a meritocracy (similar in some ways to the debates about mobility in Britain) but the sociological consensus has largely been that both achieved and ascribed factors continue to be important (see, for example, Saunders, 1995; Lampard, 1996; Marshall and Swift, 1996).

As part of the ISSP module we asked a number of questions that tapped the extent to which the public (as opposed to sociologists) believes that various achieved and ascribed characteristics affect people's chance of getting ahead. We asked the following:

> *To begin, we have some questions about opportunities for getting ahead ... Please tick one box for each of these to show how important you think it is for getting ahead in life ...*
>
> *How important is ...*
> *... coming from a wealthy family?*
> *... having well-educated parents?*
> *... having a good education yourself?*
> *... having ambition?*
> *... hard work?*
> *... knowing the right people?*
> *... having political connections?*
> *... giving bribes?*
> *... a person's ethnicity?*
> *... a person's religion?*
> *... being born a man or a woman?*

The response codes are "essential", "very important", "fairly important", "not very important", "not important at all", and "can't choose". Most of these questions had also been asked in the three previous rounds of the ISSP module.

The various items correspond to different theories about what are the main influences on who gets ahead. One theory is the classic meritocratic theory, which corresponds to the ideals of a liberal society such as contemporary Britain, to which we have already alluded. The items "having a good education" and "hard work" clearly belong to the meritocratic theory as, perhaps, does "ambition".

A second set of items, "knowing the right people", "having political connections" and "bribes" corresponds to sociological theories about the role of contacts and connections in obtaining desirable occupations (see, for example, Granovetter, 1973; Lin *et al,.* 1981). These would generally be seen as non-meritocratic factors which give insiders an advantage in the competition for top jobs and which serve to exclude outsiders or people from non-elite backgrounds. In the British context we would not expect bribery to be seen as a major factor, and its inclusion in the list is more because the ISSP is also conducted in countries where bribery and corruption are seen to be endemic.

Thirdly we have the items "coming from a wealthy family", "well-educated parents", "ethnicity", "religion" and "being born a man or a woman" which would normally be seen as ascriptive factors. That is, these are all largely matters connected with the family that one is born into and over which one has no choice oneself. Religion does not fit all that well into this group, since one can, of course, choose to convert to or leave a religion, although in general there is strong tendency for people to 'inherit' their religions from their families of origin.

To be sure, these theories are not mutually exclusive. For example, social connections might be one of the main mechanisms which explain why white men from wealthy backgrounds tend to be advantaged when competing for jobs, or why women or ethnic minorities are excluded from such positions. Furthermore, some sociologists would argue that the chances of obtaining a good education are crucially dependent upon one's family background, and in that sense is not nearly so 'meritocratic' as it appears at first sight. Indeed, as we noted above, most sociologists would tend to argue that, in a country like Britain, all three sorts of explanation have a role to play in explaining 'who gets ahead', although they disagree about the relative importance of the different factors. Table 2.3, then, shows what people think about their importance.

Table 2.3 Perceptions of what is important for getting ahead, 1987–2009

	1987	1992	1999	2009
% saying factor is essential or very important				
Meritocratic factors				
Hard work	84	84	n/a	84
Good education	72	74	n/a	74
Ambition	79	74	n/a	71
Non-meritocratic factors				
Knowing the right people	39	35	41	33
Having political connections	7	7	n/a	6
Giving bribes	n/a	n/a	n/a	2
Ascriptive factors				
Well-educated parents	27	28	n/a	31
Wealthy family	21	15	19	14
A person's religion	5	3	n/a	9
A person's race/ethnicity	16	15	n/a	8
Being born a man or a woman	11	12	n/a	8
Base	*1212*	*1066*	*804*	*958*

n/a = not asked

The great majority of people see the meritocratic items, namely "having a good education oneself" and "hard work", as either essential or very important. Over three-quarters think these are crucial, and the figure has stayed fairly constant over time. There is no sign in Table 2.3 that these two meritocratic principles are perceived to be on the decline in Britain, although there is some decline in the perceived importance of ambition. Possibly this decline reflects the circumstances at the time of the 1987 survey when Thatcherism, with its emphasis on opportunities for the aspirational members of society, was at its height.

However, many people feel that meritocracy is not the only game in town. Family background – "having well-educated parents" – is also seen to be crucial by around a third of people, as is "knowing the right people". However, there is little sign that these elements of privilege are seen to be more important today than they were previously. In fact, there have been slight declines in the percentage who think that "coming from a wealthy background" or "knowing the right people" is essential or very important, although this is balanced by a slight increase in the percentage who think that "having well-educated parents" is essential or very important. And it is reassuring that very few people see political connections, and even fewer see bribes, to be very important.

Markedly less important, too, in the eyes of the public are the other ascriptive factors – ethnicity (termed race in the two earlier surveys), religion and gender. Indeed, there is something of a decline in the percentage of people who think that ethnicity and gender are very important for getting ahead.

If we carry out a factor analysis (further information on factor analysis can be found in Appendix I of this report) of these items,[5] in essence checking how the people's answers about different items are correlated, we find three main dimensions only one of which corresponds perfectly to one of the three sociological theories described above. One dimension corresponds to the classic 'meritocratic' principles of a good education and hard work, together with ambition. A second dimension might be interpreted as one focusing on 'privilege', broadly defined. This dimension includes coming from a wealthy background, having well-educated parents (although this particular item is also quite strongly related to the meritocratic dimension) as well as the non-meritocratic factors of knowing the right people, and having political connections. A third dimension covers the 'ascribed' characteristics of race/ethnicity, gender and religion.

It is interesting that people tend to link coming from a wealthy background and having well-educated parents with knowing the right people and political connections, rather than with ethnicity, religion or gender. Possibly people believe that different obstacles, such as discrimination, are faced by women or ethnic minorities and that the issues around these ascribed factors amount to more than (as could be the case for coming from a wealthy background and having well-educated parents) simply a matter of lacking the right connections. This would not be an unreasonable interpretation, although we do not have the data to investigate it further in this chapter. (For details of the factor analyses see Tables A1 and A2 in the appendix to this chapter.)

So the perception of British society which people have is one of qualified meritocracy: most people think that effort, ambition and education are important, but many also think that privilege in the form of family background and/or connections are important, too. In this respect our respondents are rather good sociologists. Standard sociological accounts indicate that education is the single most important influence on one's success, but that family background is also important – even among people with similar educational levels (e.g. Heath *et al.*, 1992). Many sociologists have also emphasised the importance of social connections in finding good jobs, while other sociologists have emphasised the barriers that ethnic minorities and women experience (Heath and Yu, 2005; Joshi, 2005).

To fully understand how people view what it takes to 'get ahead', we need to know the relative weight that people place on the importance of each of these three dimensions. Who thinks that only one of these dimensions explains why some people get ahead and others do not, and who thinks that the mechanisms are more nuanced? To look at this issue, we classified people into three main types:

- Utopians: who think that the meritocratic factors of education and effort (or ambition) are the only ones that are either essential or very important, and who do not give so much weight to the non-meritocratic factors.

- Realists: who think that in addition to the meritocratic factors, at least one of the main non-meritocratic factors (wealthy family, well-educated parents, knowing the right people, political connections, ethnicity, religion or gender) is also essential or very important.

- Cynics: who think that none of the meritocratic factors are either essential or very important.

What we find is that the realists are the most numerous group amounting to 53 per cent of the sample in 2009, with a fair number of utopians (41 per cent) and very few cynics (only 6 per cent). In line with the detailed results of Table 2.3, there is rather little change over time in the percentages of utopians, realists and cynics. In 1987 there were fewer utopians (only 37 per cent) and more realists (59 per cent), but in 1992 the percentages were almost identical to those from the most recent survey.

Our next question is whether people's own mobility experiences colour their perceptions of what it takes to get ahead. Are the upwardly mobile more likely to adopt the utopian view, while the downwardly mobile are more likely to be[come] cynics? Theorists have often suggested that people who have done well out of the current system will take a more favourable view of it, whereas those who have not done so well will be more cynical about it. Table 2.4 gives us our answer.

Table 2.4 Subjective intergenerational mobility for utopians, realists and cynics

		Utopians	Realists	Cynics	Base
Level/status of job is ...					
... much higher than father's	%	43	53	4	111
... higher than father's	%	45	53	3	259
... about equal	%	40	50	10	269
... lower than father's	%	40	53	7	160
... much lower than father's	%	33	60	7	69
All	%	41	53	6	868

Table 2.4 suggests that subjective mobility experiences have only a weak relationship with people's perceptions of what it takes to get ahead. As had been expected, there is a tendency for the upwardly mobile to be somewhat more utopian and less cynical in their views, and for the downwardly mobile to be less utopian and more realistic. But the differences are very modest and certainly do not suggest any especial crisis in the legitimacy of British institutional arrangements.

Further analysis of other possible drivers of these perceptions, such as people's 'objective' mobility experiences, their occupational standing, their educational level and their wealth, all produce similarly modest relationships in the expected direction. People who have missed out are indeed slightly more cynical, while those who have got to the top take a somewhat rosier view, but there is no great gulf in perceptions between those at the top and the bottom. People differ in their perceptions of what it takes to get ahead, but the differences in perception are only weakly structured by one's own social position in society.

Outcomes

So far, then, we find that the declining rates of subjective social mobility have not been associated with a perception that meritocracy is waning, and we have seen no sign of a growing groundswell of discontent about the avenues for getting ahead. However, as we emphasised earlier, a perception that meritocracy is the major determinant of who gets ahead should not necessarily be taken to indicate that the distribution of outcomes will also be regarded as fair and legitimate. People may be reasonably happy with what it takes to climb the ladder, but they may not be so happy about the height of the ladder. This is an empirical matter to which we now turn.

We have regularly asked the following question about the actual and the appropriate level of earnings of a range of jobs, covering both highly paid positions such as company chairmen or cabinet ministers and lower-paid jobs such as unskilled factory workers or shop assistants.

We would like to know what you think people in these jobs actually earn. Please write in how much you think they usually earn each year before taxes

First, about how much do you think a doctor in general practice earns?
The chairman of a large national corporation?
A shop assistant?
An unskilled worker in a factory?
A cabinet minister in the UK government?

Next, what do you think people in these jobs ought to be paid – how much do you think they should earn each year before taxes, regardless of what they actually get?

In Table 2.5 we show the median answers to these questions. (That is, half the respondents gave an amount below the figure shown in the table, and half gave an amount above it.)

Table 2.5 Median perceptions of what job earnings actually are and what they should be, 1987–2009

	1987		1992		1999		2009	
	Earns	Should earn	Earns	Should earn	Earns	Should earn	Earns	Should earn
	£	£	£	£	£	£	£	£
Chairman, large national company	75,000	45,000	100,000	60,000	125,000	75,000	200,000	100,000
Cabinet minister	35,000	25,000	50,000	40,000	60,000	45,000	85,000	60,000
GP	20,000	20,000	30,000	34,000	35,000	40,000	70,000	69,000
Owner, small shop	10,000	11,000	17,000	20,000	n/a	n/a	n/a	n/a
Skilled factory worker	10,000	10,000	12,500	15,000	15,000	18,000	n/a	n/a
Unskilled factory worker	6,000	7,000	8,000	10,000	10,000	12,000	13,000	16,000
Farm worker	6,000	8,000	9,000	12,000	n/a	n/a	n/a	n/a
Shop assistant	n/a	n/a	7,500	10,000	9,000	12,000	12,000	16,000
Base (minimum)	*1024*	*995*	*943*	*908*	*660*	*623*	*1709*	*1661*

Figures are not adjusted for inflation
n/a = not asked

There are several striking findings. First, we can see that people clearly accept the notion of higher pay for 'top' jobs. There is a clear hierarchy with respondents feeling that the chairman of a large national company should get paid more than a cabinet minister or GP, with a skilled factory worker or owner of a small shop coming in the middle of the earnings hierarchy, and a shop assistant, farm worker or unskilled factory earning rather less.

Second, it is equally clear that, in all four years in which these questions have been asked, people felt that the actual earnings of people in these jobs were considerably more unequal than they ought to be. For example, in 1987, the median perceived earnings of the chairman of a large national company were 12.5 times that of a farm worker or unskilled factory worker (£75,000/£6000), whereas the appropriate or fair ratio was thought to be slightly over 6:1 (£45,000/£8000). In fact, in all four years people on average felt that the earnings of the top jobs should be reduced while those of the bottom jobs should be raised (see the chapter by Rowlingson *et al.* in this report for an examination of attitudes to income inequality and redistribution).

It is also worth recording that people almost certainly underestimate the actual salaries of the top earners. Getting reliable estimates of top salaries is almost as contentious as measuring social mobility, but we can at least get authoritative measures of cabinet ministers' pay. In 2009, for example, the actual salaries of cabinet ministers were, at £144,500, over 50 percent higher than the £85,000 estimated by our median respondent.[6] And in 2006/7 (the latest year for which data have been published) GPs in England typically earned around £110,000, over 50 per cent higher than people's median estimate of £70,000.[7] We are not brave enough to try and estimate the actual salaries of chairs of large national companies (partly because of the uncertainty of who exactly is included in this category). However, the National Equality Panel reported that, in 2008, the average remuneration of the chief executive officers (CEOs) of the FTSE top 100 companies was £2.4 million a year, while that of the next largest 250 companies was £1.1 million. To be sure, a CEO technically is a different position from the Chair of the Board, while the FTSE top 100 companies include many multinational companies (such as BP, for example) and not just large national companies. We would guess, then, that people substantially underestimate these salaries, probably to an even greater extent than they have underestimated the salaries of GPs and cabinet ministers.

At the lower end, in contrast, people's perceptions appear to be more accurate. From the 2009 Labour Force Survey[8] we have been able to estimate that the average hourly earnings of women in the 'routine' class (which would include shop assistants) were £6.55. This would gross up (assuming a 36-hour working week and payment for all 52 weeks of the year) to somewhere around the £12,000 estimated by our median respondent for shop assistants (whom people might typically assume to be women). Average earnings are rather higher for male routine workers, which people have therefore probably underestimated. However, they are probably as not as far out as they are with the GPs and cabinet ministers. Our estimate (from the Labour Force Survey) of hourly earnings for male routine workers in 2009 was £8.29, which would gross up to around £15,000 per annum compared with our median respondent's estimate of £13,000 for unskilled factory workers (shown in Table 2.5). But this would still represent an overestimate of only 15 per cent. So the 'true' ratios between the earnings of different occupations are very likely to be considerably larger than those perceived by people, and reported in Table 2.6.

The third striking point that we take from Table 2.5 involves changes in people's perceptions over the time period. There is a clear pattern for earnings inequalities to be perceived to be larger in 2009 than in any of the previous years. Table 2.6 shows how the ratios (taking the unskilled factory worker's median perceived earnings as the base) have changed over time. In particular the ratio between top (chairman of large national company) and bottom (unskilled worker) is perceived to have widened from 13:1, where it had been in all three previous surveys, to 15:1 in 2009. Similarly the cabinet minister:unskilled worker ratio in 2009 is the highest that it has been in any of the four surveys (up to nearly 7:1 from the approximately 6:1 that it had been in the three previous surveys), and so is the GP:unskilled worker ratio (up to over 5:1 compared with less than 4:1 in the previous surveys). So there is very clearly a perception in 2009 of widening differentials.

It is difficult to determine the extent to which people's perceptions of increased inequalities between 1999 and 2009 are borne out in reality. The salaries of cabinet ministers are readily available and are shown to have increased by 30 per cent between 1999 and 2009, rather less than our median respondent's estimate of an increase of 42 per cent over this period.[9] It is very likely that the MPs, expenses row and the media attention on MPs, remuneration led people to feel that cabinet ministers, too, had gained excessively over this period. On the other hand, there can be little doubt that GPs' salaries did increase very substantially over this period following the renegotiation of their contracts.[10] And the National Equality Panel shows very clearly that, in real terms, the remuneration of CEOs of large companies rose by very much more between 1999 and 2008 than did those of the average employee.[11]

Table 2.6 Perceived earnings ratios relative to those of an unskilled factory worker, 1987–2009

	1987		1992		1999		2009	
	Earns	Should earn	Earns	Should earn	Earns	Should earn	Earns	Should earn
	(ratio)	(ratio)	(ratio)	(ratio)	(ratio)	(ratio)	(ratio)	(ratio)
Chair, large national company	13	6	13	6	13	6	15	6
Cabinet minister	6	4	6	4	6	4	7	4
GP	3	3	4	3	4	3	5	4
Unskilled factory worker	1	1	1	1	1	1	1	1
Base (minimum)	1024	995	943	908	660	623	1709	1661

Overall, then, the public is probably not too far off the mark in thinking that differentials had increased between 1999 and 2009. But it probably greatly under estimates the true extent of the increase.

The fourth and final striking point is how stable people's views have been on what the income differentials *should* be (Table 2.6). For example, the ratio for what a company chairman should earn was six times that of the unskilled factory worker in 2009, the same as it had been in 1987, 1992 and 1999. Similarly, the ratio for what cabinet ministers should earn was the same in 2009 as it had been in the three previous surveys. Only in the case of GPs do we see a marked change, with an increase in the acceptable ratio between 1999 and 2009.

Overall, then, it would seem that people's judgements about what the differentials in pay should be have remained remarkably stable over time, despite the recent turmoil over the excessive wages of bankers, and MPs, expenses. There is a clear acceptance of differentials, and a clear and stable understanding of what those differentials should be. There is also a long-standing perception that actual differentials are substantially larger than the ones that *should* prevail. In 2009 there has been a clear change, with the public perceiving that the gap between 'is' and 'ought' has widened, with top earners' salaries pulling away.

A key question is whether people's views about the salary differentials are related to their views about the extent to which a privileged background or connections are important for getting ahead. In other words, was the National Equality Panel right to argue that:

> ... the crucial test of whether inequalities in outcomes are seen as fair or unfair will depend on whether they reflect choices ... [that] stem from aspects of their lives over which they have manifestly little control. (NEP, 2010: 4)

We do this by comparing the views of our utopians, realists and cynics on the salary levels of different occupations (Table 2.7). What are the views of each about whether the chairman of a large national company, a cabinet minister, a GP and an unskilled manual worker are paid 'about right' or 'too little'? We might expect, given the arguments of the National Equality Panel, that people who think that merit is the crucial factor in getting ahead (the people whom we have termed 'utopians') might find the pay of the high earners more acceptable, while people who think that getting ahead depends partly on privilege or on ascribed factors that are outside people's control (whom we have termed 'realists') will take a more negative view.

For Table 2.7, the proportion of people saying that a particular occupation is paid 'about right' or 'too little' has been calculated by comparing the salary that people say that the occupation is paid with what they say they ought to be paid (for more detail, see note 12). So, as we can see, the vast majority of people feel that unskilled factory workers earn about right or too little. There is, then, a very clear gradient, with fewer and fewer people thinking that GPs' earnings, cabinet ministers' earnings and chairmen of large companies earnings are about right or too little.

Table 2.7 Perceptions of different occupational pay levels, by perceptions of meritocracy[12]

	Utopians	Realists	Cynics	All
% saying that the occupation is paid about right or too little				
Chairman, large national company	21	18	33	20
Cabinet minister	25	34	29	30
GP	67	58	69	63
Unskilled factory worker	96	95	96	96
Base (minimum)	*340*	*425*	*51*	*816*

Table 2.7 does not support the arguments of the National Equality Panel posed above. In fact we see little or no sign of utopians finding the pay of high earners more acceptable or of realists taking a more negative view. There is pretty general disapproval of the earnings of the chairmen of large national companies, and the difference between the utopians and the realists is not statistically significant. In the case of cabinet ministers' earnings, it is the realists not the utopians who find their level of pay more acceptable. Only in the case of GPs do we find the expected pattern, with utopians taking a more favourable view of their level of earnings. Meanwhile all three groups are united in thinking that unskilled factory workers earn too little or about right.

So perceptions of the role of privilege in 'getting ahead' do not, on this evidence, show any consistent or strong relationship with the acceptability of the rewards accruing to holders of high-level positions. While there is broad acceptance that meritocratic factors are important in getting ahead, there is also very broad rejection of the extent of the earnings differentials secured by those who have got ahead. And we should remember that the extent of the 'true' earnings differentials is almost certainly a great deal larger than the ones that people believe to be the case. In short, most people in Britain believe that there is, to a greater or lesser extent, a measure of equality of opportunity. But they do not believe that the outcomes are fair. In this respect, we cannot support the arguments of the National Equality Panel that inequalities in outcomes are acceptable to those who believe that society is meritocratic.

We must, however, admit one possible objection to our argument and analysis. The questions about what is important for 'getting ahead' did not specify particular types of occupation. It may well be that our respondents, when they answered this question, were thinking about rather broader occupational categories, such as our category of the 'salariat' (in which, as it happens, GPs are located) rather than about 'elite' occupations such as cabinet ministers and the chairmen of large national companies. While apologists for the extraordinary earnings of captains of industry and finance routinely tell us that these salaries are necessary in order to retain the 'best' people, we should not take it for granted that the general public agrees. It is an open question whether the general public 'buys' this argument, a question to which unfortunately our data do not contain an answer.

Conclusions

On the basis of our analysis, we can conclude, with reasonable confidence, that perceived social mobility has declined somewhat over time, more in line with economists' than with sociologists' analyses of the trends, but this has not been accompanied by any growing cynicism about the openness of routes for 'getting ahead'. In general, British people remain either 'utopians' or 'realists', believing that meritocratic factors are a major (or in the case of utopians the primary) route for getting ahead, although family background, connections and other ascriptive factors are also believed by the majority (the 'realists') to be equally important. There is no sign of an increase in cynicism. However, there has been a perception that earnings differentials have risen sharply between 1999 and 2009, especially for cabinet ministers and the chairmen of large national companies, and that they should not have done. Finally, there is little evidence that people's perceptions of the fairness of these outcomes is related to their perceptions of how meritocratic are the channels for getting ahead.

Our provisional conclusions, then, are that politicians and policy makers are probably wrong to assume that a socially mobile society is one that will necessarily be regarded as fair and socially just. The National Equality Panel is probably wrong to suggest that:

> ... the crucial test of whether inequalities in outcomes are seen as fair or unfair will depend on whether they reflect choices made against a background where the opportunities open to people were equal to start with. (NEP, 2010: 4)

While we do not have quite enough evidence to refute the NEP's argument entirely, since we do not know how fair access to those elite positions whose rewards have grown so disproportionately is perceived to be. We suspect that the British public does not agree that equality of opportunity necessarily justifies very large inequalities of outcome.

People in Britain, then, are not only rather good sociologists; they may also be rather good political philosophers and recognise that equality of opportunity is indeed not the same thing as equality of outcome.

Notes

1. Erikson and Goldthorpe (2010) have also shown that the family income variable in the 1958 data on which Blanden and Machin based their research is not of a comparable standard to that found in the 1970 data.

2. Answering using a five-point scale from "agree strongly" to "disagree strongly". The figures quoted combine the proportions who "agree strongly" and those who "agree".

3. Goldthorpe (1987) collapses his seven-class schema into three broad classes for the same kind of purpose. The major difference from our approach is that he classified class VI, the skilled manual class, together with his class VII (the semi- and unskilled manual class), whereas we have classified it as one of the intermediate classes. Our reason for doing so is that, as Goldthorpe explains elsewhere, his seven-class schema is not strictly ordered and that his classes III, IV, V and VI cannot be placed in any straightforward ordering. Movement between these classes would therefore be regarded as 'sideways'. It therefore seems desirable, when measuring rates of upwards and downwards mobility, to put them at the same level. We have, however, checked our findings about trends over time, re-classifying class VI into the lowest of our three classes. See Table A2 in the appendix to this chapter. As we can see, rates of long-range upwards mobility are as a result greater than those shown in Table 2.2, while rates of short-range upwards mobility are lower.   Table A2 also shows a high degree of stability over time, exactly in line with Goldthorpe and Mills' conclusions.

4. We coded father's and respondent's classes in all datasets on the basis of the Social-Economic Groups (SEG) using the conversion programme by Heath and McDonald (1987) but with the category for the armed forces removed due to the lack of ranking information (see also Goldthorpe and Mills, 2008). GHS 2005 does not have SEG for fathers. We coded the 35-category NsSEC derived from the original SOC codes (soc2kf) into the Goldthorpe classes according to Rose and Pevalin (2003: 8–10).

5. Using all four years of data.

6. The figure of £144,500 includes cabinet ministers' full parliamentary salaries. For full details see House of Commons Information Office (2009).

7. See NHS Information Centre for Health and Social Care (2009). However, we should note that this figure is more contentious and that salaried GPs earn considerably less than the figure quoted, which is for 'contractor' GPs, i.e. partners.

8. More information on the Labour Force Survey can be found at: http://www.ons.gov.uk/about-statistics/user-guidance/lm-guide/sources/household /lfs/index.html

9. The salaries of cabinet ministers increased from £111,300 in 1999 to the 2009 figure of £144,500.

10. The NHS Information Centre provides figures for the period 2002/3 to 2007/8 which show an increase of 46 per cent, and the increase is likely to have been much greater for the full 1999 to 2009 period covered by *British Social Attitudes*.

11. The NEP concluded: "For all employees, real earnings were roughly static between 2003 and 2008 …, but between 1999 and 2007 the real earnings of the CEOs of the top 100 companies more than doubled (reaching £2.4 million per year)" (NEP 2010: 42).

12. We constructed this variable as follows: people who gave a higher value for the actual earnings of a given occupation than they gave for what it ought to earn were classified as believing that the occupation was paid too much. Those who gave the same figures for actual earnings and for what ought to be earned were classified as

thinking the earnings were 'about right', while those who gave a lower figure for the actual earnings than for the earnings that members of the occupation ought to earn were classified as thinking that it earned too little.

References

Blanden, J. and Machin, S. (2007), *Recent Changes in Intergenerational Mobility: Report for the Sutton Trust*, London: Sutton Trust

Breen, R. (2004), *Social Mobility in Europe*, Oxford: Oxford University Press

Cabinet Office (2008), *Getting on, getting ahead: A discussion paper: analysing the trends and drivers of social mobility*, London: Cabinet Office

Erikson, R. and Goldthorpe, J. (2010), 'Has social mobility in Britain decreased? Reconciling divergent findings on income and class mobility', *British Journal of Sociology*, **61(2)**: 211–230

Ermisch, J. and Nicoletti, C. (2007), 'Intergenerational earnings mobility: changes across cohorts in Britain', *The B E Journal of Economic Analysis and Policy,* 7

Goldthorpe, J.H. (1987), *Social Mobility and Class Structure in Modern Britain*, 2nd edition, Oxford: Oxford University Press

Goldthorpe, J.H. and Mills, C. (2008), 'Trends in intergenerational class mobility in modern Britain: evidence from national surveys, 1972–3005', *National Institute Economic Review*, **205**: 83–100

Granovetter, M. (1973), 'The strength of weak ties', *American Journal of Sociology*, **78(6)**: 1360–1380

Harman, H. (2010), 'Introduction', in National Equality Panel, *An Anatomy of Economic Inequality in the UK: report of the National Equality Panel*, London: Government Equalities Office

Heath, A. F. and McDonald, S.K. (1987), 'Social change and the future of the Left', *The Political Quarterly*, **58**: 364–377

Heath, A.F., Mills, C. and Roberts, J. (1992), 'Towards meritocracy – new evidence on an old problem', in Crouch, C. and Heath, A.F. (eds.), *Social Research and Social Reform: Essays in Honour of A.H. Halsey*, Oxford: Oxford University Press, pp. 217–243

Heath, A.F. and Yu, S. (2005), 'The puzzle of ethnic minority disadvantage', in Heath, A.F., Ermisch, J. and Gallie, D. (eds.), *Understanding Social Change*, Oxford: Oxford University Press, pp. 187–234

House of Commons Information Office (2009), *Ministerial salaries*. Factsheet M6, Members Services. Appendix A

Joshi, H. (2005), 'Gender and pay: some more equal than others', in Heath, A.F., Ermisch, J. and Gallie, D. (eds.), *Understanding Social Change*, Oxford: Oxford University Press, pp. 151–186

Kelley, S. and Kelley, C. (2009), 'Subjective social mobility: data from 30 nations', in Haller, M., Jowell, R. and Smith, Tom W. (eds.), *Charting the Globe: The International Social Survey Programme 1984–2009*, London: Routledge, pp. 106–124

Li, Y. and Heath, A. (2010), 'Struggling onto the ladder, climbing the rungs: employment status and class position by minority ethnic groups in Britain (1972–

2005)', in Stillwell, J., Norman, P., Thomas, C. and Surridge, P. (eds.), *Spatial and Social Disparities*, Dordrecht: Springer, pp. 83–97

Lin, N., Ensel, W. and Vaughn, J. (1981), 'Social resources and the strength of ties: structural factors in occupational attainment', *American Sociological Review*, **46**: 393–405

National Equality Panel (2010), *An Anatomy of Economic Inequality in the UK: report of the National Equality Panel*, London: Government Equalities Office

NHS Information Centre for Health and Social Care (2009), *GP Earnings and Expenses Enquiry 2006/7: Final Report*, available at http://www.ic.nhs.uk/webfiles/publications/

Rose, D. and Pevalin, D. (2003), *A Researcher's Guide to the National Statistics Socio-economic Classification*, London: Sage

Young, M. (1958), *The Rise of the Meritocracy, 1870–2023: an essay on education and equality*, London: Thames and Hudson

Acknowledgements

The *National Centre for Social Research* is grateful to the Economic and Social Research Council (grant number RES-062-23-1671) for their financial support which enabled us to ask the questions reported in this chapter. The views expressed are those of the authors alone.

The authors would like to thank Jane Roberts of the Nuffield College data library for her invaluable assistance in accessing and organising the *British Social Attitudes* data.

Appendix

Table A1 Factor analysis of the 'getting ahead' items, 2009 (N=892)

	Factor 1	Factor 2	Factor 3
Wealthy family	0.76		
Well-educated parents	0.58		0.39
Good education yourself			0.70
Ambition			0.80
Hard work			0.79
Knowing the right people	0.73		
Having political connections	0.73		
Giving bribes	0.48	0.40	
A person's race/ethnicity		0.78	
A person's religion		0.83	
Being born a man or a woman		0.73	
Eigenvalue	3.31	1.86	1.20

'Not answered' excluded but 'can't choose' included in base
Principal components extraction and varimax rotation

Table A2 'Objective' rates of intergenerational occupational mobility, 1987–2005, with skilled manual assigned to the lowest of the three classes

	1987	1992	1999	2009
	%	%	%	%
Long-range upwards	9.0	10.0	13.5	10.4
Short-range upwards	24.2	25.7	26.2	24.8
Stable	45.1	44.7	42.5	41.6
Short-range downwards	17.8	15.5	14.4	18.6
Long-range downwards	3.8	4.2	3.5	4.5
Base	1212	1066	804	958

3 One school of thought? Reactions to education policy

*Elizabeth Clery and Natalie Low**

What do the public think about the education system in Britain? In this chapter, we seek to answer this question, focusing on five key dimensions of compulsory school-level education. Firstly, to what extent should education be a priority for government spending, and on which particular elements of education should government focus its funds? Secondly, at what ages should compulsory school start and finish? Then, what topics and skills should schools teach as part of compulsory education, and what should the balance be between academic qualification and 'life skills'? Fourthly, how should children be assessed on what they have learnt? And lastly, how effectively do people think that secondary schools are currently performing?

Given the importance of the state education system in Britain, these questions are of perennial interest. All young people in Britain have the opportunity to receive 11 years of state-funded education, with education currently accounting for 13 per cent of central and local government spending.[1] And at the end of 13 years of Labour administration, it is particularly timely to take a look at public attitudes to compulsory education, and explore how these have changed over this period. They were last examined in *The 20th Report*, using data from the 2002 survey (Wragg and Jarvis, 2003). At that point, public attitudes on most issues around education policy had remained remarkably stable since the 1980s. However, despite this stability, and a marked lack of enthusiasm about the proliferation of exams, levels of public *satisfaction* with schools had increased. In the eight years that have elapsed since that last chapter, the Labour government introduced a variety of educational initiatives in England, with ambitions for a wider role for schools in the lives of the young people who attend them. Also, in recent years there have been high-profile debates – involving policymakers, academics, teaching staff, the media and the public – in several key areas of education policy, including when children should start and finish compulsory schooling and the role of examinations in assessing pupils.

* Elizabeth Clery and Natalie Low are both Research Directors at the *National Centre for Social Research*. Elizabeth Clery is Co-Director of the *British Social Attitudes* survey series.

So, in 2009, do people's attitudes reflect, endorse or sit at odds with educational policy under the Labour administration? And how is the public likely to react to a refocusing by the Coalition government of schools on the traditional spheres of curricular education and academic attainment?

In exploring what people think about compulsory education, a key consideration is how attitudes vary across different sections of the population. Are people's attitudes related to their own, or their children's, experiences of education, or by the recency of this experience? Or can attitudes be explained on the basis of broader socio-economic and cultural factors? By addressing these questions in relation to the five components of compulsory education examined in this chapter, we can begin to understand what underpins public attitudes to compulsory education and, thus, if and how we might expect these to change in the future.

Education policy under Labour and the future

Here we provide the policy backdrop against which public attitudes to compulsory education can be understood and interpreted. What have the policy developments in compulsory education been over the past decade in relation to the five dimensions we introduced at the start of the chapter – that is, its funding, duration, content, pupil assessment processes and schools' performance? And, what direction might the new government take on each of these elements of education policy?

Since public attitudes to education were last analysed in 2002, the UK as a whole has seen an increase in absolute spending on education, and education has remained a key priority across England, Scotland, Wales and Northern Ireland.[2] However, this situation is likely to change. While certain areas of education have been ring-fenced from the general cuts in spending announced by the Coalition government in 2010, it is already clear that this will not apply to major initiatives under the previous government's education policy, such as the Building Schools for the Future programme. Given this context, the first issue that this chapter will address is the extent to which the public sees education, and its various components, as priorities for government spending, and whether public views on spending appear to link to the relatively high levels of spending on education experienced over the last decade.

The ages at which a child should start and finish schooling has been a hotly debated topic. In England and Wales, children start school in the academic year in which they turn five (in practice, generally starting when they are aged four), while five is the legally enforceable compulsory age for starting school. In general, children start school on a full-time basis, although some local authorities offer initial part-time places or deferred starts for younger children.[3] Recently, the Cambridge Primary Review recommended a delay in the start of formal schooling to the age of six (Cambridge Primary Review, 2009), a practice that is adopted in many other European countries.

Currently, a young person can complete their compulsory education as early as age 16. However, the option to extend compulsory education or training to the age of 18 has been the subject of much discussion, generated in part by a focus on (and targets around) reducing the number of young people not in education, employment and training (so-called 'NEET's). The Labour government legislated to raise the participation age to 18 (a policy which extends beyond the option of simply staying in full-time education to include other forms of training such as apprenticeships and part-time education and training alongside employment). Current legislation requires the age to be raised from 2013 in England and Wales. The second issue that this chapter addresses is when the public thinks a young person should start and finish their compulsory education, examining how far people's views tally with current government policy and the proposed alternatives.

Government educational initiatives frequently focus on the content of what schools teach, and public attitudes on this issue form the third topic which the chapter considers. In England and Wales, the content of what schools teach has been determined by the statutory National Curriculum, although there has been a drift in recent years towards greater freedom in the classroom and less central prescription. Within the National Curriculum, the content of school-level education has expanded significantly in recent years, with an increased focus on non-academic areas. In England, this was influenced by wider changes in the provision of services for children and young people. The introduction of 'Every Child Matters' (ECM) agenda – developed in response to the death of Victoria Climbie and the subsequent inquiry – aimed to provide a more coherent network of support for children (Department for Education and Skills, 2003). The Children Act 2004 sought to create more 'joined up' services, allying health and social care agencies with schools and other relevant bodies. The involvement with schools in ECM and its associated key outcomes (for children to be healthy, stay safe, enjoy and achieve, make a positive contribution to society and achieve economic well-being) encouraged schools to consider their wider role in the lives of the young people whom they taught. In practical terms, this was manifested through key educational initiatives such as the Every Child programmes as well as ones such as the extended schools programme (now the extended services programme) which pushed schools beyond the traditional remit of academic achievement. However, recent efforts by the previous Labour administration to extend the compulsory curriculum to include personal, social and health education (which would have included sex and relationships education) were not successful. Moreover, the clear signal from the newly-elected Coalition government is that schools will need to re-focus on their traditional remit, with the newly renamed Department for Education's priority being one of "supporting teaching and learning".[4]

There have also been efforts to raise the status of vocational qualifications and training. In 2004, the Tomlinson report recommended the bringing together of academic and vocational qualifications into a single qualification for 14 to 19 year olds (Department for Education and Skills, 2004). The subsequent introduction of vocational diplomas alongside the existing GCSEs and A levels was at best a partial realisation of this recommendation, which sought to provide an alternative route for those groups traditionally less well served by existing qualifications. However, plans to introduce academic diplomas have now been scrapped by the Coalition government. Given this context, it will be interesting to see, in the section below on curriculum content, how far the public is in favour of the recent broader focus of schools – or of a return to a more focused academic remit – particularly its views on the balance between the teaching of academic qualifications *versus* practical skills and training.

One aspect of compulsory education which has received particular attention, and been the subject of much debate in recent years, is the methods used in the assessment of pupils. There have been moves away from the use of formal, external tests (referred to in this chapter as SATs (Standard Assessment Tests)), which have been abandoned in England for certain ages and subjects in favour of greater elements of teacher assessment. Continuing debate over the use and validity of the remaining SATs led to a partial boycott of the tests for 11 year olds in 2010. The call for reform of the testing procedures has been echoed in a number of areas, including the Report of the Expert Group in Assessment for the Department of Education (Department for Education and Skills, 2009), the Conservative Party (then in opposition) and teaching unions. Although future trends would seem to favour further reductions in the use and scale of external formal testing, it seems equally likely that some core testing will be maintained. The fourth question we address in the chapter is how far moves away from formal examination are in tune with public preferences for pupils' assessment.

The final question that we will consider is how effectively the public feels that secondary schools are currently performing in relation to their various remits. A key consideration will be the extent to which people assess the performance of secondary schools on the basis of personal experience. Do those with recent experiences of secondary-level education, either themselves or through their children, have particular views?

By definition, the *British Social Attitudes* survey series explores the attitudes and values of those living in England, Scotland and Wales. While Scotland has long had a separate education system, Scottish and Welsh devolution in 1999, which saw responsibility for schools and education being devolved to the two countries, has resulted in further differences emerging between the three countries in terms of education policies and their implementation. For instance, in Scotland there is more flexibility than elsewhere in the age at which children start school, while Wales has a reduced focus on examinations compared to the other two countries, having abandoned both SATs and performance tables in 2002. So, throughout the chapter, although we largely report on the views of 'the British public', where we have found that people in England, Scotland and Wales have different views on the education system, or indeed similar views despite having quite different systems, we have highlighted this in our discussions.

Education as a spending priority

The amount of funding allocated to compulsory education, and to particular elements within it, can be seen as the necessary pre-cursor for the decisions made around the policies that we explore in subsequent sections in this chapter – that is, the duration and content of compulsory education and the assessment of pupils' performance. For this reason, we begin by examining how important the public considers the funding of education and its various aspects to be within the realistic context in which it operates – as one of a number of competing social policy areas which might attract government attention and investment.

Since the inception of the *British Social Attitudes* survey series in 1983, the interview has in most years included the following question:

> *Here are some items of government spending*
> *Which of them, if any, would be your highest priority for **extra** spending?*
> *Please read through the whole list before deciding*
>
> *And which next?*

People are presented with a list of options from which to choose, as detailed in Table 3.1 below. The table presents the proportions of people who, at regular intervals since 1983, selected each option as their first or second choice for extra government spending.

What is striking about the answers provided over the past three decades is the degree of stability in public priorities for extra government spending. Health and education have always been the highest two priorities. In 2009, more than seven in ten people identify health as their first or second spending priority and almost six in ten ascribe this importance to education.

While the order of people's priorities has remained largely unchanged over time, there have been changes in the degrees of importance attached to different areas of government spending. In the early 1980s, education was regarded by around half of the British public to be one of the government's two main spending priorities. This proportion increased to seven in ten in 1997, coinciding with the election of the New Labour government and the widely publicised focus of Tony Blair on a policy of "education, education, education". Since then, the importance attached to government spending on education has declined a little, though not yet to the levels seen in the early 1980s. This may reflect the fact that, with sustained rises in government spending on education, people now perceive less of a need to provide extra spending on top of this. (Indeed, public reactions to shifts in public spending have been shown to be associated with its experiences of changes in spending levels, rather than with fluctuations in their actual abstract preferences for spending (Wlezien, 1995)).

Alternatively (or additionally), the decline in the proportion of people choosing education as a priority may reflect a rise in levels of support for other areas of government spending, arguably as a result of ongoing international and economic developments. In particular, 11 per cent of the public in 2009 highlight "help for industry" as their first or second priority for extra spending, a level of support that has not been witnessed since 1993 and may result from the impact of the recession on the fates of British companies. Moreover, defence, traditionally only a priority for a small minority, has rapidly been attracting more support: the proportion selecting defence as their first or second priority for extra government spending tripled between 2004 and 2009 – a trend likely to result from the ongoing presence of the British army in Iraq and Afghanistan and the widely publicised terrorist threat from Al-Queda. In other words, it seems likely that these very timely concerns are reducing the importance attached by the public to extra government spending in the traditional social policy fields of health and education. Certainly, we might expect the priority attached to spending on education and health to rise, as cuts to the comparatively high levels of spending provided in recent years are made in the coming years. Nevertheless, the data below make it clear that any spending re-prioritising will take place, not in isolation, but within the context of developments in a wide range of areas of government policy.

Table 3.1 First or second priorities for extra government spending, 1983–2009

	1983	1987	1990	1993	1997	2000	2003	2006	2009
	%	%	%	%	%	%	%	%	%
Health	63	79	81	70	78	81	79	75	73
Education	**50**	**56**	**63**	**57**	**70**	**64**	**63**	**60**	**59**
Housing	21	24	20	22	11	11	10	12	14
Police and prisons	8	8	7	11	10	10	12	17	12
Help for industry	29	12	6	14	8	5	4	4	11
Defence	8	4	2	3	3	3	3	6	9
Public transport	3	1	6	4	6	10	13	11	8
Roads	5	3	4	4	3	6	6	5	6
Social security	12	12	13	13	9	7	6	5	4
Overseas aid	1	1	1	2	1	1	1	3	2
Base	*1761*	*2847*	*2698*	*2945*	*1355*	*3426*	*4432*	*3240*	*3421*

Note: As the table adds together first and second priorities for extra spending, columns sum to 200 per cent

The priority ascribed by the public to extra spending on education therefore appears to link to the government's own publicised priorities and actual spending levels, as well as to wider socio-economic and international developments. But to what extent do individuals' personal experiences, values and concerns play a part in determining their spending priorities? While 59 per cent of the public select education as their first or second priority for extra spending in 2009, this proportion is much higher among certain groups who could be viewed as having particularly close links to the field of education – the young, those with a greater number of educational qualifications and those with children of current or recent school age. Two-thirds (66 per cent) of those aged 18 to 34 identify education as a priority area for extra spending, compared with half (49 per cent) of those aged 65 and over. Similarly, three-quarters (73 per cent) of those with children of current or recent school-age (aged 5 to18 years) prioritise education, compared with 55 per cent of those without children in this age group. For this group, as well as for younger respondents, compulsory education is an experience to which they are much closer than their counterparts (and possibly one about which they have a better memory of deficiencies which extra spending could address). In terms of qualifications, 70 per cent of those with a degree select education as one of their first two priorities for extra spending, compared to 45 per cent of those with no qualifications. Those with higher-level qualifications will have necessarily spent a longer period in education (albeit not all compulsory), meaning it is a life-stage in which they have invested more time than others (and potentially feel they have benefited more from).

While public support for education as an area for extra government spending appears to have declined as actual spending levels have risen, differences in spending levels on education in England, Scotland and Wales do not affect people's likelihood of prioritising it for extra spending. Specifically, despite Wales spending less on compulsory education per pupil than England (a fact which has received considerable media coverage in recent times), the priority given to education as an area for extra government spending in 2009 is almost identical in each of the three countries.

When considering whether to prioritise education for extra government spending, people could potentially be thinking about 'education' as a whole, or about one or more specific areas within it. To disentangle where people think extra spending within education should be directed, *British Social Attitudes* has included the following question throughout the lifetime of the survey series:

> *Which of the groups on this card, if any, would be your highest priority for extra government spending on education?*

The groups available as options for extra spending on education are shown in Table 3.2, alongside the proportions of people who selected each as their highest priority.

As with the previous question on government spending, it is striking that the order of people's priorities for extra government spending within education has remained relatively constant over time. The three elements of compulsory education attract more support than non-compulsory nursery and higher education. Among compulsory education, more often than not, secondary school children attract the highest level of support. In 2009, levels of support for extra spending on secondary school children are almost identical to those witnessed in 1983, with three in ten people identifying this as their first priority. However, levels of support have fluctuated in the intervening three decades – and specifically have risen by five percentage points since 1998. Over the decades, funding of education for children with special needs has most often been people's second most popular choice for extra spending. However, support for extra spending here is now at a comparatively low level, whereas support for extra spending on primary school children is at a level only previously reached in 1998.

   These levels of support broadly mirror the priorities of the Labour administration, which initially focused much of its attention on primary schools, following the 1997 General Election. This suggests that the public's spending priorities to some extent mirror those of the government. However, it is unclear whether the public is influenced by the widely publicised priorities of the government, or whether the government has simply picked up on the public mood.

Table 3.2 Highest priority for extra government spending on education, 1983–2009

	83	85	87	90	93	95	98	00	02	06	09
	%	%	%	%	%	%	%	%	%	%	%
Secondary school children	29	31	37	27	29	32	24	28	29	27	30
Children with special educational needs	32	34	29	29	34	19	21	26	27	28	21
Primary school children	16	13	15	15	16	18	24	22	18	19	23
Nursery/pre-school children	10	10	8	16	11	21	17	13	10	9	11
Students at university	9	9	9	9	7	9	9	9	14	10	9
Students in further education (FE)	n/a	n/a	n/a	n/a	n/a	n/a	n/a	n/a	n/a	4	4
Base	*1761*	*1804*	*2847*	*1400*	*1484*	*1227*	*1035*	*1133*	*3435*	*3240*	*3421*

n/a = not asked

So, in 2009, public support for prioritising education over other areas for extra government spending is at its lowest level since the start of the Labour administration. Clearly, this may be attributed to some extent to satisfaction with the existing comparatively high levels of spending and the emergence of more urgent and deserving areas of priority, prompted by economic and international developments. However, it might also be symptomatic of a widespread satisfaction with the ways in which compulsory education is currently administered and the levels at which schools are performing – a range of issues which the chapter turns to examine next.

Compulsory school starting and leaving ages

At what age does the public think that compulsory education should start? And when is the earliest that young people should be able to leave schooling? To explore what people think about this, a number of questions were asked for the first time on the 2009 *British Social Attitudes* survey:

> *When children start compulsory education do you think they should initially attend full-time or part-time?*

> *At which age do you think children should start to attend compulsory education full-time?*

> *Until what age do you think young people should have to stay in compulsory education or training?*

As shown in Table 3.3, the attitudes of the majority reflect the *status quo* in terms of when children should start school. Three-quarters (73 per cent) of people think that children should start full-time school at age four or five, which is what currently happens. However, given that compulsory schooling is legally enforced at age five, it could be argued that only a slight majority (56 per cent) explicitly endorse this. While very few people (four per cent) think that full-time compulsory education should begin before the age of four, one in five (19 per cent) feel it should start at an age later than five, reflecting the recent recommendations of the Cambridge Review. Two-thirds of the public (67 per cent) feel that children should start compulsory education on a full-time basis (which is what generally happens), with 28 per cent preferring initial attendance to be part-time and around one in twenty (four per cent) indicating it should depend on the individual child.

In terms of when compulsory education should finish, public attitudes are far more divided. Around half (48 per cent) support the *status quo* and think that 16 years is the ideal age to which young people should remain in compulsory education or training. A third (33 per cent) feel that 18 would be a more appropriate age, reflecting support for legislation to raise the participation age to 18. So, only in relation to the finishing date of compulsory education does a sizable proportion support a specific alternative to current educational practice.

Younger people are more likely than older people to hold a view which differs from current practice. As shown in Table 3.3, those aged between 18 and 34 are the least likely age group to think compulsory education should begin at the age of five (just 47 per cent express this view, compared to 66 per cent of those aged 65 years and over). That said, younger people are not consistently more likely to support the idea of children starting younger or older than age five:

those who dissent from current practice are as likely to support starting younger than five (27 per cent, compared with 17 per cent of those aged 65 and over) as they are to support starting older (20 per cent, compared with 14 per cent). In addition, younger respondents are the least likely to endorse the current practice for young people being able to leave school at age 16: just 42 per cent think that this is what should happen, compared with 60 per cent of those in the oldest age group. There is much wider support among the youngest age group for extending compulsory education to age 18, a view endorsed by 41 per cent of those aged 18 to 34, compared with just 17 per cent of those aged 65 and over.

Table 3.3 Attitudes to when compulsory education should begin and end, by age

	18–34	35–49	50–64	65+	All
	%	%	%	%	%
Children should initially attend compulsory education					
Full-time	71	67	64	66	67
Part-time	26	29	31	28	28
Depends on the child	4	4	5	5	4
Compulsory full-time education should begin					
Before age 4	6	3	2	2	4
At age 4	21	20	14	15	18
At age 5	47	52	61	66	56
After age 5	20	20	20	14	19
Compulsory education should finish					
Before age 16	2	3	3	7	4
At age 16	42	40	54	60	48
At age 17	10	10	9	6	9
At age 18	41	40	27	17	33
After age 18	4	3	2	1	2
Some other time	1	3	3	7	3
Base	*748*	*1051*	*862*	*792*	*3421*

Those with higher educational qualifications are also more likely to express a view that is at odds with current practice, compared with those with few or no qualifications. A third (34 per cent) of people with a degree think that children should begin their compulsory education part-time, compared to 28 per cent of those with no qualifications. Twenty eight per cent of people with a degree think that children should begin their education at age six or later, compared with 16 per cent of those with no qualifications. And, most markedly, 35 per cent of those with a degree think compulsory education should be extended to age 18, compared with just 25 per cent of those with no qualifications.

Although we might anticipate that people with children who are currently or recently in compulsory education would have particular views on compulsory school ages, this is in fact only the case in relation to the end date of compulsory education. People with children of current or recent school age are more likely to think compulsory education should last until age 18 rather than age 16. Forty-four per cent of those with children aged between five and 18 years thought this, compared with 29 per cent of those without children in this age group.

Clearly, sizeable proportions, albeit not always a majority, of the public support current practices about the age at which children should start and can leave compulsory education. Interestingly, it is those with the greatest level of exposure to and potential interest in education – through having completed their own schooling recently, having obtained a greater number of qualifications or with children in this life-stage – who are the most likely to favour an alternative approach. This implies that recent experience of these practices may encourage the view that an alternative approach is more optimal. Certainly, if the views of the younger generation reflect an upward trend in support for a leaving age of 18, then the legislation to raise the participation age introduced by Labour may be in line with public opinion.

Content of compulsory education

In recent years, the parameters of compulsory education have widened, with an increased range of options for vocational study and a wider emphasis on children's lifestyles and community involvement, manifested, for example, by the introduction of Citizenship Education in 2002.

The survey has traditionally included the following question, which was repeated in 2009:

> *In the long-run, which do you think gives people more opportunities and choice in life ... READ OUT ...*
> *... having good practical skills and training,*
> *... or, having good academic results?*

Although this question does not ask explicitly about the purpose of compulsory education, if the aim of education is to give people more opportunities and choice in life, then we would expect it to act as a barometer for what the public thinks are the areas upon which compulsory education should focus.

As shown in Table 3.4, the view that it is good practical skills and training which provide people with more opportunities and choice in life has consistently been more popular than the view that opportunities and choice come from having good academic results. However, while in 1983, there was a 14 percentage point difference between those thinking that practical skills and training would provide the most and those who thought that academic results would do so, this gap has increased to 42 percentage points in 2009. The size of this gap started to increase from 2002 onwards. The view that good practical skills and training gives more opportunities and choice in life now attracts the support of six in ten people, compared with around four in ten in 1993. Conversely, the proportion of people holding the view that good academic results give people more opportunities and choice has declined from three in ten in 1993 to slightly less than two in ten in 2009. If compulsory education is to be seen as a vehicle for giving people opportunities and choice in life, these findings suggest that the public thinks that education should have a focus on practical skills and training, rather than simply pupils' attainment of good academic results. This shift in views may reflect a perceived gap between what young people are learning (perhaps with an excessive focus on academic attainment) and the requirements of potential employers. It has occurred in a time of expansion of post-16 and higher education, with the difficulties of many graduates in securing suitable employment receiving widespread media coverage. Certainly, it suggests that recent attempts to boost the profile of vocational qualifications, which occurred after the data collection for the 2009 survey began, are broadly in tune with the public's pre-existing priorities.

Table 3.4 Options which give people more opportunities and choice in life, 1993–2009

	1993	1995	2002	2005	2009
Options which give more opportunities and choice	%	%	%	%	%
Good practical skills and training	44	43	38	45	60
Good academic results	30	32	32	22	18
(Mixture/depends)	25	25	30	33	22
% difference (between proportion selecting good practical skills and training and good academic results)	14	11	6	23	42
Base	*1484*	*1227*	*3435*	*2092*	*3421*

In addition to promoting vocational training and qualifications, educational policy has recently sought to broaden the role of schools beyond the traditional academic sphere, to include a focus on young people's lifestyles and wider community involvement. To measure the importance that the public places on such initiatives relative to the teaching of the traditional curriculum, the 2009 *British Social Attitudes* survey included a new question. Specifically, respondents were asked to identify which of the following two statements came closest to their views:

> *Schools should **only** be judged on how well they teach subjects in the curriculum, such as English, Maths, Music, Art, etc. ...*

> *Schools should **also** be judged on how well they teach children skills for life, such as social skills, developing self-esteem and how to live a healthy lifestyle, even if this means that less emphasis will be paid to judging curriculum subjects*

People's responses suggest widespread public support for the broadened remit of schools promoted by the Every Child Matters agenda and related initiatives. Almost three-quarters (72 per cent) of people say that the second statement best reflects their views: that is, they feel that schools should be judged on how well they teach children skills for life, even if less emphasis is paid to judging their teaching of curriculum subjects. Just one in five people (20 per cent) think that the focus should only be on how well schools teach the subjects in the curriculum.

Clearly, attempts by the previous Labour administration to incorporate vocational skills and broader life skills within the compulsory curriculum appear to be in tune with public perceptions regarding the importance of these two areas. However, to understand precisely which subjects and issues the public thinks that compulsory education should cover, and the relative priority it ascribes to each, the 2009 survey fielded two new questions, each of which was asked of a random half of the sample. One half was asked the following question, in relation to each of the options detailed in Table 3.5 below:

The following are qualities that young people may have developed by the age of 16. In your view, how important is it that schools aim to develop such qualities?
(Essential, very important, fairly important, not very important, not at all important)

The other half was asked about the same set of qualities and were presented with the same answer options, but with the following preceding question, encouraging them to focus on primary schools:

In your view, how important is it that primary schools aim to develop the following qualities in children?

As shown in Table 3.5, the public is in favour of schools developing a broad range of qualities in children. Sizeable majorities view each of the qualities listed as ones which it is "essential" or "very important" for schools to develop. The qualities which are most widely viewed as being "essential" for schools to develop are skills and knowledge to get a job (48 per cent), understanding about drugs and alcohol (45 per cent) and being a good citizen (39 per cent). Notably "gaining qualifications or certificates of achievement" is less widely viewed as being an essential quality for schools to develop – with just under one quarter thinking this is the case. These data reflect the greater priority attached by the public to good practical skills and training noted previously – and lend further support to the view that the focus of the previous Labour administration on vocational skills and training was largely in tune with public priorities for compulsory education. These findings also suggest considerable support for the Every Child Matters agenda in general and the specific programmes developed as a result, with large majorities of the public regarding as essential or important drugs and alcohol education, being a good citizen and knowledge of how to deal with personal finances.

As we might expect, the public has a slightly different profile of priorities when asked to consider the qualities to be developed specifically by primary schools. The qualities most frequently identified as "essential" for primary schools to develop are an enthusiasm to continue learning (40 per cent), understanding about drugs and alcohol (40 per cent) and how to be a good citizen (39 per cent). Certain qualities, such as the skills and knowledge which help to get a good job, would inevitably be less immediately required, and thus perceived as less essential for a child of primary school age, and the order of the public's priorities reflects this. However, there is widespread support for primary school pupils' acquisition of many of the key "life skills" emphasised by the Every Child Matters agenda. This includes teaching about issues relating to sex and relationships and drug and alcohol use, about which there has been considerable debate about the appropriate age to introduce such subjects within the school context. Our data certainly suggest that the majority of the public thinks it is important that they are covered from the primary school stage.

Table 3.5 Qualities viewed as essential or very important to develop at schools and at primary schools

	Schools		Primary schools	
	Essential	Essential or very important	Essential	Essential or very important
Qualities schools should develop	%	%	%	%
Skills and knowledge which help to get a good job	48	94	33	74
An understanding of the facts about drug and alcohol use	45	89	40	78
Being a good citizen	39	87	39	87
An understanding of sex and relationships	38	82	26	62
How to deal with personal finances	37	84	23	56
How to live among people from different backgrounds	32	78	31	75
A lifestyle which promotes good health	31	81	35	88
Social skills	30	80	30	81
Gaining qualifications or certificates of achievement	24	72	16	54
A desire to continue studies or training (An enthusiasm to continue learning)[+]	15	66	40	90
Base	*1681*		*1681*	

The table has been ordered on the basis of qualities identified as essential to be developed by primary schools

[+] The option in brackets was presented to those respondents who answered the question about primary schools

People's responses to the four questions reported above suggest strong public support for compulsory education to maintain or develop a focus both on the practical skills required to attain a job and on a range of non-academic life skills, in addition to the traditional academic curriculum. But are these views widely held across all sectors of society, or are certain types of people more or less in favour? The answer is that those with no or fewer educational qualifications and those from routine occupational groups are more likely than others to think that good practical skills and training give people more opportunities in life than do good academic results. Two-thirds (64 per cent) of those with no qualifications feel this, compared to half (49 per cent) of those with a degree. And 62 per cent of those from a routine occupational group think this, compared with 54 per cent of those from a professional occupational group. As was the case with attitudes to compulsory school ages, it seems likely that people's attitudes are influenced by their own experiences and circumstances.

However, the picture in relation to people's views on whether schools should be judged in part on their teaching of life skills is less clear. People in the youngest age group, those from a professional occupational group and those with greater experience of education (in terms of finishing their compulsory education later and attaining a large number of qualifications) are slightly, though significantly, more likely to favour schools being judged on their teaching of life skills, in addition to their traditional academic remit. This is despite being more likely than others to believe that academic results ultimately yield more opportunities and choice in life, as noted previously. These views are not necessarily contradictory: the more highly educated group may feel that academic results are ultimately the most useful, while recognising that a range of non-academic skills are also essential. Ultimately, a considerable majority of people in every socio-demographic group adhere to the view that schools should be judged on their teaching of life skills, even if it leads to less priority being given to academic subjects.

Assessment

We have seen thus far that there is wide support for the idea of a broader role for schools in young people's lives, focusing on areas beyond academic attainment. But how does the public think that pupils should be assessed on what they have learnt? When attitudes to education were last explored in *The 20th Report* in 2002, a lack of public enthusiasm for the proliferation of examinations and formal assessments was one of the most notable trends to emerge. Since then, there have been moves away from the formal assessment of pupils – and it is against this backdrop that we consider whether public attitudes to methods of assessment, including examinations, tally or are at odds with current educational practices.

The 2009 survey included three different questions on this issue, two of which have featured in the study since the late 1980s, with the third introduced in 2009. People were asked to indicate whether they agree or disagree with each of the following statements:

> *Formal exams are the best way of judging the ability of pupils*

> *So much attention is given to exam results that a pupil's everyday classroom work counts for too little*

> *Schools focus too much on tests and exams and not enough on learning for own sake*

The proportions of people agreeing with each of these statements, both in 2009 and (for the first two) at a range of points over the past two decades are shown in Table 3.6 below. Clearly, the public is divided on the issue of whether formal examinations are the best way to judge the ability of pupils, with 43 per cent of people subscribing to this view, 30 per cent disagreeing and 22 per cent not expressing a clear view (neither agreeing nor disagreeing with the statement). Regardless of whether examinations are regarded as the best method of assessment, it seems that the public thinks that they currently have too much priority and status. Around six in ten people agree with the view that "so much attention is given to exam results that a pupil's everyday classroom work counts for too little" and that "schools focus too much on tests and exams and not enough on learning for its own sake".

Moreover, there is some evidence that public attitudes to formal examinations as a method of assessment have become more negative in recent years, possibly in response to actual developments in this area. The proportion of people who feel that formal exams are the best way of judging the ability of pupils is at its lowest since the time-series began – and while it is not significantly different to that observed in 1987, it has fallen by 12 percentage points since 1994. On the other hand, adherence to the view that so much attention is given to exam results that a pupil's classroom work counts for too little has fluctuated since this question was first asked in 1987 and has fallen by three percentage points since 2002 – perhaps in reaction to the gradually declining focus on examinations in England, Scotland and Wales. All in all, these data suggest that the decreasing focus on examinations as a method of assessment is a development that is in tune with public perceptions and priorities – though the public does not necessarily feel that this has gone far enough.

Table 3.6 Attitudes to examinations as a method of assessment, 1987–2009

% agree	1987	1990	1993	1994	2002	2009
Formal exams are the best way of judging the ability of pupils	45	48	53	54	47	43
So much attention is given to exam results that a pupil's everyday classroom work counts for too little	70	62	60	59	64	61
Schools focus too much on tests and exams and not enough on learning for own sake	-	-	-	-	-	64
Base	*1243*	*1233*	*1306*	*984*	*2900*	*2942*

When we look at the views of people in different socio-demographic groups or people with different personal experiences of education, we do not find many differences in what people think about exams. However, one factor that is associated with holding more or less positive views on the issue is age: younger people (those aged 18 to 34) are less likely than others to see formal exams as the best way to judge the ability of pupils. Four in ten (39 per cent) 18 to 34 year olds agree that formal exams are the best methods of assessment, compared with half (50 per cent) of those aged 65 and over. Similarly, 68 per cent of those aged 18 to 34 agree that so much attention is given to exam results that a pupil's everyday classroom work counts for too little, compared with around six in ten of those aged 35 and over (59 per cent, 58 per cent and 59 per cent of those aged 35 to 49, 50 to 64 and 65 years and older respectively). Those in the 18 to 34 age group will have experienced the rapid proliferation of formal examinations in the 1990s, suggesting their markedly negative attitudes may represent a generational effect, rather than a particular standpoint which we can expect the young to adhere to at any given point in the future.

How well are schools performing?

So, we now know that the majority of the public supports the educational policies and practices introduced by the Labour government in relation to what, when and how schools should teach children. But how well does the public think that schools are currently performing to fulfil their various remits? Have public perceptions improved over the period in which the Labour government has introduced these changes?

The *British Social Attitudes* survey has traditionally used the following three questions to assess public perceptions of the performance of *secondary* schools – focusing on their teaching of the 'three Rs' (reading, writing and arithmetic), the preparation of young people for work, and the extent to which they bring out pupils' natural abilities:

> *From what you know or have hard, please tick one box on each line to show how well you think state secondary schools nowadays ...*
> *... prepare young people for work?*
> *... teach young people basic skills such as reading, writing and Maths?*
> *... bring out young people's natural abilities? (very well, quite well, not very well, not at all well)*

How the public rated schools on these three measures in 2008, when they were most recently asked, and at key points throughout the previous two decades are presented in Tables 3.7, 3.8 and 3.9 below. The public is somewhat divided in its views on how secondary schools are currently performing, on each of these three measures. Secondary schools do best, in public perceptions, on their teaching of basic skills such as reading or writing: three-quarters (73 per cent) of people think that schools perform "very" or "quite" well on this measure. In comparison, six in ten (58 per cent) people think schools do "very" or "quite" well in bringing out pupils' natural abilities. Public assessment of the effectiveness of schools in preparing young people for work is the least positive: just half (49 per cent) of people think that schools are doing "very" or "quite" well at this, with an identical proportion feeling that they are doing "not very" or "not at all" well. Given the priority ascribed by the public to the role of schools in preparing young people for work, and the perceived importance of vocational skills and training highlighted previously, such a mixed assessment on this measure should be viewed as a cause for concern.

That said, the picture to emerge in relation to the performance of secondary schools over the period of the Labour government is a positive one. The proportion of people who think that secondary schools teach basic skills "very" or "quite well" has increased by 17 percentage points since 1996, the year before the Labour government came to power. The bulk of this increase occurred in the late 1990s and has remained at a stable level ever since. The perceived success of secondary schools in preparing young people for work has also increased since 1996, by 12 percentage points (although the more major changes on this measure occurred between the late 1980s and late 1990s). However, it is in public perceptions on the performance of secondary schools in bringing out pupils' natural abilities that we witness the most substantial change: the proportion of people thinking that secondary schools do this "very" or "quite well" has risen by 18 percentage points since 1996, and, at 2008, is at its highest recorded level to date.

Table 3.7 Success of state secondary schools teaching three Rs, 1987–2008

	1987	1990	1993	1995	1996	1998	1999	2000	2001	2002	2008
	%	%	%	%	%	%	%	%	%	%	%
Very well	10	9	12	11	10	12	13	16	12	15	18
Quite well	46	48	53	49	46	53	55	59	61	56	55
Not very well	31	33	25	30	33	28	24	20	21	22	22
Not at all well	11	8	7	6	8	5	7	3	4	4	3
Base	*1281*	*1233*	*1306*	*1058*	*1038*	*847*	*833*	*972*	*941*	*2900*	*2994*

Table 3.8 Success of state secondary schools preparing young people for work, 1987–2008

	1987	1990	1993	1995	1996	1998	1999	2000	2001	2002	2008
	%	%	%	%	%	%	%	%	%	%	%
Very well	2	2	5	5	4	6	6	5	5	4	6
Quite well	27	35	38	35	34	40	43	50	45	44	44
Not very well	54	50	47	49	51	45	41	39	44	43	44
Not at all well	15	11	8	7	8	6	7	5	4	6	7
Base	*1281*	*1233*	*1306*	*1058*	*1038*	*847*	*833*	*972*	*941*	*2900*	*2994*

Table 3.9 Success of state secondary schools bringing out pupils' natural abilities, 1987–2008

	1987	1990	1993	1995	1996	1998	1999	2000	2001	2002	2008
	%	%	%	%	%	%	%	%	%	%	%
Very well	3	4	6	5	5	8	7	7	4	6	10
Quite well	32	32	40	37	35	43	42	44	44	41	48
Not very well	49	50	42	44	46	38	38	41	43	41	34
Not at all well	15	12	10	10	11	10	10	6	7	8	6
Base	1281	1233	1306	1058	1038	847	833	972	941	2900	2994

Public perceptions of the performance of secondary schools could be shaped by a number of factors – an individual's own experience of secondary schools or those of their friends or family or the coverage of this issue in the media. The extent to which people feel that state secondary schools are performing well differed markedly across different sections of the population. Those with a close proximity to their own or their children's secondary-level education tend to view the performance of secondary schools much more positively than others. Most specifically, more than eight in ten (83 per cent) 18 to 34 year olds feel that secondary schools teach basic skills very or quite well, compared with two-thirds (65 per cent) of those aged 65 and over. Those with children of or close to secondary school age (aged 11 to 18 years) also view the performance of secondary schools more positively than those without children at this life-stage. Eight in ten (78 per cent) of those with children in this age group think secondary schools teach basic skills well, compared with seven in ten (72 per cent) of those without children of this age. And 65 per cent of people with children in this age group feel that secondary schools do very or quite well at bringing out pupils' natural abilities, compared with 57 per cent of those without children in this age group. These differences should not necessarily come as a surprise. There is wide-ranging evidence from the *British Social Attitudes* survey series that those with more recent or direct experience of an institution or type of institution tend to hold more positive views about its performance or express greater levels of satisfaction in it (Appleby and Phillips, 2009.

While people's proximity to school-level education (through one's own experiences or those of one's children) is associated with positive attitudes on the performance of secondary schools, there is not the same relationship between positive attitudes and having higher educational qualifications. In fact, the reverse is true, with those with higher-level qualifications and who left school later being the least positive. Forty-three per cent of those with a degree feel secondary schools do very or quite well at preparing young people for work, compared with 53 per cent of those with no educational qualifications. Similarly, 52 per cent of those with a degree and 62 per cent of those with no educational qualifications feel that secondary schools do well at bringing out pupils' natural abilities. Comparable patterns exist for those who completed their full-time education at different ages, with those who finished at age 19 or later being the least likely to express a positive view. It may be that experiences of post-compulsory education, including higher education, colour individual views of secondary-level education, by providing individuals with another educational sector against which to draw comparisons in terms of their effectiveness. Alternatively, it could be that those with a greater number of qualifications simply have higher expectations of what secondary schools should be providing, for instance in terms of reading and writing, where they themselves would have attained a comparatively high level of proficiency.

Unsurprisingly, social class, known to be associated with education levels, also makes a difference to people's perceptions. Forty-four per cent of those from a professional occupational group feel secondary schools do very or quite well at preparing young people for work, compared with 55 per cent of those from a routine occupational group. Finally, those living in Scotland and Wales are more positive than those living in England on each of the three measures. Most markedly, 47 per cent of those living in England feel that secondary schools do very or quite well at preparing young people for work, compared with 60 per cent in Wales and Scotland. This is despite the fact that we found few differences in attitudes between those living in England, Wales and Scotland on the substantive areas of educational policy and practice discussed earlier in the chapter.

Conclusions

The public is broadly supportive of current practices in compulsory education, and of the range of initiatives introduced and proposed by the Labour government in the past decade. In particular, there is strong support for the expansion of the compulsory curriculum to cover a range of life skills, as well as options for vocational study and training. People's attitudes are more mixed on the age at which compulsory education should start and finish, and on the assessment of pupils. Sizeable proportions of people oppose the current (albeit reduced) focus on examinations and the traditional legally enforceable duration of compulsory education from age five to age 16. Despite this, the public feels that the performance of secondary schools has improved markedly over the past decade across a wide range of measures.

Attitudes to education are clearly linked to personal experiences of education – with those who are young (who will have recently completed their own compulsory education) frequently expressing relatively distinct views. The same is often true of those who have acquired a large number of educational qualifications, completed their full-time education comparatively late or have children of current or recent school age. These differences strongly suggest that attitudes to education, rather than being primarily grounded in a particular set of values or beliefs, tend to be mediated by personal experience. Perhaps this is unsurprising: education is one area of social policy of which we will all have substantial experience, meaning that personal experience has a greater potential than in other areas to contribute to the formation of attitudes.

Nevertheless, public attitudes to education do not operate in isolation. The importance attached to education as a spending priority has clearly been influenced by the relatively high levels of spending received in recent years and the emergence of arguably more pressing considerations, as a result of the recent recession and international events. It is likely that the former has also prompted the public to attach increasing importance to the practical purpose of education, in preparing young people for work – and it is clear that, on this measure, the public feels that secondary schools could be doing much better. Over the coming years, this may be an aspect on which educational policy will increasingly need to focus, if compulsory education is to continue to be viewed relatively positively by the public.

Notes

1. This figure is an estimate of the proportion of government spending on education in the financial year 2010, available at http://www.ukpublicspending.co.uk/index.php.
2. Data on government expenditure, available at http://www.ukpublicspending.co.uk/downchart_ukgs.php?chart=20-total&state=UK, shows that central and local government spending on education has risen from £37.2 million in 2007 to £85.6 million in 2010. In addition to inflation, this reflects an overall increase in government spending over the past decade. As an absolute proportion of government spending, however, spending on education has not risen substantially in the past decade (equating to between 12 per cent and 14 per cent of total government spending for each year between 1997 and 2010
3. This statement originally appeared in an e-mail, which subsequently received considerable media coverage see for example http://news.bbc.co.uk/1/hi/uk_politics/8679749.stm
4. The 2011/12 School Admissions Code has been revised to make the option of a flexible start date for compulsory schooling more widely available in England.

References

Appleby, J. and Phillips, M. (2009), 'The NHS: Satisfied now?', in Park, A., Curtice, J., Thomson, K., Phillips, M. and Clery, E. (eds.), *British Social Attitudes: the 25th Report*, London: Sage

Cambridge Primary Review (2009), *Children, their World, their Education: final report and recommendations of the Cambridge Primary Review*, Abingdon and New York: Routledge

Department for Education and Skills (2003), *Every Child Matters* Green paper

Department for Education and Skills (2004), *14–19 Curriculum and Qualifications Reform. Final Report of the Working Group on 14–19 Reform*

Department for Education and Skills (2009), *Report of the Expert Group on Assessment*

Wlezien, C. (1995), 'The Public as Thermostat: Dynamics of Preferences for Spending', *American Journal of Political Science*, **39**: 981–1000

Wragg, T. and Jarvis, L. (2003), 'Pass or fail? Perceptions of education', in Park, A., Curtice, J., Thomson, K., Jarvis, L. and Bromley, C. (eds.), *British Social Attitudes: the 20th Report* – Continuity and change over two decades, London: Sage

Acknowledgements

The *National Centre for Social Research* is grateful to the Department for Education (formerly the Department for Schools, Children and Families) for their financial support which enabled us to ask the questions reported in this chapter, although the views expressed are those of the authors alone.

4 A healthy improvement? Satisfaction with the NHS under Labour

John Appleby and Ruth Robertson[*]

The consequences of the economic recession on government spending, combined with the change in administration from 13 years of a Labour government to the new Conservative–Liberal Democrat coalition government place the NHS at a potential crossroads. As the UK's economy begins to recover from its worst recession in many decades, with a loss of economic output in 2009 of around six per cent of GDP, a number of banks in public ownership or in receipt of billions of pounds of financial support from the taxpayer, the hangover for the public finances looks dire. For the NHS – the largest spending department, consuming around 18 per cent of government spending (equivalent to education and defence combined) – the historically unprecedented boom years of additional funding are now ending as part of the exigencies of the financial crisis. The new government promises real increases in funding for the NHS over the next few years. However, given the economic imperative to deal with the country's structural deficit and the difficult trade-offs necessary with other departments' spending, there is little expectation of increases to rival those of the last decade. Tighter budgets but increasing demand and aspirations to improve the quality of services mean the NHS will need to significantly improve productivity over the coming years (Appleby *et al.* 2009), together with further organisational and structural reform (Secretary of State for Health, 2010).

Here, we take the opportunity of being at this 'crossroads' to review Labour's time in office. What impact did Labour's policies on health have on the public's views and attitudes towards the NHS? Have people perceived any changes in the 'service' they receive from the NHS since Labour came to power in 1997? One expectation is that extra spending, coupled with a reform programme focused in part on dealing with the public's concerns about waiting times, along with a more consumerist approach (through patient choice in England and

[*] John Appleby is Chief Economist at the King's Fund. Ruth Robertson is a Research Officer at the King's Fund.

through cooperation and integration in Scotland and Wales) will have had a positive impact on patient and public satisfaction. But is this actually the case?

We use *British Social Attitudes* survey data, largely from the mid-1990s to 2009, to address these questions. More specifically, we show how people's satisfaction with the NHS – both overall and in particular areas – changed over the period of the last Labour government, and how these trends parallel changes in government policy on health. We report on how satisfaction levels have varied between population groups, for example, between age groups and supporters of different political parties, and consider why this might be the case. We look for associations between people's perceptions of whether NHS services have been improving and their satisfaction with the NHS. We look specifically at waiting times, given that they were a high-profile focus within Labour's policy on health care. Given devolution, health policy in Wales and Scotland has not been an exclusive Labour domain. This means that England is the main focus in the chapter.[1] However, towards the end of the chapter, we do compare people's satisfaction with health care across England, Scotland and Wales. In our concluding comments we consider, with a colder financial climate ahead, what we can surmise from people's views during the last administration about the prospects for future trends in satisfaction.

Before we go further, we provide a brief overview of Labour's policies towards the NHS from its election in 1997 up to 2010, to set the policy context for the rest of the chapter.

Labour's health policies: 1997–2010

When Labour came to power in May 1997, it inherited an NHS with a number of issues. Inpatient waiting lists in England stood at nearly 1.2 million. One in four patients on waiting lists had been waiting over six months, and four per cent (nearly 47,000 patients) had been waiting for over a year (Department of Health, 2010).[2] Public concern about the NHS was also high. In an opinion poll conducted by MORI in June 1997, 51 per cent of those surveyed stated that the NHS was the most important issue facing Britain at that time (Ipsos-Mori, 2010). Between 1994 and 1997, NHS spending had fallen as spending increases lagged behind general economic growth.[3] By 1997, following a small real reduction in funding – the first time this had happened since the mid-1970s – spending had slipped back to its level at the beginning of the decade (Appleby *et al.*, 2009).

It is perhaps of no surprise, then, that the *British Social Attitudes* survey in 1997 recorded the lowest level of public satisfaction with the NHS since the survey series began in 1983. And, hyperbole aside, Labour's 1997 General Election manifesto reflected the mood, promising not just to save the NHS but to '… rebuild the NHS, reducing spending on administration and increasing spending on patient care' (Labour Party, 1997).

Despite some of the detailed pledges at the time – ending waiting for cancer surgery, taking 100,000 people off waiting lists, introducing targets for improvement in the quality of hospital care – it would have been hard to predict then the course of Labour's policy towards the NHS over the ensuing years – in particular, the policy journey from a promise to abolish the market-type arrangements[4] set up by the previous Conservative administration in 1991, to the adoption of competition and choice as means to drive up the performance of the NHS.

In hindsight, the trajectory of policy, and stages in its development, can be discerned, or at least constructed. On this, Simon Stevens – a former policy adviser to two Secretaries of State for Health and one Prime Minister – has provided a coherent account (Stevens, 2004), at least from 1999 when Alan Milburn took over from Frank Dobson as Secretary of State for Health. The period from 1997 to 1999 saw small growths in funding for the NHS and the beginnings of Labour's implementation of its manifesto pledges – significantly, the abolition of GP fundholding (in which GPs could opt to hold budgets to spend on care of their patients) and a start on reducing waiting lists. But from 1999, according to Stevens, Labour's health policy began to develop over the years in three, albeit overlapping, phases. The first phase, from 2000, recognised public concern that the NHS had been under-funded historically, not only relative to other countries, but in relation to its own wealth. After more or less sticking to its 1997 commitment to work with the previous administration's public spending plans for two years, towards the end of 1999 and the beginning of 2000, the political decision was taken to find significantly more money for the NHS. This decision was accompanied by the commissioning of a detailed long-term review of the future funding needs of the NHS (Wanless, 2002) and a revamped plan of action for reform and investment (*The NHS Plan* – Secretary of State for Health, 2000). *The NHS Plan* lay particular emphasis on what the extra money pledged would buy: more doctors, more nurses, more equipment and, as staff contracts throughout the NHS were renegotiated, higher pay, too.

Between 2000/01 and 2009/10, funding indeed increased substantially, more than doubling in real terms. Over this period, this enabled the NHS to increase its workforce by over a third and to meet much of the *NHS Plan*'s goals to increase equipment and infrastructure (Wanless et al., 2007).

However, as Stevens argues, more money and more resources in general were not seen as enough, by themselves, to achieve all the ambitions set out in the *NHS Plan*. In its second stage from 2002, policy development was characterised in particular by the imposition by the Department of Health of targets coupled with tough sanctions (including the sacking of managers failing to meet targets) to improve, for example, waiting times. It also involved the setting up of new regulatory bodies to monitor and publicly report on the performance of local NHS organisations as well as national service frameworks designed to introduce best practice in the treatment of, for example, cancer and diabetes.

'Targets and terror' (Bevan and Hood, 2006) proved quite an effective means to focus the NHS on a few key aspects of its performance, most notably, again, on the reduction in waiting times. But while such tactics had their successes (cf. Propper *et al.*, 2008), they engendered criticism from clinical professionals and examples of excessive managerial zeal bordering, and in some cases encompassing, outright fiddling of the figures (National Audit Office, 2001).

In part it was the recognition by policy makers of the limits of the target regime – especially one run remotely from the Department of Health and seen as an imposition on professional practice – that led to the third and so far continuing stage: the introduction of more 'automatic' incentives designed to change the NHS into a 'self improving' organisation.

This third stage, emerging from around 2004, emphasised greater autonomy and independence for hospitals through foundation trust status. Greater, more formalised choice of hospital by patients which was linked to a payment system for hospitals (Payment by Results) ensured money followed the patient. And while the previous Conservative administration's introduction of an internal market had never been completely abolished (despite Labour's 1997 manifesto pledge) the third phase involved a much greater focus on competition between health care providers and a deliberate effort to inject competitive pressure through positive encouragement to the independent health care sector to compete for NHS business.

The expressed aims of Labour's reforms were not only to improve the efficiency and effectiveness of the NHS. Importantly, they included the improvement of health outcomes for patients, and patients' experience of the care and treatment they received.

Trends in satisfaction

So over this period, what happened to levels of public satisfaction with the NHS and its services? Since 1983, *British Social Attitudes* has asked:

> *All in all, how satisfied or dissatisfied would you say you are with the way in which the National Health Service is run nowadays?*
>
> *[Very satisfied, quite satisfied, neither satisfied nor dissatisfied, quite dissatisfied, very dissatisfied]*

This single question can be seen as an overarching measure of health service performance, and one which arguably captures many of the multiple outcomes that the reforms were designed to produce. As we mentioned above, when Labour came to power in 1997, levels of public satisfaction with the NHS, as measured by this question, were lower than at any time since 1983 (when the *British Social Attitudes* survey series began). In 1997, just 34 per cent of people said they were satisfied with the way that the NHS was being run, and 50 per cent expressed dissatisfaction (Figure 4.1). Satisfaction with the NHS rose by 12 percentage points in Labour's first two years to 46 per cent in 1999. However, this looks like it may have been a honeymoon effect as satisfaction fell again in the following two years. But from 2001 onwards, we have seen a steady increase in levels of public satisfaction so that, by 2009, satisfaction levels reach 64 per cent, their highest level since the *British Social Attitudes* survey series began. In 2009, the proportions expressing satisfaction with the NHS are almost double to that when Labour came to power in 1997. And with the proportion expressing dissatisfaction reducing to 19 per cent (the *lowest* since 1983), net satisfaction also reaches its highest level.

Figure 4.1 Satisfaction with the way that the NHS is run, 1983–2009

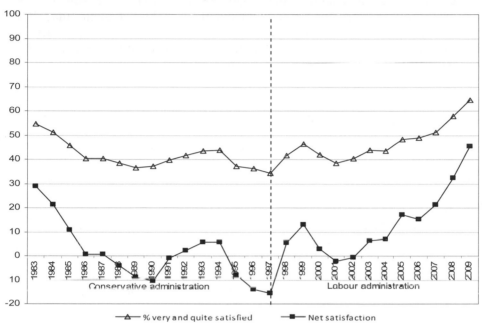

'Net satisfaction' = (very + quite satisfied) minus (very + quite dissatisfied)
The data on which Figure 4.1 is based can be found in the appendix to this chapter

In addition to the question above, *British Social Attitudes* includes questions which ask people how satisfied or dissatisfied they are with a number of NHS services (each of which uses the five-point scale described above):

> *From your own experience, or from what you have heard, please say how satisfied or dissatisfied you are with the way in which each of these parts of the National Health Service runs nowadays:*
> *... local doctors or GPs?*
> *... National Health Service dentists?*
> *... being in hospital as an inpatient?*
> *... attending hospital as an outpatient?*
> *... Accident and Emergency departments?*
> *... NHS Direct/NHS 24, the telephone or internet advice service?*
> *... diagnostic services, for example x-rays, scans, hearing tests or heart tests?*
> *... private dentists?*

In the period preceding the Labour administration, levels of public satisfaction with all four aspects had fallen (Figure 4.2). In 1996,[5] a year before Labour came to power, fewer people were expressing satisfaction with GPs (77 per cent), dentists (52 per cent) and inpatient services (53 per cent) than at any time since 1983. And satisfaction with outpatient services, at 52 per cent in 1996, was also only one percentage point higher than its lowest point since 1983. However, the trajectory since 1997 for satisfaction levels for the four services has been quite different. Unpicking the reasons for this is difficult, and is likely to involve a number of factors particular to each area.

Figure 4.2 Satisfaction with GPs, dentists, inpatients and outpatients, 1983–2009

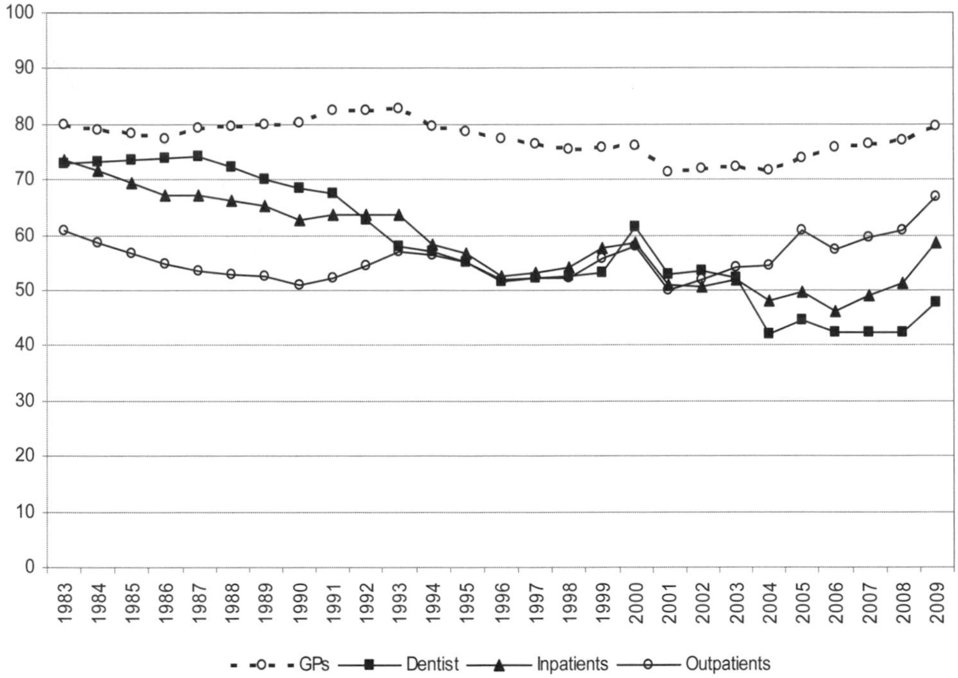

The data on which Figure 4.2 is based can be found in the appendix to this chapter

Although traditionally high, levels of satisfaction with GP services fell throughout the 1990s. There was a (small) recovery in satisfaction levels in 2000, but this may reflect a honeymoon period for Labour, also evident in trends in satisfaction with the NHS overall and in satisfaction rates for other services. In 2001 satisfaction dropped five percentage points and only started to recover in 2005, rising each subsequent year to 80 per cent in 2009. The rising levels of satisfaction with GPs over the last six years may be explained in part by the imposition of maximum waiting time targets to get an appointment.

In contrast, the long-term decline in levels of satisfaction with dentists since 1983 was only arrested in 2004, remaining flat until 2009 when the proportion of people expressing satisfaction with dentist services rose to just less than half (48 per cent). These low satisfaction levels probably reflect continuing problems over the last few years for people in many parts of the country able to get treatment on the NHS.

Levels of public satisfaction with outpatient services, which historically most closely mirror changes in satisfaction with the NHS overall, have now risen to their highest level since 1983, reaching 67 per cent in 2009. Outpatient services have performed the best out of all four services in terms of improvement in satisfaction levels since 1996 with a 15 percentage-point increase in the number of respondents who were satisfied with the service between 1996 and 2009. In contrast, levels of satisfaction with inpatient services have been in decline for most of the Labour administration, and only started to recover in 2007. In 2009, six in ten (59 per cent) people say that they are satisfied with inpatient services, a proportion still lower than in the 1980s and early 1990s. A likely explanation for this recent rise in satisfaction levels is the public perception that people are waiting less time for hospital appointments. This is an issue to which we return below.

There was a greater increase in satisfaction levels with the NHS overall than with individual services during Labour's time in power. Although satisfaction with some services increased between 1996 and 2009, reflecting the success of service-specific initiatives such as outpatient waiting time targets, overall satisfaction with the NHS has risen at a faster rate. Part of the explanation for this is probably the low starting point for satisfaction with the NHS overall: historically this has been 10 to 20 percentage points lower than for individual services and so had greater scope to achieve larger percentage point improvements. In contrast, for example, satisfaction with GP services has traditionally been very high – between 75 and 80 per cent – and so, statistically, has had less scope for similarly large improvements. But part of the explanation may also reflect an increased public optimism in the NHS as an institution and a greater confidence in its continued future – confidence in part based on the success of the NHS in dealing with key public concerns such as excessive waiting times.

Variations in satisfaction levels between population groups

While levels of satisfaction with the NHS and its services have risen markedly in comparison with levels in 1996, we know from past analysis of the *British Social Attitudes* data (e.g. Appleby and Phillips, 2009) that different population groups – the elderly and the young, households with different levels of income, those with educational qualifications and those with none, and so on – can vary significantly in their levels of satisfaction. Moreover, historically, the elderly, the less well off and those with no educational qualifications have been more satisfied with the NHS than the young, the well off and those with higher qualifications. So, a question arises here as to whether the increase in levels of public satisfaction during the Labour administration have been driven primarily by increases in satisfaction among those sections of the population who have traditionally been more satisfied with the NHS, or whether Labour succeeded in reaching those who not only are historically less disposed to express satisfaction with the NHS, but are also important groups to win over given the funding base of the NHS. Retaining and improving support for the NHS from the middle classes has always been a concern in relation to possible tax resistance and the potential rise in the attitudes that higher spending could be throwing good money after bad.

Age, income, party identification and education

Table 4.1 (last column) shows that between 1996 and 2009, levels of satisfaction have increased among all population groups. Not only that, but the largest increases have been among those traditionally with comparatively low levels of satisfaction. For example, satisfaction levels among 18–34 year olds have increased between 1996 and 2009 by 32 percentage points, to 61 per cent in 2009, while levels among people over the age of 65 have risen by only 24 percentage points over the same period (at 75 per cent in 2009). As a result, the gap between the views of the younger and older age groups narrowed by an average of 0.4 per cent a year between 1997 and 2009, whereas it actually *increased* by 0.6 per cent a year over the previous period from 1983 to 1996.

A similar trend is evident between households in different income quartiles. With proportionately larger increases in levels of satisfaction among the better off (those in the highest and second highest quartiles), the gap in satisfaction levels between the lowest and highest income quartile has reduced from 13 percentage points in 1996 to seven percentage points in 2009. Likewise, the gap in satisfaction levels between those with higher educational qualifications and those with no qualifications narrowed slightly from 11 per cent in 1996 to nine per cent in 2009. There is some evidence that the gap in satisfaction levels between the highest and lowest income quartiles was already reducing between 1983 and 1996. The change from 1997 onwards was the speed in which the gap was closing (0.6 per cent per annum, compared to 0.3 per cent per annum in the previous period). The story is different for education, where the gap in satisfaction between those with higher educational qualifications and those with no qualifications had *increased* by an average of around 0.2 per cent per annum from 1986 to 1996, whereas between 1997 and 2009 it *fell* by 0.4 per cent per year on average.

Table 4.1 Trends in satisfaction with the NHS overall, by population group, 1983–2009[6]

% satisfied with the way in which the NHS is run nowadays	1983	1987	1990	1993	1996	1999	2003	2007	2009	Change 1983 – 1996	Change 1996 – 2009
Age											
18–34	50	39	30	34	29	40	42	43	61	-21	+32
35–54	52	36	37	41	33	44	38	49	62	-19	+29
55–64	48	44	38	50	40	47	43	52	63	-8	+23
65+	70	49	47	61	51	58	58	64	75	-19	+24
Political affiliation											
Conservative	57	48	47	55	49	46	38	46	61	-8	+12
Lib Dem/Alliance	44	31	30	33	33	39	45	55	66	-12	+34
Labour	56	35	28	37	28	50	50	57	73	-28	+46
Household income (quartiles)											
Lowest quartile	63	45	39	51	43	55	47	55	68	-21	+25
2nd lowest quartile	55	45	37	46	38	48	44	55	66	-17	+29
2nd highest quartile	52	38	36	41	29	44	41	45	65	-23	+36
Highest quartile	45	34	30	37	30	39	39	50	60	-15	+31
Educational attainment (highest level)											
Higher education	n/a	32	31	34	32	41	40	49	63	0	+31
A level	n/a	35	27	36	33	40	41	48	60	-2	+27
O level/CSE	n/a	42	37	43	34	47	41	48	64	-8	+30
No qualifications	n/a	44	43	52	43	53	51	57	72	-2	+29

n/a = not asked

Previous analyses have suggested that there is a link between political affiliation and satisfaction with the NHS, with satisfaction rising among Labour supporters during Labour's period in office and falling for Conservative supporters (cf. Mulligan and Appleby, 2001, Appleby and Alvarez, 2003). However, the findings in Table 4.1 suggest that, while there was a jump in levels of satisfaction among Labour supporters between 1996 and 1999 (from 28 per cent to 50 per cent), satisfaction levels among this group fluctuated between 40 and 50 per cent until 2003, since when, they have been rising, with particularly steep increases from 2007. True, levels of satisfaction among Conservative supporters fell during the early years of the Labour administration.

But, since 2007, they, like their Labour counterparts, have been expressing increasing satisfaction with the NHS. This makes the turnaround in satisfaction with the NHS since 1997 perhaps all the more remarkable, with even Labour's opponents recognising something positive going on.

So, given there has been a degree of convergence in views across different population groups, what factors (age, political affiliation, and so on) are still important in explaining people's *propensity* to express satisfaction with the NHS? As the population categories we have examined above overlap (possibly in systematic ways such that the reason for the satisfaction levels expressed by Conservative supporters may be due to the income levels of this group rather than their political affiliation) we used multivariate analysis (reported in detail in Model 1 in the appendix) to disentangle the association between these different factors and people's levels of satisfaction with the NHS. This shows that despite the convergence in levels of satisfaction, most of the traditional divides between population groups still hold true.[7]

Perceptions of improvement in the NHS and satisfaction

Clearly, increases in levels of satisfaction with the NHS over recent years show that the public has noticed something different about the NHS – but what exactly? Six questions explore whether people think that particular elements of the NHS have improved or got worse over the preceding five years, a number of which have a specific focus on waiting times. Four of these questions have been asked in four years – 1995, 2001, 2008 and 2009:

> *Please say how much better or worse you think each of these things has been getting over the last five years ...*
> *the general standard of health care on the NHS?*
> *the time most people wait to get **outpatients' appointments** in NHS hospitals?*
> *the time most people wait in **outpatients'** departments in NHS hospitals before a consultant sees them?*
> *the time most people wait at their **GP's surgery** before a doctor sees them?*

The other two were asked only in 2009:

> *Please say how much better or worse you think each of these things has been getting **over the last five years**...*
> *the time most people would have to wait between being **referred by their GP** for hospital treatment and that treatment starting?*
> *how much say NHS patients have in decisions about their treatment and health care?*

As Table 4.2 shows, the majority public view is that the general standard of NHS care has improved a lot since 1995, and particularly since 2008. In 1995, 18 per cent of people felt that NHS care had improved over the previous five years, but by 2009, 40 per cent of people think this. The decline in the numbers of those who feel it has got worse is even more marked, from nearly half of people in 1995 to 18 per cent in 2009.

Table 4.2 Trends in perceptions of improvements in the NHS in last five years, 1995–2009

Change over the last five years in …	1995	2001	2008	2009	Change 95 –09
… general standard of NHS care	%	%	%	%	
Better	18	22	32	40	+23
Same	32	37	38	39	+7
Worse	49	40	27	18	-31
Net improvement	-32	-18	+5	+22	+54
… wait *for* outpatient appointment					
Better	17	12	28	37	+19
Same	38	39	37	32	-6
Worse	39	45	26	25	-14
Net improvement	-22	-33	+1	+11	+33
… wait *in* outpatient department					
Better	10	11	21	27	+9
Same	39	42	41	41	+2
Worse	38	42	29	26	-13
Net improvement	-20	-31	-9	+1	+21
… wait in surgery to see a GP					
Better	28	23	34	39	+11
Same	49	51	48	44	-5
Worse	21	24	15	15	-0
Net improvement	+7	-1	+19	+24	+17
… referral to treatment times					
Better	n/a	n/a	n/a	36	
Same	n/a	n/a	n/a	35	
Worse	n/a	n/a	n/a	21	
Net improvement				+14	
… say in treatment decisions					
Better	n/a	n/a	n/a	38	
Same	n/a	n/a	n/a	43	
Worse	n/a	n/a	n/a	11	
Net improvement				+27	
Base	*2399*	*2188*	*3358*	*3421*	

n/a = not asked
Better = "much better" or "better"; worse = "worse" or "much worse"

In terms of specific aspects of NHS care, people's perceptions were that things got worse between 1995 and 2001, but have been getting steadily better since then. In people's minds, there has been more improvement regarding the amount of time most people have to wait to get an appointment than in the amount of time they have to wait to see a doctor once they arrive for their appointment. The proportion of people who feel there has been an improvement in the amount of time that most people have to wait to get an outpatient appointment more than doubled between 1995 and 2009, from 17 per cent to 37 per cent. In 2009, these views are similar to what people think about the time it takes between getting a GP referral and getting treatment: 36 per cent of people feel that there have been improvements in the last five years. In contrast, the rise in the proportion of people thinking that waiting in outpatient departments has improved is more modest, rising from 18 per cent to 27 per cent over the period. Views about waiting in GP surgeries follow a similar trend.

As might be expected, there is a strong association between people perceiving improvements in specific areas of the NHS and their perception of improvements in the overall care provided by the NHS (see Model 2 in the appendix). However, the converse is not always true for those who feel things have got worse. It seems that people's views about improvements in NHS care overall are associated more with their views on hospital treatment than they are with their views on the service provided by GPs or the amount of say that they have in decisions about treatment. Although those who feel that the wait from referral to treatment or the wait in outpatient departments has worsened in the last five years are less likely to think that standards of care in the NHS have improved over the same period, this is not true for those who feel there has been a decline in standards in other specific areas: waiting in GP surgeries and having a say in decisions about treatment.[8]

Table 4.2 shows the 'net improvement' in each area, according to public perception. It takes account of the difference in the proportion of people perceiving things to have improved and the proportion of those who think they have not. It is clear that since 1995, increases in the perceived net improvement in the general standard of NHS care and in the time that people wait to get an outpatient appointment are greater than increases in the perceived net improvement in waiting times in outpatient departments and GP surgeries. Could this be explained by the fact that the former have been subject to direct government policy – either through the target regime or by other performance management tactics? Well, very likely. While the 'general standard of NHS care' is a rather broad measure, arguably it has been the overarching goal of Labour's NHS reforms and subject to a variety of targets, performance management and, of course, extra resources. More specifically, the waiting time to get an outpatient appointment has been subject to direct targets set by the Department of Health which, from 2004, were rolled into the 18 week maximum waiting time target which measured the complete waiting time from GP referral, through outpatients and diagnostics to an inpatient stay (if required). An 'improvement' question relating to this latter target was only asked in 2009, but the results, as noted above, are very similar to the responses to the question concerning waiting times for an outpatient appointment. Also in 2009 for the first time, respondents were asked if they felt there had been an improvement in the amount of say patients have about their treatment and health care. This question shows the highest level of net improvement (27 per cent), due mainly to the small number who felt things had worsened.

For those improvement areas where there are hard data, the public's views would appear to coincide with what actually happened: the median wait for an inpatient admission in England fell from 13.4 weeks in 1997 to around 4.2 weeks in 2009. (Department of Health, 2010). And now, between 90 and 95 per cent of patients wait fewer than 18 weeks from GP referral to treatment at hospital compared with 1997 when around 50 per cent of those admitted to hospital and 75 per cent of those treated in outpatients waited that long (Thorlby and Maybin, 2010).

So, at least for those aspects of improvement explored by the *British Social Attitudes* survey, there is good news for the NHS – and possibly a positive impact from Labour's policy to target waiting times. The fact that public perceptions are quite closely linked with reality, at least as far as waiting times go, cannot be explained solely in terms of people's own experiences of NHS care. True, those with recent contact tend to be more satisfied and to feel that NHS care has improved over time than those who have not had recent contact. However, the rise in satisfaction levels and perceived improvements have happened across all population groups, regardless of contact with the NHS. Does this, perhaps, suggest that, over the last decade, the NHS has started to overcome some of its public image problem?

Views on improvements in the NHS and satisfaction

Perhaps unsurprisingly, people's perceptions about whether there have been improvements in NHS care are associated with their levels of satisfaction with it. Table 4.3 shows the proportions of people who are "satisfied" or "dissatisfied" with the NHS who think that there have been improvements in different areas of NHS care over the last five years. As we might expect, a much higher proportion of those who express satisfaction with the NHS feel there have been improvements, compared with the views of those who are dissatisfied with the NHS. This is particularly strong in relation to perceptions of improvements in NHS care in general. However, the table reveals some nuances to this general finding. Firstly, while few of those satisfied with the NHS say that any individual areas have got worse in the last five years, the converse is less true for those dissatisfied with the NHS. Quite substantial proportions of those dissatisfied with the NHS still think that there have been improvements in waiting times in GP surgeries and having a say in treatment. Moreover, some areas of improvement are more strongly associated than others with levels of satisfaction. For example, only 34 per cent of those who are satisfied with the NHS feel waiting times in outpatient departments have improved, compared with 43 per cent who feel referral to treatment times have improved. And 52 per cent who express *dis*satisfaction with the NHS think waiting times in outpatient departments have got *worse*, compared with 41 per cent who think referral to treatment times have worsened.

Table 4.3 Satisfaction and views about improvements in the NHS in the last five years

Improvement in the last five years in ...	Satisfaction with NHS overall	
	Satisfied[+] %	Dissatisfied %
... general standard of NHS care		
Better	51	16
Worse	7	52
Net improvement	+44	-35
... wait from referral to treatment		
Better	43	19
Worse	14	41
Net improvement	+29	-21
... wait in outpatients		
Better	34	11
Worse	16	52
Net improvement	+18	-41
... wait in the GP surgery		
Better	45	28
Worse	10	27
Net improvement	+34	+1
... say in decisions and treatment and health care		
Better	44	24
Worse	5	25
Net improvement	+39	-1
... wait for outpatient appointment		
Better	45	20
Worse	16	52
Net improvement	+30	-33
Base	*2206*	*656*

[+] Satisfied = "very satisfied" or "quite satisfied"; dissatisfied = "quite dissatisfied" or "very dissatisfied"; better = "much better" or "better"; worse = "worse" or "much worse"

Controlling for other factors (as in Model 1 in the appendix), those who felt there had been improvements in waiting times in outpatient departments were more likely to be satisfied, compared with those who felt there had been improvements in any other areas.[9] However, statistically, the differences in the tendency to be satisfied were not significant (as indicated by the overlapping confidence intervals for the value of the coefficients (Exp[B]) for each of the improvement area variables). It is therefore hard to be conclusive about which is the most important improvement factor except to say they are, statistically at least, all significant.

Country variation in policy and views about the NHS

While the NHS is a UK-wide institution, like some other public services (education for example) there have always existed some variations in structure and policy between the four territories. But since devolution in 1999, health policy has started to take, in some important respects, more divergent paths in the four countries. In England, there has been choice, competition, and increased use of the independent sector for NHS work; in Scotland and Wales, there has been cooperation, integration and a rejection of competition (Greer and Trench, 2008). There has been less divergence with respect to funding levels, as Figure 4.3. shows in terms of per capita spending on the NHS. Noticeable, however, is the fact that both Scotland and Wales have and continue consistently to spend more on health care than England.

Figure 4.3 Per capita NHS funding in England, Scotland and Wales, 1998–2010

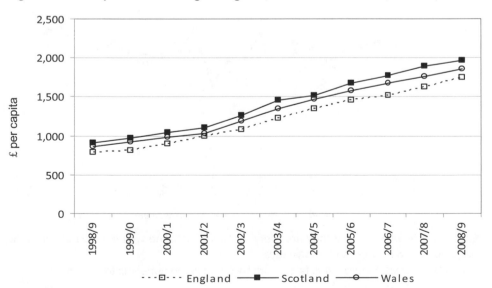

Source: Authors' construction from PESA data (HMT, 2010)

Given the different policy routes taken in the different countries, we report here on the extent to which there has been a divergence between the countries in relation to public satisfaction with the NHS and individual services, and public perceptions about improvements over the last five years. While we do not see our analyses as a definitive test of the comparative performance of the NHS between countries,[10] we are interested in whether *British Social Attitudes* data imply that attitudes in the countries have been affected by policy divergence. A key area on which policy has differed is around patient choice and involvement. As a result, we take a particular look at this issue.

Satisfaction and perceptions of improvements

Trends in levels of public satisfaction with the NHS, in particular those from 2000 to 2009, are very similar in England and in Scotland/Wales (Figure 4.4). (Because of the relatively small number of people interviewed in Scotland and Wales, we have combined the responses of people in the two countries, to compare England against the two devolved states.[11])

Figure 4.4 Trends in satisfaction with the NHS overall, by country, 1983–2009

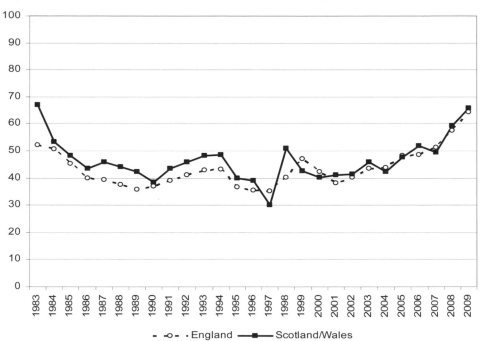

Satisfied = % who say that they are "very" or "quite" satisfied with the way in which the National Health Service is run nowadays
The data on which Figure 4.4 is based can be found in the appendix to this chapter

However, while there seems very little difference in views on satisfaction between the countries, there is a noticeable gap between the countries when it comes to people's views about *improvements* in services over the last five years. Table 4.4 shows that, across all the aspects of NHS performance that people were asked about, a higher proportion of people in England think that things have got better (and conversely, a lower proportion who think things have got worse) than people in Scotland or Wales. It is particularly noticeable that Scotland and Wales lag further behind England in terms of the perceived net improvements in waiting times from referral to treatment and for an outpatient appointment – both areas in which the English NHS has put considerable effort in improving over the last five to 10 years.

Table 4.4 Perceptions of changes in the NHS, by country

Change over the last five years in …	England	Scotland/Wales	Difference (England minus Scotland/Wales)
	%	%	
… general standard of NHS care			
Better	41	34	+7
Worse	18	22	-4
Net (Better–worse)	+23	+13	+11
… say patients have in treatment decisions			
Better	39	30	+9
Worse	10	13	-3
Net (Better–worse)	+28	+17	+12
… wait from referral to treatment			
Better	37	30	+7
Worse	20	29	-9
Net (Better–worse)	+16	+1	+16
… wait for an outpatient appointment			
Better	38	28	+10
Worse	24	33	-9
Net (Better–worse)	+14	-5	+19
… wait in GP surgery			
Better	39	38	+1
Worse	14	18	-3
Net (Better–worse)	+24	+20	+4
… wait in outpatients			
Better	27	23	+4
Worse	25	28	-3
Net (Better–worse)	+2	-5	+7
Base	2917	504	

As we saw from the spending figures in Figure 4.3, these perceived improvements in England, compared with Scotland/Wales cannot be explained by comparatively faster growth in spending in England. Between 1999 and 2009, per capita NHS spending has grown at very similar rates in all countries and spending in England has remained around 10 to 15 per cent less than in Wales and Scotland respectively.

So, it would appear that the NHS in England has secured satisfaction rates on a par with Scotland and Wales at lower per capita spending. A more likely explanation is differences in policy foci between England and the other countries. The two areas of improvement where, according to public opinion, Scotland and Wales perform particularly poorly in comparison with England – namely the wait for an outpatient appointment and the wait from referral to treatment – have been, as noted earlier, areas of arguably greater policy focus in England than in Scotland and Wales. It is notable that the upward trend in perceived improvements in both the general standard of NHS care and in the time taken to get an outpatient appointment has been much steeper for England than for Scotland and Wales. From a similar level in 1995 when, for instance, around 17 per cent of people in all countries felt that outpatient waiting times had improved in the previous five years, the proportion of people saying this in England in 2009 is 38 per cent, compared with 28 per cent of those in Scotland/Wales (Table 4.5)

Table 4.5 Perceptions of whether time that most people wait to get outpatient appointment has got better over the last five years, by country, 1995–2009

	1995	2001	2008	2009
% agree has got better over last five years				
England	17	12	29	38
Base	*2052*	*1837*	*2898*	*2917*
Scotland/Wales	17	10	21	28
Base	*347*	*351*	*460*	*504*

Patient choice

Another area of policy divergence between England and Scotland and Wales has been in relation to patient choice. Giving people more choice has been a major focus of government policy in England since 2002, with patients now entitled to choose any NHS or eligible non-NHS hospital when referred by their GP. In Scotland and Wales, on the other hand, while a degree of choice exists, it has not been formalised in the same way as in England within the context of a competitive market for care.

British Social Attitudes includes a question which asks people:

> *Imagine a patient was due to have hospital treatment and that this*
> *treatment was being paid for by the NHS. Which of the statements on*
> *this card best describes the choice this patient would have over where*
> *to have their treatment?*
> *Patients do not have any choice of hospital*
> *Patients can choose between different NHS hospitals only*
> *Patients can choose between both NHS and private hospitals*

Table 4.6 shows that, while a substantially greater proportion of people in England than in Scotland and Wales think that patients can choose their hospital (76 per cent, compared with 53 per cent), a fifth (21 per cent) do not think they have a choice and half (51 per cent) think their choice is restricted to NHS hospitals only.

Table 4.6 Views on patient choice of hospital, by country

	England	Scotland or Wales
	%	%
Patients do not have any choice of hospital	21	44
Patients can choose NHS hospitals only	51	32
Patients can choose NHS and private hospitals	25	21
Base	*2917*	*504*

While there is, to an extent, greater recognition by English residents of their right to choose, compared with Scottish and Welsh residents, such an understanding does not appear to be linked with a greater propensity to be satisfied with the NHS: awareness of choice was not found to be a significant factor with regard to NHS satisfaction when controlling for other variables (see Model 1 in the appendix to this chapter).

Conclusions

The turn of the democratic wheel at the May 2010 General Election closed a significant period for the NHS since Labour's 1997 victory. Policy towards the NHS had developed and evolved over this time and, to a certain extent, diverged in England, Scotland and Wales. Health funding in all these countries has increased substantially over the period, bringing the UK close to the European Union countries' average, as pledged by the former Prime Minister, Tony Blair. And so, too, since its nadir in 1997, has the public's satisfaction increased with the NHS overall and its services – from just 34 per cent in 1997 to 64 per cent in 2009.

So, to answer the first part of this chapter's title, on the headline figures it would seem that Labour did very well indeed. Our analyses have shown improvements in satisfaction levels which, over the last six or seven years, have been expressed by those population groups (Conservative Party supporters, the young, the well off and those with higher education qualifications) who have historically been less inclined to report satisfaction with the NHS. Although all four of these groups are still less likely to be satisfied than their counterparts at the other end of the scale, the gap between the extremes in all these groups has narrowed somewhat since 1996 (less so for different educational groups). So not only have satisfaction levels increased, there seems to be a growing consensus regarding satisfaction across the population. This is a real achievement and, for a universal public service funded from general taxation, is of particular significance given the need for the NHS not only to serve all sections of society but to demonstrate its worth to those who pay for it.

The second part of this chapter's question is much harder to answer. How *did* Labour improve the public's satisfaction with the NHS so dramatically? The intuitive (if slightly circular) answer is that satisfaction increased because the NHS improved in ways which were recognised and appreciated by the public and patients. And indeed, this, in part, is the answer from our modelling of those statistically significant factors explaining the propensity to be satisfied with the NHS overall. Along with certain socio-demographic characteristics – educational qualifications, political affiliation and age – perceived improvements in various aspects of the NHS were the other main set of significant factors associated with satisfaction. And when we looked at those factors associated with a propensity to state that the general level of care in the NHS had improved, waiting time from referral to treatment was significant (along with a number of other improvement areas).

This, perhaps, provides more of a clue to the 'how' question. A key policy – particularly in England over the last decade or so – has been to reduce waiting times. And as we have shown earlier, waiting times for inpatients, outpatients, and, more recently, the combined referral to treatment time have all reduced substantially over the last five to 10 years. It can be hard to remember now, but in the 1990s and earlier, barely a week passed without a report in the media of personal tales of huge delays in receiving hospital treatment or even getting an outpatient appointment in the first place. The stories escalated in winter with reports of bed shortages, queues and patients left on trolleys in corridors. Today, such stories are a rarity. Of course, other concerns and headlines rise to the top, and now the media and the public's concerns tend to be about hospital – acquired infection and access to expensive cancer drugs deemed not to be cost – effective by NICE. Nevertheless, regardless of such worries, the survey headlines show satisfaction to have increased.

However, other areas of improvement – the wait in outpatient departments as well as the say patients have in their treatment decisions – were also significant factors associated with a propensity to be satisfied with the NHS. On these it is harder to make a direct connection with policy action or, indeed, to say whether there were actually any improvements in these areas, as few objective statistics are collected.[12] Nevertheless, there may be outcomes of increased investment (and perhaps reform) that have led to improvements in these areas which some people have noticed.

Another aspect of Labour's policy towards the NHS, and one less emulated in Wales and Scotland, has been the promotion of a more formalised offer of choice of hospital for NHS patients in the context of a more competitive health care market. Our analysis shows, however, that choice *per se* was not a statistically significant factor in either satisfaction with the NHS overall or with perceptions of improvements in the general level of NHS care over the last five years. This is not to say that the public does not want or value choice (previous *British Social Attitudes* surveys have shown the opposite Appleby and Alvarez-Rosete, 2003), or that choice has not played some part in improving the things the public cares about. But it does suggest that the link between choice and, say, reductions in waiting times, is not recognised by the public or seen as important (if, indeed, such a link exists).

This is in part confirmed by our analysis of satisfaction and improvements in the NHS across England, Scotland and Wales where policy on, for example, patient choice has differed. We found no significant regional element in explaining the propensity to express either satisfaction or the view that general standards of care in the NHS had improved over the last five years.

One broad conclusion from this analysis is that the public is very results and less policy oriented; improvements in the things the public cares about are important in influencing satisfaction. Exactly how improvements are brought about are perhaps, naturally enough, of less interest or importance.

Is there a message here for the new coalition administration? The new government's health policy (in England) is now laying even greater emphasis on patient choice and more disaggregated purchasing of care by GPs (rather than primary care trusts) as the main mechanisms for improving the NHS (Secretary of State for Health, 2010), but against a virtual zero real growth in funding for the next four years and the rejection (at least overtly) of a target regime (shown to have been instrumental in improving waiting times). If such policies fail to deliver improvements in the things the public cares about (or at least maintain improvements over the last five years) it will be hard to see future *British Social Attitudes* surveys reporting continued upward trends in satisfaction with the NHS.

Notes

1. With the exception of the final section ('Country variation in policy and views about the NHS'), where we analyse the survey by country, all analyses are for the whole survey dataset.
2. The Conservative government had had some success during the early 1990s in reducing the numbers of people waiting over a year for admission to hospital.

3. Before that, NHS spending as a proportion of GDP had risen during the first few years of the 1990s.
4. These were known as the 'internal market' which involved separating the purchasing of hospital care from its provision in order to encourage competition between hospitals to win contracts from health authorities.
5. In the *British Social Attitudes* survey in 1997, questions on satisfaction with the individual services were not fielded.
6. Bases for Table 4.1 are as follows:

		1987	1990	1993	1996	1999	2003	2007	2009
Age	18–34	885	848	862	1035	828	579	709	747
	35–54	1024	1016	1040	1261	1080	842	1113	1297
	55–64	451	382	350	451	450	338	500	580
	65+	482	537	679	858	783	533	753	792
Political affiliation	Conservative	1095	986	964	1012	785	568	786	961
	Labour	824	1074	1101	1528	1333	867	1083	905
	Lib Dem/Alliance	533	220	368	391	323	245	280	330
	Other	40	136	104	122	123	95	201	332
	None	205	229	232	354	416	377	491	616
Household income quartiles	Lowest quartile	627	592	755	1008	815	638	778	733
	2nd lowest	442	623	588	906	778	475	706	834
	2nd highest	753	532	666	646	563	437	575	650
	Highest quartile	672	491	551	622	612	414	569	690
Educational attainment	Higher education	592	605	563	911	797	626	857	991
	A level	255	305	316	429	365	289	427	521
	O level/CSE	765	821	885	1020	901	689	692	847
	None	1207	1038	1124	1184	1014	631	799	746

7. Recent experience of the NHS continues to be associated with higher levels of satisfaction with the NHS. Controlling for a range of socio-demographic factors (see Model 1 in the appendix), we found that recent personal contact with inpatient services was associated with a propensity to express satisfaction with the NHS.
8. Views on improvements in the wait *for* outpatient appointments were not included in the model due to their similarity to views on referral to treatment waits.
9. Views on improvements in the wait for outpatient appointments were not included in the model due to their similarity to views on referral to treatment waits. Views on improvements in the general standard of the NHS were not included due to their similarity to the outcome variable, general satisfaction with the NHS.
10. The analyses in this section do not include Northern Ireland, as the *British Social Attitudes* survey is not carried out there.
11. Country of residence is included in Model 1 in the appendix. We find it has no significant impact on satisfaction with the NHS overall. This means that the small

difference in satisfaction levels seen in Figure 4.4 is explained by characteristics other than the respondents' country of residence.

12. Some data on these issues are collected through the National Patient Survey Programme. More information on this programme is available at: http://www.dh.gov.uk/en/Publicationsandstatistics/Publications/PublicationsPolicyA ndGuidance/Browsable/DH_5578969

References

Appleby, J. and Alvarez-Rosete, A. (2003), 'The NHS: keeping up with public expectations?' in Park, A., Curtice, J., Thomson, K., Jarvis, L. and Bromley, C. (eds.), *British Social Attitudes: the 20th Report – Continuity and change over two decades* London: Sage

Appleby, J., Crawford, E., Emerson, C. (2009), *How cold will it be? Prospects for NHS funding 2011/12 to 2016/17*, London: King's Fund/Institute for Fiscal Studies

Appleby, J. and Phillips, M. (2009), 'The NHS: satisfied now?', in Park, A, Curtice, J., Thomson, K., Phillips, M. and Clery, E. (eds.), *British Social Attitudes: the 25th Report*, London: Sage

Bevan, G., and Hood, C. (2006), 'Have targets improved performance in the English NHS?', *BMJ*, **332**:419–22.

Department of Health (2010), *Historic waiting times data* available at http://www.dh.gov.uk/en/Publicationsandstatistics/Statistics/Performancedataandstatis tics/HospitalWaitingTimesandListStatistics/index.htm

Greer, A. and Trench, S. (2008), *Health and intergovernmental relations in the Devolved United Kingdom,* London: Nuffield Trust

HMT (2010) Public Expenditure Statistical Analyses (PESA) (various years), available at http://www.hm-treasury.gov.uk/pespub_index.htm

Ipsos-Mori (2010) Political and social trends, available at http://www.ipsos-mori.com/researchspecialisms/socialresearch/specareas/politics /trends.aspx

Labour Party (1997), Labour Party manifesto, available at http://www.labour-party.org.uk/manifestos/1997/1997-labour-manifesto.shtml

Mulligan, J.-A. and Appleby, J. (2001), 'The NHS and Labour's battle for public opinion', in Park, A., Curtice, J., Thomson, K., Jarvis, L. and Bromley, C. (eds.), British Social Attitudes: the 18th Report – Public policies, social ties, London: Sage

National Audit Office (2001), Inappropriate Adjustments to NHS Waiting Lists, London: The Stationery Office

Secretary of State for Health (2000), The NHS Plan: A plan for investment, a plan for reform, Cm 4818-I, The Stationery Office London:

Secretary of State for Health (2010), Equity and Excellence: Liberating the NHS, Cm 7881, London: TSO

Stevens, S. (2004), 'Reform Strategies for the English NHS', Health Affairs, **23(3)** 37–44

Thorlby, R. and Maybin, J. (eds.) (2010), A high-performing NHS? A review of progress 1997–2010 London: The King's Fund

Wanless, D. (2002), *Securing our future health: taking a long term view. Final Report,* London: Treasury

Wanless, D., Appleby, J., Harrison, A., Patel, D. (2007), Our Future Health Secured? A review of NHS funding and performance, King's Fund: London

Acknowledgements

The *National Centre for Social Research* is grateful to the Department of Health for their financial support which enabled us to ask the questions reported in this chapter. The views expressed are those of the authors alone.

Appendix

Multivariate analysis

Two logistic regressions were undertaken on the 2009 survey data. The first analysed various factors – age, sex, party identification etc – to assess the propensity to express satisfaction (very + quite) with the NHS overall. The second logistic regression model analysed factors associated with a propensity to state that over the last five years the general standard of care in the NHS had got better (much better + better).

Model 1: Overall satisfaction with the NHS

Backward stepwise variable exclusion produced nine significant factors (with four related to various aspects of improvement over the last five years). The final model results are shown in Table A.1.

Variables initially included in the regression (italics indicates variables dropped by the stepwise procedure): Age group, political identification, level of education, contact in the last 12 months with inpatients, improvements in: wait from GP referral to treatment, wait in GP surgery, wait in outpatient department, say patients have in decisions about their treatment and health care, reasonable wait for a hip replacement, *income, occupational class, country of residence (England v Scotland and Wales), gender, awareness of choice, contact in the last 12 months with: dentist, A and E, outpatients, GP.* Views on improvements in the wait for outpatient appointments were not included in the model due to their similarity to views on referral to treatment waits. Views on improvements in the general standard of the NHS were not included due to their similarity to the outcome variable, general satisfaction with the NHS.

The first column reports the odds ratio for each factor in relation to the reference group (in parentheses) where a coefficient of >1 indicates a greater propensity than the reference group to express satisfaction with the NHS overall, with a coefficient of < 1 indicating the converse. So, Labour supporters are 1.8 times more likely to be satisfied with the NHS than those with no political identification and those with higher educational qualifications are less likely to be satisfied than those with no qualifications, for example. The second and third columns show the 95 per cent confidence intervals for the coefficent values. The last column shows the level of statistical significance for each factor in the model (where for $p < = 0.05$ the factor is considered significant at the five per cent level and at $p = < 0.01$ significant at the one per cent level).

Table A.1 Overall satisfaction with the NHS (very + quite satisfied)

	Coefficient	95% confidence interval		p value
		Lower	Upper	
Age group (65 and over)				
18–34	0.84	0.62	1.14	.263
35–54	*0.74	0.56	0.97	.030
55–64	**0.66	0.49	0.90	.007
Education (no qualifications)				
Higher education	**0.60	0.45	0.80	.001
A level or equivalent	*0.71	0.51	0.97	.034
O level/CSE or equivalent	0.77	0.57	1.02	.071
Political identification (none)				
Conservative	1.06	0.82	1.38	.643
Labour	**1.82	1.39	2.39	0.000
Liberal Democrat	1.35	0.97	1.89	0.077
Other party	1.13	0.81	1.58	0.464
Inpatient contact (no contact)				
family member or friend	1.18	0.96	1.45	0.107
personal experience	**1.80	1.39	2.34	0.000
Improvements in last five years Referral to treatment waiting time (about the same)				
Better	*1.31	1.05	1.62	0.015
Worse	**0.69	0.55	0.88	0.002
Improvements in last five years Wait in outpatients (about the same)				
Better	**1.80	1.42	2.29	0.000
Worse	**0.47	0.38	0.57	0.000
Improvements in last five years Wait in GP surgery (about the same)				
Better	1.20	0.99	1.46	0.060
Worse	*0.72	0.56	0.94	0.014

Table continued on next page.

Improvements in last five years
Say in decisions about treatment
(about the same)

Better	**1.35	1.11	1.64	0.003
Worse	**0.49	0.37	0.65	0.000

Reasonable wait for a hip operation
(0–2 weeks)

>2–6 weeks	1.19	0.95	1.50	0.129
>6–18 weeks	1.23	0.96	1.56	0.098
>18 weeks	*1.54	1.10	2.15	0.011
Constant	1.83			0.003

Base 2889

* = significant at 95% level
** = significant at 99% level
Response categories used in model but not reported in the table include:
> Educational attainment: Foreign qualifications, don't know, refused, not answered.
> Household income: Don't know, refused
> Political identification: Don't know, refused, other
> Inpatient contact: Not answered
> Improvements in the last five years: Don't know

Views on improvements in the wait for outpatient appointments were not included in the model due to their similarity to views on referral to treatment waits

Model 2: Improvements in NHS care over the last five years

Backwards stepwise variable exclusion initially produced eight significant factors (with four related to various aspects of improvement over the last five years). One factor – household income – was subsequently excluded as the only significant result was for those who did not know or refused to answer. This exclusion had little impact on the final model results shown in Table A.2.

Variables initially included in the regression (italics indicates variables dropped by the stepwise procedure): Age, sex, party identification, improvements in: wait from GP referral to treatment, wait in GP surgery, wait in outpatient department, say patients have in decisions about their treatment and health care, *occupational class, level of education, income, country of residence (England v Scotland and Wales), awareness of choice, contact in the last 12 months with: dentist, A and E, outpatients, inpatients, GP, reasonable wait for a hip replacement.*

The interpretation of the odds ratio is as in Model 1.

Table A.2 Improvements in the general standards of NHS care over the last five years (much better + better)

	Coefficient	95% confidence interval		p value
		Lower	Upper	
Age (65+)				
18–34	1.22	0.94	1.57	0.131
35–54	*0.76	0.60	0.97	0.025
55–64	*0.70	0.53	0.93	0.015
Sex (female)				
Male	**1.44	1.22	1.71	0.000
Political identification (none)				
Conservative	0.98	0.75	1.28	0.897
Labour	**1.70	1.30	2.22	0.000
Liberal Democrat	1.21	0.87	1.69	0.265
Other party	0.94	0.66	1.33	0.718
Improvements in last five years Referral to treatment waiting time (about the same)				
Better	**2.18	1.78	2.66	0.000
Worse	**0.57	0.43	0.74	0.000
Improvements in last five years Wait in outpatients (about the same)				
Better	**1.98	1.61	2.43	0.000
Worse	**0.48	0.38	0.61	0.000
Improvements in last five years Wait in GP surgery (about the same)				
Better	**1.64	1.36	1.97	0.000
Worse	1.08	0.81	1.44	0.607
Improvements in last five years Say in decisions about treatment (about the same)				
Better	**1.56	1.29	1.88	0.000
Worse	0.85	0.61	1.19	0.334
Constant	0.32			0.000

Base 2889

* = significant at 95% level; ** = significant at 99% level
Response categories used in model but not reported in the table include:
      Political identification: Don't know, refused, other
      Improvements in the last five years: Don't know

Table A.3 Satisfaction with the way that the NHS is run, 1983–2009

	83	84	86	87	89	90	91	93	94	95	96	97
	%	%	%	%	%	%	%	%	%	%	%	%
Very/quite satisfied	55	51	40	40	37	37	40	44	44	37	36	34
Very/quite dissatisfied	26	30	40	40	46	47	41	38	38	45	50	50
Net	29	21	1	1	-9	-10	-1	6	6	-8	-14	-15
Base	*1761*	*1675*	*3100*	*2847*	*3029*	*2797*	*2918*	*2945*	*3469*	*3633*	*3620*	*1355*

	98	99	00	01	02	03	04	05	06	07	08	09
	%	%	%	%	%	%	%	%	%	%	%	%
Very/quite satisfied	42	46	42	39	40	44	43	48	49	51	58	64
Very/quite dissatisfied	36	33	39	41	41	37	37	31	34	30	25	19
Net	5	13	3	-2	-1	6	7	17	15	21	32	46
Base	*3146*	*3143*	*3426*	*2188*	*2287*	*2293*	*3199*	*3193*	*2143*	*3078*	*3358*	*3421*

Table A.4 Satisfaction with GPs , dentists, inpatients and outpatients, 1983–2009

	83	86	87	89	90	91	93	94	95	96	98
GPs	%	%	%	%	%	%	%	%	%	%	%
Very/quite satisfied	80	77	79	80	80	83	83	80	79	77	75
Dentists											
Very/quite satisfied	73	74	74	70	69	68	58	57	55	52	53
Inpatients											
Very/quite satisfied	74	67	67	65	63	64	64	58	57	53	54
Outpatients											
Very/quite satisfied	61	55	54	52	51	52	57	56	55	52	52
Base	*1761*	*3100*	*2847*	*3029*	*2797*	*2918*	*2945*	*3469*	*3633*	*3620*	*3146*

	99	00	01	02	03	04	05	06	07	08	09
GPs	%	%	%	%	%	%	%	%	%	%	%
Very/quite satisfied	76	76	71	72	72	72	74	76	76	77	80
Dentists											
Very/quite satisfied	53	62	53	54	52	42	45	42	42	42	48
Inpatients											
Very/quite satisfied	58	58	51	51	52	48	50	46	49	51	59
Outpatients											
Very/quite satisfied	56	58	50	52	54	54	61	57	60	61	67
Base	*3143*	*3426*	*2188*	*2287*	*2293*	*3199*	*3193*	*2143*	*3078*	*3358*	*3421*

BRITISH SOCIAL ATTITUDES

Table A.5 Trends in satisfaction with the NHS overall, by country, 1983–2009

	83	84	86	87	89	90	91	93	94	95	96	97
England	%	%	%	%	%	%	%	%	%	%	%	%
Very/quite satisfied	52	51	40	39	36	37	39	43	43	37	36	35
Base	*1494*	*1407*	*2623*	*2402*	*2571*	*2395*	*2490*	*2503*	*2959*	*3100*	*3072*	*1153*
Scotland and Wales												
Very/quite satisfied	67	53	43	46	42	38	43	48	49	40	39	30
Base	*267*	*268*	*477*	*445*	*458*	*402*	*428*	*442*	*510*	*533*	*548*	*202*

	98	99	00	01	02	03	04	05	06	07	08	09
England	%	%	%	%	%	%	%	%	%	%	%	%
Very/quite satisfied	40	47	42	38	40	43	44	48	49	51	58	64
Base	*2695*	*2718*	*2887*	*1837*	*1924*	*1917*	*2684*	*2721*	*1824*	*2635*	*2898*	*2917*
Scotland and Wales												
Very/quite satisfied	51	42	40	41	41	46	42	48	52	49	59	66
Base	*451*	*425*	*539*	*351*	*363*	*376*	*515*	*472*	*319*	*443*	*460*	*504*

5 The evolution of the modern worker: attitudes to work

Alex Bryson and John Forth[*]

The world of work has undergone a transformation since the first *British Social Attitudes* survey was conducted over a quarter of a century ago. A technological revolution has redesigned job tasks around computer and information technologies, leading to greater demand for skilled labour and the rapid decline of easy-to-automate jobs. The same technological revolution has facilitated the globalisation of product and labour markets by reducing the costs of inter-connectedness. International trade has boomed and market competition is tougher than ever. As a consequence, mature western economies such as Britain have seen an increasing percentage of manufactured goods come from abroad, resulting in a substantial decline in the relative size of the manufacturing sector in Britain and a decline in the prevalence of manual jobs. At the same time, the demographic profile of employees in Britain has changed markedly.

Many of these key changes are illustrated in Table 5.1. It shows, for instance, that the proportion of employees working in the manufacturing sector has more than halved, from 27 per cent in 1985 to 12 per cent now. One in ten employees now belongs to a minority ethnic group, a contributing factor to this increase being the rise in immigration to the UK, a further reflection of the internationalisation of markets. And there are now nearly as many women in the workforce as there are men. Many women have also broken through the 'glass ceiling' which once prevented them from doing jobs in the higher echelons of the labour market (Blackburn, 2010).

Finally, as Table 5.1 shows, just over a quarter of employees now belong to a trade union, down from nearly half in 1985.

Of course, alongside changes in the real economy, there have been numerous important policy shifts in the UK which have also affected the nature of employment. *Laissez-faire* policies in the 1980s saw rapid de-industrialisation, high levels of unemployment, and unprecedented growth in wage inequality in Britain, with statutory interventions aiming to increase the flexibility of the

[*] Alex Bryson is a Senior Research Fellow and John Forth a Research Fellow at the National Institute of Economic and Social Research (NIESR).

labour market and pin back the power of trade unions. The first half of the 1990s continued in the same vein, but the advent of a Labour government in 1997 marked a profound shift in policy (Dickens and Hall, 2009). It ushered in a period of labour market 're-regulation' perhaps best epitomised by the introduction, for the first time in Britain's history, of a national minimum wage. A huge expansion in higher and further education was intended to meet the big growth in demand for highly skilled labour, and contributed to a substantial rise in the proportion of graduate employees, from a quarter in 1985 to 40 per cent now. The public sector, which had shrunk in size in the 1990s, also grew again under Labour as a result of the policy focus on education and health.

Table 5.1 The changing character of employees, 1985–2009

% of employees with specified characteristics	1985	1989	1995	1999	2005	2009
Workplace characteristics:						
Manufacturing	27	25	18	22	17	12
Public sector	34	33	n/a	26	30	32
Job characteristics:						
Manual occupation	44	43	38	39	37	35
Union member	47	44	36	32	29	27
Employee characteristics:						
Female	44	46	51	49	48	47
Ethnic minority	3	3	4	4	8	10
Degree-level qualification	25	27	32	34	39	40
Base	*857*	*1462*	*1448*	*1364*	*1952*	*1594*

Base: all employees
The *British Social Attitudes* sample of employees only includes those working 10 or more hours per week

There has also been much talk of a revolution in the management of employees. Firms have adopted 'employee engagement' practices, such as team working, encouraging efforts on the part of workers to participate in the creation of high-quality goods and services which can compete in increasingly competitive markets (Wood and Bryson, 2009). The ways in which firms are created and governed have also undergone a radical overhaul. Mergers and acquisitions are commonplace, facilitated by new international rules governing corporate structures. Corporate decision making at companies such as Cadbury (recently acquired by Kraft of the US) – traditionally thought of as British-owned – takes place in other parts of the world where the 'global brand' is key.

Some of the effects of these changes are well-known. There has been a polarisation in the rewards from working, with skilled workers commanding a large wage premium (Autor *et al.* 2008; Machin, forthcoming). This is nowhere more evident than the market for the best paid 'super-stars' (chief executives, bond traders and the like) where rewards are often heavily geared to individual or company performance (Bell and Van Reenen, 2010). At the other end of the labour market, cost pressures on firms have led to the adoption of more flexible employment practices, such as the introduction of temporary contracts, intended to minimise labour costs and deliver 'flexible firms' capable of responding through 'just-in-time' production to increasingly uncertain patterns of demand for goods and services.

In this chapter we explore how employees' *experiences of, and attitudes to, work* have changed over the last quarter of a century. A previous examination of the period 1983–96 found that the quality of working life deteriorated between the early 1980s and early 1990s, a time which not only encompassed the economic and policy upheavals we have already mentioned, but also the deep recession of 1990/91 (Bryson and McKay, 1997). Since then, Britain first experienced 12 years of uninterrupted economic growth, and then the most severe recession since the 1930s. So we will examine how employees' experiences of, and attitudes towards, work have changed since then. Has there been further deterioration in the most recent decade, or did the years of economic prosperity and the introduction of many new minimum standards lead, instead, to an improvement? Further, what effect has the most recent recession had on employees' attitudes to work?

We begin by examining employees' perceptions to two of the most critical aspects of any employment relationship: the degree of job security and the amount of pay on offer. We then move on to consider more qualitative features of the employment relationship: the degree of trust or conflict between employees and their employers, and the degree of involvement that employees consider themselves to have over decision making at their workplace.

Exploring changes in attitudes to work

In trying to explain trends in employee attitudes we need to distinguish between three possible explanations for change. The first stems from *compositional changes*; changes in the composition of the workforce. For example, if the proportion of employees who are women is growing, and women are more likely than men to hold a particular view, then – all other things being equal – the proportion of employees holding this view will grow. A second possible reason for change is linked to *the economic cycle*. It may be, for example, that some attitudes vary depending on whether the economy is in a period of upturn or downturn – so some changes may simply reflect fluctuations in the economy. As noted above, there have been two major recessions since 1983; Bryson and McKay (1997) observed only the first of these, so we are in a better position to identify cyclical trends. The third possible reason for change is an *underlying time trend*, that is, a change over time which is independent of the economic cycle and does not reflect the changing nature of the workforce. Such developments might be prompted by changes in societal norms, for instance. These different possible trends not only have different implications for policy makers, but may also counteract and mask one another – making simple year-on-year data difficult to interpret.

We explore these issues through both descriptive and multivariate analysis.[1] The multivariate analysis uses regression models to assess the importance of certain factors after taking account of (controlling for) all others. Changes in the *composition* of the workforce are accounted for by including in our models a number of factors relating to the demographic characteristics of employees, their jobs and the workplace within which they work. The models then account for changes in the *economic cycle* by including variables indicating the level of unemployment in each year and the changes in unemployment levels (and, in some models, changes in gross domestic product (GDP)). Once these various factors have been controlled for, dummy variables which identify each of the survey years serve to indicate the extent to which attitude change has occurred over time *above and beyond* what would be expected as a result of changes in workforce composition and economic changes. (Further details of the regression analysis that has been carried out can be found in the appendix to this chapter, and a more general explanation of regression techniques can be found in the Appendix to this report). Our analysis will indicate whether any overall changes we find in employees' attitudes to work reflect changes in workforce composition, the economic cycle or other trends.

Job security

It is already known that feelings of job security tend to follow the economic cycle to some degree (see Green, 2006). Employees feel more secure when the economy is growing and less secure when economic downturns begin to lead to job losses. But there is also a general perception that job security has seen a secular decline over the past quarter century, as increased competition (partly arising from the globalisation of product markets and supply chains, but also extending into the public sector) has all but eliminated the 'job for life'. To examine perceptions of job security, we ask employees:

How likely or unlikely is it that you will leave this employer over the next year for any reason?

This question has appeared in most years of the series and the pattern of results is shown in the line at the top of Figure 5.1. Our last reading shows that just under a quarter (23 per cent) think they will leave their employer within the next year, a proportion which has fluctuated considerably since the mid-1980s. However, there does appear to be a gradual upward trend since 1983 in the proportion of people who think it likely they will leave their job within the next year. This corresponds with other data which suggest that average job tenure fell in the 1980s and 1990s (Gregg and Wadsworth, 2002).[2]

Of course, for some employees the end of the current employment relationship will come voluntarily, as they look for a new challenge or better terms and conditions in another organisation. However, from the point of view of job insecurity, we are most interested in people who are leaving involuntary. We identify them by asking respondents who say that they are "very" or "quite" likely to leave their employer why they think this will happen. Here we focus on those employees who say either that "my firm will close down" or that "I will be made redundant"; the percentage of all employees giving either response is shown on the dashed line towards the bottom of Figure 5.1.

One would expect this second series to rise as the economy falters and firms begin to consider layoffs, and then to fall as the economy recovers. However, the series was surprisingly stable throughout the period from 1983 to 1991, although unemployment fell sharply between 1983 and 1989. Once unemployment began to rise after the recession of 1990/91, however, the two series began to move upwards in tandem. The response to the recent recession has been much less pronounced – at least up until the time of writing. The percentage of employees saying that they are likely to leave their current job because of redundancy or the closure of their firm now stands at four per cent, with no significant change since 2008. Similarly, when employees were asked in 2005 and 2009 "how secure do you feel your employment is with your present employer?", the proportion saying either "insecure" or "very insecure" was the same (nine per cent) in both years. The only indication of an increase in insecurity was a fall in the percentage saying they felt "very secure" (from 37 per cent in 2005 to 30 per cent in 2009) and an equivalent rise in the percentage saying they felt either "secure" or "neither secure nor insecure" (see Curtice and Park in this volume). This relatively muted response to the recent recession no doubt reflects the lower rate of actual job loss when compared with its predecessors, despite the comparatively larger fall in GDP (Gregg and Wadsworth, 2010). This has been attributed to higher rates of firm profitability going into the current recession, which reduced the pressure on firms to shed jobs, and to supportive monetary and fiscal policies (*ibid.*).

Figure 5.1 Feelings of job insecurity and ILO unemployment rate[+], 1983–2009

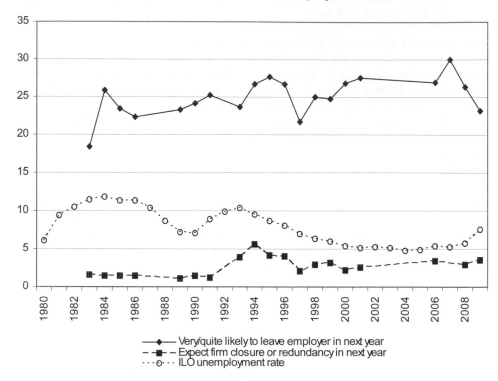

Base: all employees
The data on which Figure 5.1 is based can be found in the appendix to this chapter
[+] Source: ONS Time Series Databank – series MGSX

Figure 5.1 does nevertheless provide some clear support for the notion of a secular increase in perceptions of insecurity since the 1980s. Even in the period of economic boom and expanding employment from 1998 through to 2005/6, the percentage of employees who thought their job would come to an involuntary end in the next 12 months remained around one and a half percentage points above the percentage seen when the economy was growing and unemployment falling in the second half of the 1980s.[3] The survey data we have cannot tell us whether this might be due to a greater proliferation of temporary or fixed-term contracts. However, the rise in insecurity since the 1980s cannot be attributed to other obvious changes in the composition of the workforce such as the decline (in the 1990s) of public sector employment, which has traditionally been seen as more secure. If we control for our standard set of compositional factors (including employee, job and workplace characteristics), the difference of around one and a half percentage points seen in Figure 5.1 is unchanged and remains statistically significant.

This suggests that the apparent increase in the 'underlying' rate of job insecurity cannot be attributed to compositional changes in the workforce. Nor does it simply reflect changes in the economic cycle. Rather, it appears that there has been a secular increase in feelings of insecurity, which can be traced back to the early 1990s and was not reversed by the labour market policies introduced by Labour during their time in office from 1997.

Wages

Wages are probably the greatest concern to employees after job security. They represent the principal pecuniary reward from employment and are the chief determinant of most employees' standard of living. So we turn now to examine employees' attitudes both to pay levels and to pay inequality, and assess how these have changed over time.

Wage growth typically falls in recessionary periods, because reductions in profits limit employers' ability to award pay increases while rising unemployment weakens employees' bargaining power. However, it does not automatically follow that employees will be less satisfied with their wages as a result: this will depend on the extent to which they take wider factors – such as the probability of job loss – into account. We can assess this by looking at responses to a question that asks employees whether they would describe the wages or salary they are paid for the job they do as being "very low", "on the low side", "reasonable" or "on the high side". On this measure, satisfaction with ones own wage seems to be loosely counter-cyclical (that is, it increases when the economy is slowing down, and falls when economic conditions improve). This is illustrated by Figure 5.2, which plots both satisfaction with wages and the unemployment rate; this shows that satisfaction was at its highest in the early 1990s and 2006/9, both periods marked by increasing levels of unemployment.

Our multivariate analysis confirms the link between wage satisfaction and the state of the economic cycle. Changes in the composition of the workforce account for almost none of the variation shown in Figure 5.2. Instead, four particular years emerge as having levels of wage satisfaction that are significantly higher (in a statistical sense) than the base year of 1985: 1991 (13 percentage points higher), 1993 (eight points), 2006 (nine points) and 2009 (nine points). These are the only four years in our estimation sample in which unemployment rose. On average, satisfaction is eight percentage points higher in years when the unemployment rate is rising, all other things being equal. An obvious explanation for this is that those employees who remain in work during these sorts of periods are glad still to be receiving some kind of wage when the aggregate risk of job loss is rising, and their views about their wage levels reflect this.

Figure 5.2 Perceptions of whether wages are reasonable and ILO unemployment rate[+], 1983–2009

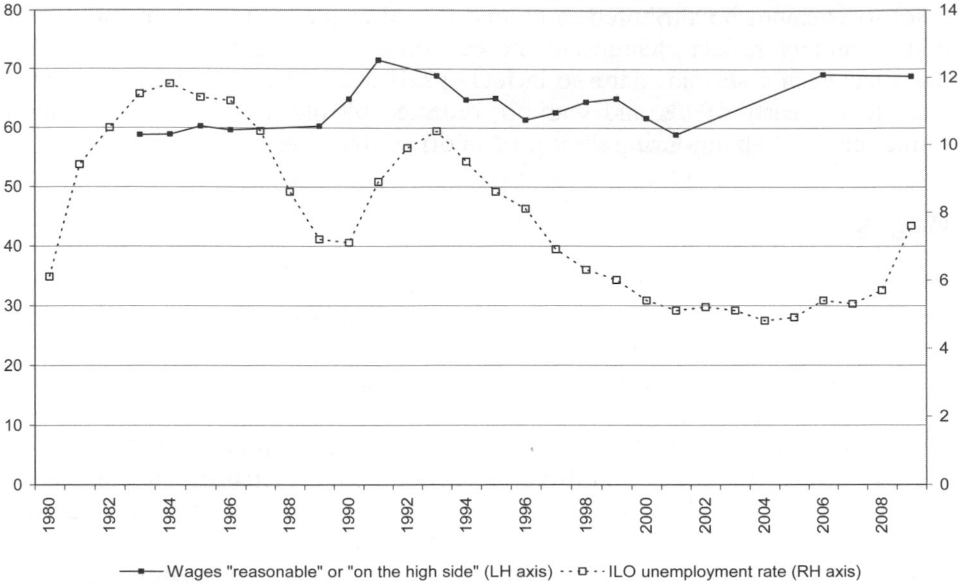

—■— Wages "reasonable" or "on the high side" (LH axis) · · ▫ · · ILO unemployment rate (RH axis)

Base: all employees

The data on which Figure 5.2 is based can be found in the appendix to this chapter.

[+] Source: ONS Time Series Databank – series MGSX

Perhaps the best-known labour market intervention of recent years is the introduction in 1999 of Britain's first national minimum wage (NMW). It seems possible that, by raising the wages of the lowest paid, the minimum wage might have had a discernible impact on wage satisfaction. However, no such effect is apparent in our data. In fact, among employees at the lower end of the wage distribution (those earning less than £12,000 per year – which would be just above the current minimum wage for a full-time worker) the percentage saying their pay was "reasonable" or "on the high side" fell from 56 per cent in 1999 to 44 per cent in 2009. This fall of 12 percentage points remained unaltered after controlling for compositional changes in the workforce. It could be that, by compressing wages at the bottom end of the distribution, the NMW has reduced satisfaction among those who were earning just above the minimum rate prior to its introduction and who now feel less distance between themselves and the lowest paid.

According to the National Equality Panel, inequalities in earnings and incomes are high in Britain by comparison with a generation ago, with most of the increase having taken place during the 1980s (Hills *et al.*, 2010). The *British Social Attitudes* survey shows that this issue is clearly of public concern. Throughout the series' lifetime, we have asked employees:

> *Thinking of the highest and the lowest paid people at your place of work, how would you describe the gap between their pay, as far as you know?*

Answer options range from "much too big", "too big" and "about right" to "too small" or "much too small". As shown in Figure 5.3, the percentage of employees saying "much too big" or "too big" increased markedly in the second half of the 1980s, reaching a peak of 56 per cent in 1994. The degree of concern has receded a little since the mid-1990s, coinciding with a cessation in the growth of inequality among female full-time employees and a slight reduction in the rate of growth among male full-timers (Hills *et al.*, 2010). However, it is striking that, despite an overall increase in inequality since the mid-1980s, the proportion who think the gap between the highest and lowest paid within their workplace is too big is remarkably similar now (47 per cent) to what it was when we first asked the question in 1983 (44 per cent). This coincides with a general decline over the last decade in public levels of concern about inequality and redistribution, as discussed in other chapters in this report (Rowlingson *et al.*; Curtice and Park). This could mean that workers – and the general public – are now more comfortable with earnings inequality, but could also suggest that they are unaware of the degree of inequality which now exists.[4]

There is very little evidence that these changes in people's perceptions of differential pay rates at work reflect the changing composition of the workforce. Indeed, the percentage of employees shown in Figure 5.3 who say that the wage gap is either "too big" or "much too big" would be slightly *higher* if there had been no compositional change since 1985.

Figure 5.3 Perceptions of the wage gap at the employees' workplace, 1983–2009

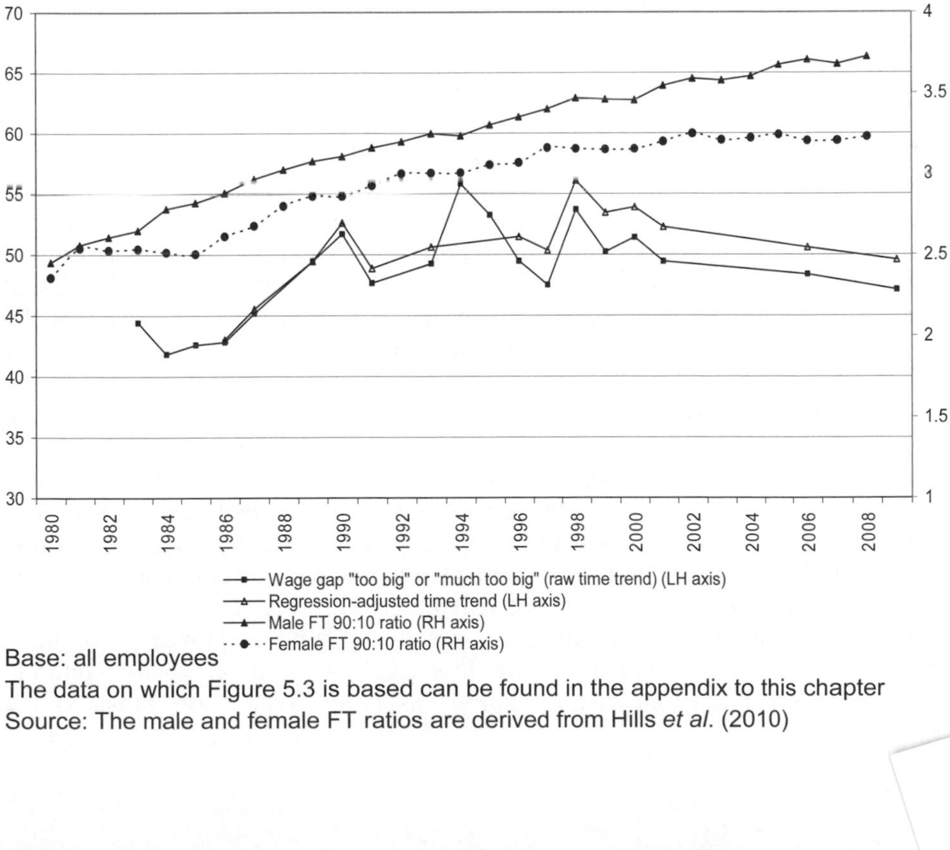

—■—Wage gap "too big" or "much too big" (raw time trend) (LH axis)
—▲—Regression-adjusted time trend (LH axis)
—▲—Male FT 90:10 ratio (RH axis)
··●··Female FT 90:10 ratio (RH axis)

Base: all employees

The data on which Figure 5.3 is based can be found in the appendix to this chapter

Source: The male and female FT ratios are derived from Hills *et al.* (2010)

The first two substantive sections of this chapter have shown a mixed picture. The increase in job insecurity noted in the mid-1990s by Bryson and McKay was clearly not temporary; there has been an increase in feelings of job insecurity over the last 25 years, which the economic growth and labour market regulation of the late 1990s and early to mid-2000s did nothing to ameliorate. In relation to wages, employees' satisfaction with their pay has risen in recent years, but this seems largely attributable to the worsening economic climate. Perceptions of whether wage inequality within the workplace is too great, however, do seem to have improved.

Employment relations

We turn now to examine employment relations, and the extent to which employees' attitudes in this area have changed over the last two decades. Notwithstanding considerable media interest in some recent strikes in the public sector and at British Airways, industrial action is lower now than at any time since 1960 (Dix *et al.*, 2009). However, while collective disputes are now relatively uncommon, measures of individual grievances (such as the number of employment tribunal cases) have been rising while others (such as absenteeism and resignations) remain high (*ibid.*). In light of these countervailing trends it is instructive to consider how employees view the relationship between management and employees. We ask:

> *In general how would you describe relations between management and other employees at your workplace?*
>
> *[Very good, quite good, not very good, or, not at all good]*

Typically around one third of employees say "very good" (34 per cent in 2009), a little under a half (48 per cent) say "quite good" and the remainder respond "not very good" (14 per cent) or "not at all good" (4 per cent). The solid line in Figure 5.4 shows the percentage of employees in each year who say that the climate of employment relations in their workplace is poor – that is, not very, or not at all, good. This shows that perceptions deteriorated in the early 1990s, with a marked increase in the proportion thinking that employment relations in their workplace were poor – from 17 per cent in 1990 to 25 per cent in 1995, but started to improve from around 2000. By 2008, employees were no more likely to report poor management/employee relations than they had been in 1983 (14 and 15 per cent respectively). This pattern appears unaffected by the economic cycle: correlations with the unemployment rate, changes in unemployment and changes in GDP are small and are not statistically significant.

Three characteristics are significantly associated with employee perceptions throughout the period: managers are less likely than other socio-economic groups to perceive employment relations as being very poor; those in the smallest workplaces have a more positive view of employment relations than those in larger workplaces; and trade union members are less sanguine about relations with management than non-members.

To what extent do changes in the composition of the workforce underpin the changing perceptions of employment relations that we have found? The dashed line in Figure 5.4 shows what we would expect employee perceptions to look like if the profile of the workforce looked the same now as it did in the 1980s. This line lies above the solid line showing actual perceptions, and the gap between the two lines widens over time. This suggests that employees increasingly exhibit traits which are conducive to more positive perceptions of employment relations, and this helps explain some of the changes we have found over time.

Figure 5.4 Perception that relations between management and other employees are "not very good" or "not at all good", 1985–2009

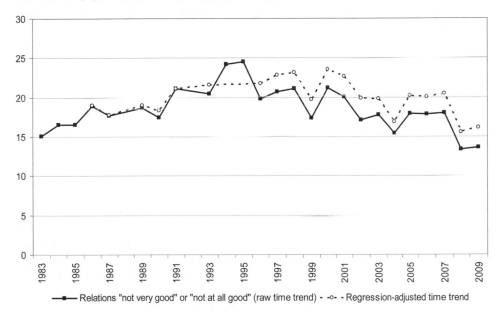

Base: all employees
The data on which Figure 5.4 is based can be found in the appendix to this chapter

A more marked improvement in workplace relations is apparent in employee perceptions about the degree of conflict between managers and workers. To assess this we asked "how much conflict is there between management and workers?" As Table 5.2 shows, the proportion saying there were "very strong" or "strong" conflicts has fallen from nearly six in ten in 1987 to four in ten in 2009. Regression analyses confirm that this decline is statistically significant, as is the decline between 1999 and 2009.

Table 5.2 Perceptions of conflict between management and workers, 1987, 1999 and 2009

Conflict between management and workers	1987	1999	2009
	%	%	%
Very strong conflicts	10	8	3
Strong conflicts	47	38	37
Not very strong conflicts	40	53	57
No conflicts	3	2	3
Base	588	328	431

Base: all employees

Like perceptions of relations between management and employees, employee perceptions of managerial competence deteriorated in the 1990s but have subsequently recovered. Employees are asked:

> *In general, would you say your workplace was very well managed, quite well managed or not well managed?*

The proportion saying "very well managed" was in the high 20s during the 1980s, falling to the low 20s in the mid-1990s. It now stands at 28 per cent, with just over half (54%) of employees feeling their workplace is "quite well managed" and under a fifth (17%) saying "not well managed". Regression analyses confirm a u-shaped time trend in the probability of employees saying their workplace is well managed: perceptions in 2009 were not significantly different to what they had been in the 1980s, having recovered from a period in the 1990s and early 2000s when employees appeared particularly concerned about how well their workplaces were being managed. Employees increasingly exhibit traits which are conducive to more positive perceptions of managerial competence but these perceptions of managerial competence are not significantly associated with measures of the economic cycle.

Employee trust in management, often touted by Human Resources specialists as the bedrock of 'partnership', is a precious commodity. Asked whether they agreed with the statement "Management will always try to get the better of employees if it gets the chance" nearly half of all employees (49 per cent) either "agreed" or "strongly agreed" in 2009. However, with the exception of 2007, when the figure was 48 per cent, this was the lowest figure recorded in the survey series since the question was first asked in 1985. Distrust in management rose in the 1980s and early 1990s, peaking in 1995 when two-thirds (67 per cent) of employees agreed with the statement, as shown by the solid line in

Figure 5.5. Distrust has fallen since then such that it is now significantly lower than it was in 1985.

Throughout the whole period there are persistent differences between individuals in terms of the trust they have in management: controlling for other factors, women, white employees, the more highly qualified, union non-members and employers and professionals tend to have more trust in management. These differences provide a clue as to what underpins the improvements in trust that we have found over time; they reflect compositional change within the British workforce. So, as the dashed line in Figure 5.5 shows, mistrust in management would be markedly higher now than it is, had the make-up of the workforce not altered since the 1980s. In contrast to perceptions of employment relations and managerial competence, perceptions that management may try to get the better of employees rise in periods of high unemployment.[5]

Figure 5.5 Agreement with the statement "management will always try to get the better of employees if it gets the chance", 1985–2009

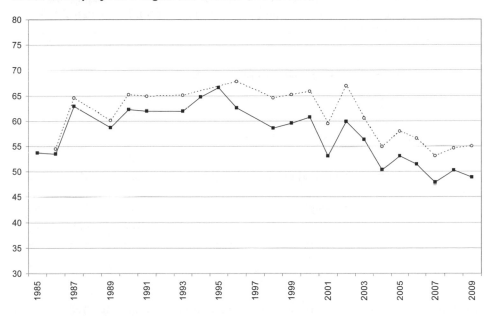

—■— Agrees management will try to get the better of employees (raw time trend) ···○··· Regression-adjusted time trend

Base: all employees

The data on which Figure 5.5 is based can be found in the appendix to this chapter

A further suite of three questions asked in 2004, 2007 and 2009 also probe trust in management but, unlike the question reported above, respondents are asked specifically about trust in management "at my workplace".[6] Table 5.3 presents the percentages agreeing or strongly agreeing with the statements. Roughly half of employees appear to trust management at their workplace on these three items, though the scores are somewhat lower with respect to management keeping promises. There is decline in trust on all three measures between 2004 and 2007 and a small upturn on two of the three between 2007 and 2009, but not to the levels experienced in 2004. The declines between 2004 and 2009 are statistically significant in the case of employers dealing honestly with employees and being sincere in their attempts to understand them, but the decline in the perceived reliability of managers to keep their promises is not statistically significant.

Once again, being female and being a manager were positively associated with higher trust while union members were less inclined to trust management than non-members. And, in contrast to what we found in relation to trust in management more generally, establishment size also matters, with those in smaller workplaces being significantly more trusting in management than their counterparts in larger establishments. However, changes like these in workforce composition do not explain the trends we have found in trust in management as, even once they are taken into account, the decline we found between 2004 and 2007 remains significant.

Table 5.3 Trust in management, 2004, 2007 and 2009

	2004	2007	2009
% agree that management at the workplace …			
… can be relied upon to keep their promises	47	43	45
… are sincere in attempting to understand employees' views	56	51	45
… deal with employees honestly	57	51	53
Base	*1164*	*1147*	*1280*

Base: all employees

In summary, employee perceptions of workplace governance, defined in terms of the climate of employment relations, good management and trust in management, deteriorated in the late 1980s and 1990s but have improved subsequently and are now largely indistinguishable from what they were in the mid-1980s. Improvements in perceived workplace governance are partly attributable to compositional change in the workforce since employees are increasingly exhibiting traits which predispose them to more positive perceptions of management and employment relations. Business cycle effects were confined to trust in management which is pro-cyclical. Some may wonder why it is, given improvements in objective conditions at work, that employee perceptions of their working environment have not discernibly improved more in over a quarter of a century. Perhaps those improvements are more apparent in relation to the content of employees' jobs, rather than in aspects of their working relationships? It is to this issue which we now turn.

Employee engagement

During the mid-1980s academics in business schools were seeking to promote the idea of employee involvement as a way to get a comparative advantage over competitors. Employees were viewed as a source of 'value' which could only be fully exploited through 'high-involvement' management practices which elicited their commitment and thus higher levels of discretionary effort (Walton, 1985). The practices have diffused through large swathes of the economy and the issue of 'employee engagement' as it has become known, has become an important political issue once again (MacLeod and Clarke, 2009). But are employees really any more 'involved' or 'engaged' than they used to be?

To assess this, we can look at responses to the following question, asked of employees since 1985:

> *Suppose there was going to be some decision made at your place of work that changed the way you do your job. Do you think that **you personally** would have any say in the decision about the change, or not?*

We then ask those who think they *would* have a say:

> *How much say or chance to influence the decision do you think you would have?*
>
> *[A great deal, quite a lot, or, just a little]*

Every year the percentage of employees saying they have a say in decisions has remained above a half, ranging between 52 per cent in 1989 and 65 per cent in 1985. The percentage in 2009 was 55 per cent, which is around the average for the whole period. Figure 5.6 shows the trends in the proportion who report having "a great deal" or "quite a lot" of say about changes to the way they do their job. The solid line shows the proportion of employees with "a great deal" or "quite a lot" of say. It averages a little above a third (37 per cent), and has ranged between 31 per cent in 1987 and 1989 to 42 per cent in 2002. Now 36 per cent say they have "a great deal" or "quite a lot" of say, one percentage point below the mean for the whole period.

Figure 5.6 Employees with "a great deal" or "quite a lot" of say in decisions about changes to one's job, 1985–2009

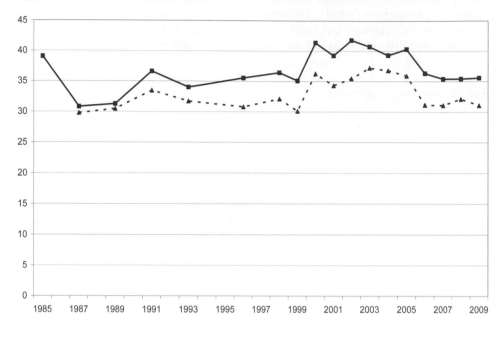

Base: all employees
The data on which Figure 5.6 is based can be found in the appendix to this chapter

Some types of worker persistently report greater influence over changes to their jobs than others. Controlling for other factors, those higher up the occupational hierarchy have greater say, with managers and employers most likely to have a lot of say followed by professionals. Those with higher academic qualifications also have greater say, while the probability of having influence is lower for young employees. Those in smaller workplaces have more influence than 'like' employees in larger workplaces; this difference has become more pronounced over time. Since the mid-1990s union members are less likely to report having a say over decisions about their jobs than otherwise 'like' non-union members. The appearance of this gap may be an indication that unions are finding it increasingly difficult to influence managerial decision-making (Bryson and Forth, forthcoming).

Employee perceptions of their decision-making influence are affected by the business cycle: "say" is lower when the unemployment rate is high. However, the current decline began in 2005–6 prior to the recent recession, so the economic cycle cannot account for the recent decline shown in Figure 5.6.

Employee influence in decision making was highest in 1985 and in the first half of the 2000s. Once again, the dashed line in Figure 5.6 presents the time trend after having accounted for our standard controls. With the introduction of control variables the decline in "say" since the early to mid-2000s becomes more pronounced. By 2009, employee "say" was significantly lower than it was at the outset in 1985 and in the first half of the 2000s, but it was not significantly different to other years. This runs counter to recent improvements in both perceptions of employment relations and trust in management. Comparing the dashed line with the solid line representing the raw time trend reveals how much the changes we have found reflect changes in workforce composition. The fact that the dashed line lies below the solid line indicates that perceptions of "say" would be lower had workforce composition remained as it was in the 1980s.

A lack of influence matters to employees. We ask: *"Do you think you should have more say in decisions affecting your work, or are you satisfied with the way things are?"* In most years between 40 and 50 per cent of employees say they want more say. There is no discernible trend over time, suggesting that the much vaunted push for greater employee involvement since the early 1980s either did not happen or, if it did happen, it failed to meet employees' aspirations. In 2009, nearly half (46 per cent of employees) wanted more say.

A further suite of three questions asked in 2005, 2008 and 2009 probes management's ability to involve employees "at your workplace". Table 5.4 presents the percentages agreeing or strongly agreeing with the statements.[7] The figures are stable over the four-year period but what is particularly noticeable is that, whereas around half of employees think managers at their workplace are good at seeking employees' views and responding to employee suggestions, only around one third think management are good at allowing employees to influence final decisions. Thus, weaker forms of employee engagement appear far more prevalent than the sort of engagement which gives employees a role in decision making.

Table 5.4 Management consultation, 2005, 2008 and 2009

	2005	2008	2009
% agree management are good at ...			
... seeking views of employees or employee representatives	54	56	55
... responding to suggestions from employees or employee representatives	50	51	52
... allowing employees to influence final decisions	35	36	34
Base	*1110*	*1260*	*1271*

Base: all employees

Policy initiatives have sought to foster limited employee engagement. Some of these, such as the Information and Consultation (I&C) Regulations 2004, implement EU Directives in UK law and are explicitly focused on improving information sharing and consultation. The I&C Regulations came into effect for businesses with 150 or more employees in April 2005 and were gradually rolled out so that by April 2008 all businesses with 50 or more employees were covered.[8]

To what extent have policy initiatives like these had an impact on employees' perceptions of what happens within their own workplace? Since 1998, we have asked employees how much they agree or disagree with this statement:

People at my workplace usually feel well-informed about what is happening there

Since 1998, the percentage agreeing has risen markedly, from 43 per cent to 52 per cent in 2003, a level at which it has remained since then. This jump is statistically significant and remains so having controlled for other factors. However, the trend has remained constant since 2003.[9]

In 2004 and 2009 employees were also asked how good they thought their employer was at keeping them informed about four facets of the workplace.[10] Table 5.5 shows the percentage saying their management was "very good" or "fairly good" at keeping them informed. Roughly two-thirds of employees think their managers are either "fairly good" or "very good" at keeping them informed and the figures have stayed roughly constant since 2004. This is confirmed in regression analyses.

Table 5.5 Management information provision, 2004 and 2009

	2004	2009
% agree management are good at keeping you informed about ...		
... plans for future employment in your organisation	69	66
... financial performance of the organisation	70	68
... training opportunities for you to advance your career	67	67
... your legal rights at work	65	62
Base	*1042*	*1189*

Base: all employees

Together, these questions suggest that there was a perceived improvement in management's ability to inform employees about what was happening at their workplace in the late 1990s and early 2000s, but there has been no change in the last five years as a result of recent legislation. Of course, it is possible that management anticipated the legislation that came into effect in 2005 by improving their practices and procedures. However, this appears at odds with the recent decline in employees' perceptions of the "say" they have in decision making at work, and the substantial unmet desire for having more "say" and influence in decision making which has been a feature of *British Social Attitudes* since the 1980s.

Conclusions

This chapter sought to examine how employees' experiences of, and attitudes towards, work have changed over the last quarter of a century, and how any developments relate to the economic cycle as well as to trends in the make-up of the British workforce. Many of our findings are broadly positive, particularly when compared with a picture of deterioration in the late 1980s and 1990s. Employees' ratings of employment relations within their workplace, and of managerial competence, have improved since the 1990s, as has the degree of trust that employees have in their managers. Satisfaction with wage levels is higher too. Employee perceptions of management's ability to keep them informed also improved in the late 1990s, although it has remained stable since then. However, other trends are more negative. In particular, there has been a secular decrease in job security which can be traced back to the early 1990s and which was seemingly impervious to the continued economic growth of the late 1990s and early 2000s. And the degree of influence which employees' report they have in decision making has also declined over the past decade.

The quality of the working environment experienced by Britain's employees therefore appears to have improved somewhat over the past decade, albeit with notable exceptions. To some extent these changes reflect the economic cycle; feelings of job security, the degree of trust in management and employee influence over decision making all tend to decline when unemployment increases. By contrast, satisfaction with wages increases as unemployment goes up, presumably reflecting employees' increased sense of good fortune at having a job. Other changes at least partly reflect trends in the socio-demographic composition of Britain's workforce, as well as longer-term changes such as the decline of manufacturing and manual work, and a fall in trade union membership. These compositional changes help account for some of the improvements we found in perceptions of employment relations, in managerial competence, trust in management and in employee involvement in decision-making. But the economic cycle and socio-demographic make-up of the workforce cannot account for all the changes over time that we have found.

The onset of a major recession in the late 2000s might have been expected to herald a fundamental shift in employees' attitudes to paid work and their working environment. In fact, none of the attitudinal series presented in this chapter have yet responded sharply to the recession. The impression, instead, is of a more muted reaction than was seen in the early 1990s – in keeping with the more muted impact of the current recession on the labour market as a whole. However, it is possible that the effects of the current recession have yet to have any pronounced impact on the attitudes that employees have towards their employers and their jobs, and so it remains to be seen whether any prolonging of the recession will result in a more pronounced reaction.

Notes

1. For both the descriptive and multivariate analysis, respondents answering "don't know" or refusing to answer a substantive item of interest have been excluded from the analysis of that item, hence their views are not accounted for in the percentages presented in the tables and figures. Theoretically, it was felt to be appropriate to exclude these groups from the binary regressions as they do not represent a definite view on the items of interest.
2. Gregg and Wadsworth show that job stability fell for men and women without dependent children. Although it rose for women with young children, this group of employees are under-represented in *British Social Attitudes* because of the focus of the survey questions on employees working 10 or more hours per week.
3. The difference between the two periods is statistically significant at the 1 per cent level.
4. This could be the case if much of the increase in inequality has taken place, not within workplaces, but between them; this is known to have been the case in the USA, for example.
5. If one adds the unemployment rate and change in unemployment to our model alongside a linear time trend and our standard controls, the unemployment rate is negative and statistically significant at a 99 per cent confidence level, whereas unemployment change is not significant.
6. These three items load together on a single factor each with factor loadings above 0.9, and a Cronbach's alpha reliability score for the three items of 0.92. These results confirm that the items are discrete measures of a single concept which we will sum up as trust in management.
7. These three items load together on a single factor each with factor loadings above 0.9, and a Cronbach's alpha reliability score for the three items of 0.92. These results confirm that the items are discrete measures of a single concept which we will sum up as management's ability to involve employees.
8. See http://www.bis.gov.uk/files/file25934.pdf
9. The percentage agreeing was 54 per cent in 2004, 53 per cent in 2005, 52 per cent in 2007 and 55 per cent in 2009.
10. These four items load together on a single factor each with factor loadings around 0.8, and a Cronbach's alpha reliability score for the four items of 0.82. These results confirm that the items are discrete measures of a single concept which might be summed up as management's ability to inform employees.

References

Autor, D., Katz, L. and Kearney, M. (2008), 'Trends in US wage inequality: re-assessing the revisionists', *Review of Economics and Statistics*, **90**: 300–323

Bell, B. and Van Reenen, J. (2010), 'Bankers' Pay and Extreme Wage Inequality in the UK', CEP Special Report No. 21

Blackburn, R. (2010), 'Vertical and Horizontal Gender Segregation; Cross-National Comparison and Analysis', report to the Economic and Social Research Council

Bryson, A. and Forth, J. (forthcoming), 'Trade Unions', in Gregg, P. and Wadsworth, J. (eds.), *The State of Working Britain'*, 3rd edition, Oxford: Oxford University Press

Bryson, A. and McKay, S. (1997), 'What about the workers?', in Jowell, R., Curtice, J., Park, A., Brook, L., Thomson, K. and Bryson, C. (eds.), *British Social Attitudes: the 14th Report*, Aldershot: Ashgate, pp. 23–48

Dickens, L. and Hall, M. (2009), 'Legal Regulation and the Changing Workplace', in Brown, W., Bryson, A., Forth, J. and Whitfield, K. (eds.), *The Evolution of the Modern Workplace*, Cambridge: Cambridge University Press, pp. 332–352

Dix, G., Sisson, K. and Forth, J. (2009), 'Conflict and Work: The Changing Pattern of Disputes', in Brown, W., Bryson, A., Forth, J. and Whitfield, K. (eds.), *The Evolution of the Modern Workplace*, Cambridge: Cambridge University Press, pp. 176–200

Fredman, S. and Morris, G. (1989), *The State as Employer: Labour Law in the Public Services*, London: Mansell

Green, F. (2006), *Demanding Work: The Paradox of Job Quality in the Affluent Economy*, Princeton, NJ: Princeton University Press

Gregg, P. and Wadsworth, J. (2002), 'Job tenure in Britain, 1975–2000, Is a job for life or just for Christmas?', *Oxford Bulletin of Economics and Statistics*, **64, 2**: 111–134

Gregg, P. and Wadsworth, J. (2010), 'The UK labour market and the 2008–2009 recession', Centre for Economic Performance, Occasional Paper No. 25, London: Centre for Economic Performance, LSE

Hills, J., Brewer, M., Jenkins, S., Lister, R., Lupton, R., Machin, S., Mills, C., Modood, T., Rees, T. and Riddell, S. (2010), *An anatomy of economic inequality in the UK: Report of the National Equality Panel*, London: Government Equalities Office

Machin, S. (forthcoming), 'Changes in UK Wage Inequality Over the Last Forty Years', in Gregg, P. and Wadsworth, J. (eds.) *The State of Working Britain'*, 3rd edition, Oxford: Oxford University Press

MacLeod, D. and Clarke, N. (2009), *Engaging for Success: Enhancing Performance Through Employee Engagement*, London: Department for Business, Innovation and Skills

Walton, R.E. (1985), 'From Control to Commitment in the Workplace', *Harvard Business Review*, **63**: 77–84

Wood, S. and Bryson, A. (2009), 'High involvement management', in Brown, W., Bryson, A., Forth, J. and Whitfield, K. (eds.) *The Evolution of the Modern Workplace*, Cambridge: Cambridge University Press, pp. 151–175

Acknowledgements

The *National Centre for Social Research* is grateful to the Department for Business, Innovation and Skills for their financial support which enabled us to ask the questions reported in this chapter, although the views expressed are those of the authors alone.

The authors gratefully acknowledge funding from the Nuffield Foundation (grant ref. OPD/37358).

Appendix

This chapter presents the results of a series of regression models. These are typically probit models of binary dependent variables. The control variables included to take account of compositional changes are: gender (dummy), ethnic minority (dummy), age (six dummies); highest educational qualification (five dummies); part-time job (dummy); socio-economic classification (five dummies); union member (dummy); recognised union at workplace (dummy); region (six dummies); industry (four dummies); public sector (dummy); and establishment size (five dummies). While many of the attitudinal series covered in the chapter begin in 1983, our regression analysis begins in 1985, when this set of control variables were first all present. The regression analysis excludes 1994 and 1995 due to the absence of the public sector variable in these years.

The data for Figures 5.1 to 5.6 are shown below.

Table A.1 Feelings of job insecurity and ILO unemployment rate

Year	Very/quite likely to leave employer in next year	Expect firm closure or redundancy in next year	ILO unemployment rate	Base
1980	n/a	n/a	6.1	n/a
1981	n/a	n/a	9.4	n/a
1982	n/a	n/a	10.5	n/a
1983	18	2	11.5	812
1984	26	2	11.8	774
1985	23	1	11.4	856
1986	22	2	11.3	1527
1987	n/a	n/a	10.4	n/a
1988	n/a	n/a	8.6	n/a
1989	23	1	7.2	1457
1990	24	1	7.1	1304
1991	25	1	8.9	1230
1992	n/a	n/a	9.9	n/a
1993	24	4	10.4	1139
1994	27	6	9.5	1429
1995	28	4	8.6	1440
1996	27	4	8.1	1508
1997	22	2	6.9	537
1998	25	3	6.3	1416
1999	25	3	6.0	1350
2000	27	2	5.4	1513
2001	28	3	5.1	1515
2002	n/a	n/a	5.2	n/a
2003	n/a	n/a	5.1	n/a
2004	n/a	n/a	4.8	n/a
2005	n/a	n/a	4.9	n/a
2006	27	3	5.4	1489
2007	30	n/a	5.3	1408
2008	26	3	5.7	1556
2009	23	4	7.6	1576

Base: all employees

Table A.2 Perceptions of whether wages are reasonable and ILO unemployment rate

Year	Wages 'reasonable' or 'on the high side'	ILO unemployment rate	Base
1980	n/a	6.1	n/a
1981	n/a	9.4	n/a
1982	n/a	10.5	n/a
1983	59	11.5	816
1984	29	11.8	771
1985	60	11.4	854
1986	60	11.3	1524
1987	58	10.4	1379
1988	n/a	8.6	n/a
1989	60	7.2	1459
1990	65	7.1	1303
1991	72	8.9	1232
1992	n/a	9.9	n/a
1993	69	10.4	1140
1994	65	9.5	1443
1995	65	8.6	1444
1996	61	8.1	1526
1997	63	6.9	544
1998	64	6.3	1425
1999	65	6.0	1361
2000	62	5.4	1520
2001	59	5.1	1532
2002	n/a	5.2	n/a
2003	n/a	5.1	n/a
2004	n/a	4.8	n/a
2005	n/a	4.9	n/a
2006	69	5.4	1495
2007	n/a	5.3	n/a
2008	n/a	5.7	n/a
2009	69	7.6	1586

Base: all employees

Table A.3 Perceptions of the wage gap at the employees' workplace

Year	Wage gap 'too big' or 'much too big' (raw time trend)	Regression-adjusted time trend	Male FT 90:10 ratio	Female FT 90:10 ratio	Base
1983	44	n/a	2.648	2.534	732
1984	42	n/a	2.782	2.513	707
1985	43	n/a	2.819	2.503	778
1986	43	43	2.880	2.613	1392
1987	45	46	2.964	2.676	1237
1988	n/a	n/a	3.023	2.798	n/a
1989	49	49	3.075	2.859	1321
1990	52	53	3.106	2.859	1196
1991	48	49	3.160	2.925	1129
1992	n/a	n/a	3.197	2.998	n/a
1993	49	51	3.247	3.002	1067
1994	56	n/a	3.233	3.004	1351
1995	53	n/a	3.301	3.052	1357
1996	49	51	3.350	3.066	1397
1997	47	50	3.400	3.158	510
1998	54	56	3.467	3.153	1327
1999	50	53	3.460	3.149	1274
2000	51	54	3.455	3.152	1434
2001	49	52	3.544	3.198	1411
2002	n/a	n/a	3.588	3.247	n/a
2003	n/a	n/a	3.576	3.208	n/a
2004	n/a	n/a	3.603	3.220	n/a
2005	n/a	n/a	3.674	3.240	n/a
2006	48	51	3.707	3.203	1400
2007	n/a	n/a	3.679	3.204	n/a
2008	n/a	n/a	3.725	3.227	n/a
2009	47	50			1501

Base: all employees

Table A.4 Perception that relations between management and other employees are "not very good" or "not at all good", 1985–2009

Year	Relations "not very good" or "not at all good"	Regression-adjusted time trend	Base
1983	15	n/a	810
1984	17	n/a	772
1985	17	n/a	851
1986	19	19	1514
1987	18	18	1372
1988	n/a	n/a	n/a
1989	19	19	1449
1990	17	18	1300
1991	21	21	1227
1992	n/a	n/a	n/a
1993	20	22	1133
1994	24	n/a	1438
1995	25	n/a	1436
1996	20	22	1515
1997	21	23	540
1998	21	23	1410
1999	17	20	1356
2000	21	24	1511
2001	20	23	1520
2002	17	20	1548
2003	18	20	1453
2004	15	17	1493
2005	18	20	1455
2006	18	20	1483
2007	18	20	1417
2008	13	16	1550
2009	14	16	1583

Base: all employees

Table A.5 Agreement with the statement "management will always try to get the better of employees if it gets the chance", 1985–2009

Year	Agrees management will try to get the better of employees (raw time trend)	Regression-adjusted time trend	Base
1985	54	n/a	738
1986	53	54	666
1987	63	64	1238
1989	59	60	1268
1990	62	65	1161
1991	62	65	1144
1993	62	65	526
1994	65	n/a	1262
1995	67	n/a	1261
1996	63	68	1332
1998	59	65	1186
1999	60	65	1065
2000	61	66	1350
2001	53	59	1317
2002	60	67	1402
2003	56	60	1624
2004	50	55	1222
2005	53	58	1609
2006	51	57	1756
2007	48	53	1582
2008	50	55	1831
2009	49	55	1371

Base: all employees

Table A.6 Employees with "a great deal" or "quite a lot" of say in decisions about changes to one's job, 1985–2009

Year	Has "a great deal" or "quite a lot" of say in decisions (raw time trend)	Regression-adjusted time trend	Base
1985	39	n/a	818
1987	31	30	1317
1989	31	30	1413
1991	37	33	1190
1993	34	32	1112
1996	36	31	1500
1998	36	32	1402
1999	35	30	1322
2000	41	36	1496
2001	39	34	1500
2002	42	35	1582
2003	41	37	1422
2004	39	37	1476
2005	40	36	1432
2006	36	31	1454
2007	35	31	1384
2008	35	32	1527
2009	36	31	1561

Base: all employees

6 A tale of two crises: banks, MPs' expenses and public opinion

John Curtice and Alison Park[*]

The final two years of the last Labour government were particularly turbulent. First of all, in the autumn of 2008, there was a serious banking crisis. The government was forced to nationalise two small banks that had got into difficulties, Northern Rock and Bradford & Bingley, to facilitate a merger between two large ones, Lloyds TSB and the Halifax Bank of Scotland, and then buy large stakes in both the newly merged bank and the Royal Bank of Scotland in order to enable them to stay afloat. Meanwhile, a coincident collapse in the stock market, the housing market, and in bank lending meant that the economy went into recession. It was not just the first recession since Labour had come to power in 1997, but the worst economic reverse since the great depression of the 1930s. Tax revenues inevitably fell, forcing the government to begin borrowing on an unprecedented scale.

No sooner had the immediate drama of the banking crisis subsided, than another crisis gripped the country. Following long-running attempts to force their publication using freedom of information legislation, the House of Commons had finally agreed to publish details of the expenses claims that had been made in recent years by MPs – but with some information, such as MPs' addresses, 'redacted'. However, shortly before publication was finally set to occur, full 'unredacted' details of the claims were acquired by the *Daily Telegraph* newspaper, which began publishing extracts in May 2009. A vivid picture was painted of MPs arranging their affairs to maximise their personal financial advantage (including avoiding taxes), and relying unduly on the taxpayer to finance a comfortable lifestyle. The public reacted with fury at what became known as the 'MPs expenses scandal', one illustration being BBC1's 2009 May 14th *Question Time* which saw audience members roundly jeering the politicians on the panel and was watched by an estimated million more viewers

[*] John Curtice is Research Consultant at the *Scottish Centre for Social Research*, part of NatCen, and Professor of Politics at Strathclyde University. Alison Park is a Research Group Director at the *National Centre for Social Research* and co-director of the *British Social Attitudes* survey series.

than usual.[1] The scandal set in motion events that led, *inter alia*, to the resignation of the incumbent Speaker of the House of Commons, Michael Martin, and an acceptance by the House of Commons that it could no longer be a self-regulating institution.

Both events dominated the news agenda for weeks. They had palpable consequences for the nation's financial and political systems, and can be expected to merit a place in the history books long after the immediate headlines are forgotten. But we might also wonder what impact they might have had on public opinion. This chapter provides an initial assessment by examining whether there are discernible differences between the public attitudes uncovered in our 2009 survey, conducted after the banking crisis and in the immediate wake of the MPs' expenses scandal, and the public's outlook in the years prior to the two events. Where there are differences, we consider whether these are likely to reflect recent events or longer-term trends. Clearly the world has changed both politically and economically in the wake of these crises; but is the same true of the public mood?

The legacy of the financial crisis

How might we expect the financial crisis to affect public attitudes? We focus here on four broad areas. The first concerns *job security*, our desire being to examine what signs there are that employees have felt the chill of the economic slowdown. Secondly, we examine the extent to which the recession has had an impact upon people's attitudes towards *welfare and inequality*. One possible expectation here is that people's views about welfare payments and welfare recipients have become more generous as times have got harder; after all, for those who do lose their jobs, their immediate financial well-being is likely to depend on the generosity of the state, through the provisions it makes for paying unemployment and other benefits. It is also possible that the financial crisis has resulted in a heighted concern about inequality in society and a wish that it be reduced. So we will also examine public attitudes towards inequality and the role that government should have in intervening to reduce it. We then, thirdly, focus on attitudes towards *the role of government* more widely. After all, the recession of 2008–9 was no ordinary recession. It saw the government intervene in an unprecedented fashion in the financial system. So we will explore whether the revelation that the state might properly have a greater role to play in the economy (and even in running some nationalised industries) may have caused some to reassess their attitudes towards the proper role of the state. Fourthly, and finally, we focus on two issues of immediate and direct relevance to the banking crisis: the extent of the *reputational damage* suffered by the banks in its wake; and whether public attitudes towards *personal credit* have become more restrictive, reflecting a view that credit should not be used as freely as it has been in the recent past.

Job insecurity

One immediate consequence of the onset of the recession was an increase in unemployment. The repercussions for those who actually lost their jobs were immediate and obvious. But the remainder of the workforce who did not lose their jobs might still wonder whether their own job was under threat, too. Thus their sense of job security might be diminished.

Certainly people's perceptions of what has been happening in their own workplace in recent months would seem to have given them some cause for concern. As many as 29 per cent of employees report that someone at their workplace has been made redundant in the last 12 months, a 10-point increase on the proportion in 2005. Similarly, 42 per cent say that there has been a reduction in the number of people employed at their workforce during the previous 12 months, a six-point increase on 2008.

Table 6.1 shows responses to the question "how secure do you feel your employment is with your present employer", and compares these with those obtained in 2005 when the question was previously asked. Fewer people do indeed feel "very secure" in their jobs nowadays as compared with four years ago – 37 per cent as compared with 30 per cent. But it would, perhaps, be more accurate to describe the change as the emergence of a sense of unease rather than a strong fear that jobs are at risk. In fact, there has not been any increase at all in the proportion feeling that their job is actually insecure. Instead there simply has been an increase in those who say their job is "secure" rather than "very secure", or else now proffering the response, "neither secure nor insecure".[2]

Table 6.1 Perceived security of employment with current employer, 2005 and 2009

	2005	2009
	%	%
Very secure	37	30
Secure	40	46
Neither secure nor insecure	13	16
Insecure	7	6
Very insecure	2	2
Base	*1477*	*1595*

That emergence of a sense of unease is also reflected in the answers to a further question (Table 6.2). When asked "how difficult or easy would it be for you to get a similar or better job with another employer if you wanted" over half now feel that they would have some difficulty. In contrast only just over one in three

(37 per cent) felt that way in 2005.[3] Here, though, there is a hint that the growth in a sense of unease had already begun to set in before the banking crisis, perhaps because unemployment had already been increasing, albeit slowly, since the beginning of 2008. In that year's survey, for which most of our interviews were conducted before the onset of the banking crisis in September, the proportion who felt that it might be difficult to find a similar job had already increased to 43 per cent.

Table 6.2 Perceived difficulty of finding a similar job, 2005, 2008 and 2009

	2005	2008	2009
	%	%	%
Very difficult	10	12	15
Difficult	26	31	38
Neither difficult nor easy	21	27	21
Easy	32	22	20
Very easy	9	7	4
Base	*1477*	*1569*	*1595*

One limitation of the survey questions that we have been examining so far, however, is that they have only been asked in recent years. In particular, they were not asked during the course of previous recessions, such as those that occurred in the early 1980s and early 1990s. So they cannot tell us whether people's sense of unease or insecurity about their jobs is any greater or less than it was during previous recessions, and thus whether the banking crisis has had any particularly marked impact on people's sense of job security. Longer-term attitudes towards job security are discussed in greater detail in the chapter in this report by Bryson and Forth; for our purposes here, we can look at the answers to one particular question asked of employees in most years since the *British Social Attitudes* survey started in 1983. This asks:

> *Over the coming year do you expect your workplace to be increasing its number of employees, reducing its number of employees, or, will the number of employees stay about the same?*

The results are shown in Figure 6.1. Here, too, we see that people are apparently less likely to feel safe and secure in their jobs now than before the crisis.[4] In particular, it is notable that the proportion anticipating a reduction in the number of employees at their workplace increased from 14 per cent in 2007 to 24 per cent now. That 10-point increase is the sharpest rise or fall ever recorded on this measure between adjacent *British Social Attitudes* surveys. So the banking crisis would appear to have had an unusually sharp impact on the public mood so far as employment prospects are concerned. However, at 24 per cent, it is notable that the proportion who anticipate a reduction in the number of employees at their workplace is still not as high as it was during the previous recessions of the early 1980s and early 1990s, while a clear majority (74 per cent) expect numbers to stay the same or even increase. This, perhaps, is a reflection of a distinctive character of the most recent recession. Although it has had a more severe impact on economic growth than those two previous recessions, to date it has occasioned less of an increase in unemployment (Gregg and Wadsworth, 2010). Thus, perhaps, the reason why it has apparently generated unease rather than widespread fear.[5]

Figure 6.1 Perceptions of future employment levels in workplace, 1983–2009

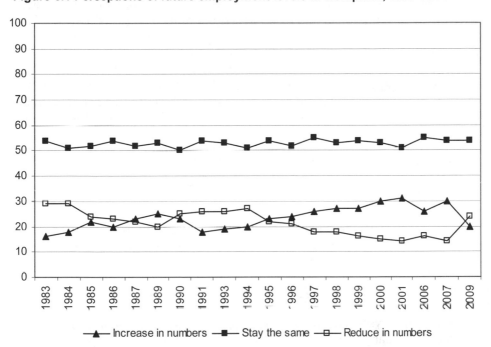

The data on which Figure 6.1 is based can be found in the appendix to this chapter

In summary, therefore, there is clear evidence that the financial crisis has affected the extent to which people feel secure in relation to their jobs, even though insecurity is not (to date) as widespread as it was during previous recessions.

Welfare and inequality

We turn now to attitudes towards welfare. In economic good times, voters might feel that those who fail to work are 'scroungers' whom they have to support through their hard-earned taxes. But when the economic climate becomes less benign, they might begin to reassess their view. After all, perhaps they themselves will be in need of the safety net provided by the state. If not, there will be a greater likelihood that they know somebody else who needs support. Certainly, *British Social Attitudes* surveys conducted during previous recessions in the 1980s and early 1990s lend credence to such an expectation (Taylor-Gooby, 2004).

We might also expect to find that the financial crisis has affected attitudes towards inequality in society and resulted in a heightened wish that it be reduced. After all, one particular feature of the banking system that attracted critical attention in the wake of the financial crisis was the payment of large bonuses to senior employees. It seemed that those who had caused the financial crisis were still being rewarded at a level few could ever hope to emulate, even though their institution had had to be bailed out at the taxpayers' expense.[6] So we will also examine public attitudes towards inequality and the role that government should have in intervening to reduce it.

We begin by considering attitudes to welfare benefits and recipients. Figure 6.2 shows responses to three questions that have been asked regularly on the *British Social Attitudes* survey during the course of the last three decades. In the first of these, respondents are asked which of two options comes closer to their view:

> *Benefits for unemployed people are too low and cause hardship, or, benefits for unemployed people are too high and discourage them from finding jobs?*

The line towards the top of the figure shows the proportion who say that unemployment benefits are too low. In the case of the remaining two items[7] respondents were asked whether they agreed or disagreed that:

> *Many people who get social security don't really deserve any help*

> *If welfare benefits weren't so generous people would learn to stand on their own two feet*

The two remaining lines show the proportion who *disagreed* with these statements and who thus might be regarded as relatively sympathetic towards welfare benefits and their recipients. This suggests that the onset of recession has had some impact on attitudes towards welfare, albeit more so in respect of unemployment benefits in particular than welfare in general.[8] Compared with 2008 there has been an eight-point increase (to 29 per cent) in the proportion who feel that unemployment benefits are too low, and a five-point increase (to 32 per cent) in the proportion who disagree that many social security recipients are undeserving, together with a more modest (and statistically insignificant) two-point increase (to 22 per cent) in the proportion who disagree that people would be more likely to stand on their own feet if welfare benefits were not so generous.[9]

However, if we adopt a longer-term perspective, attitudes towards unemployment and welfare benefits still appear relatively harsh. For example, the 29 per cent who state that unemployment benefits are too low is well below the levels that were obtained in the wake of previous recessions – as many as 53 per cent took that view in 1993, as did just under half (49 per cent) in 1984. Equally, at 32 per cent and 22 per cent respectively, the proportions who disagree with our two statements about welfare benefits are well below the levels obtained in the early 1990s, when around a half disagreed with both statements. Overall, there has been a considerable change in the public mood since the 1980s and early 1990s, partly reflecting New Labour's ideological repositioning on issues such as equality and government action (Curtice, 2010).

Figure 6.2 Attitudes towards unemployment and welfare benefits, 1983–2009

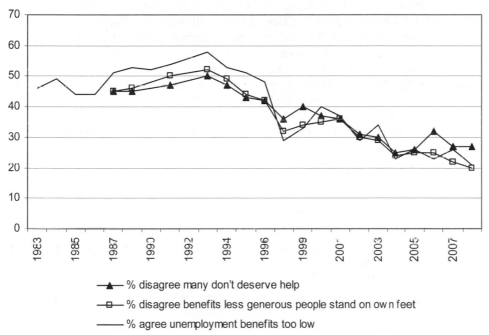

—▲— % disagree many don't deserve help

—☐— % disagree benefits less generous people stand on own feet

——— % agree unemployment benefits too low

The data on which Figure 6.2 is based can be found in the appendix to this chapter

We also speculated earlier that, in addition to increasing sympathy for the unemployed and those on benefits (something for which we have found some limited evidence), the financial crisis might have resulted in a heightened concern about inequality in society and a wish that it be reduced. We can examine this by looking at responses to the following long-running question:

Government should redistribute income from the better off to those who are less well off

The first row of Table 6.3 shows the proportion who agree with this proposition. This is actually one of five items that the survey asks each year and which between them are designed to form a scale measuring where people stand on a 'socialism versus laissez-faire' spectrum that captures people's underlying attitudes towards inequality and the role that government should play in trying to reduce it. (Full details of these items are to be found in Appendix 1.) The second row of Table 6.3 shows the proportion who can be regarded as being on the 'socialist' or 'left-wing' end of this spectrum.[10]

Previously, we have argued that one of the key trends in public opinion following the advent of New Labour under the leadership of Tony Blair has been a marked drift in attitudes towards the 'right' (Curtice, 2010). Indeed, one feature of Table 6.3 that is immediately apparent is a decline from 1994 onwards (the year in which Tony Blair became Labour's leader) in the proportion agreeing that the government should redistribute income and who more generally might be regarded as left-of-centre. This falls further still from 1998, after New Labour took office. There is no sign that the decline has been reversed significantly in the wake of the banking crisis; at 36 per cent, the proportion favouring redistribution in particular is actually (a statistically insignificant) two points below the previous reading in 2008 and is much the same as it has been in most years since 1998. Moreover, at 48 per cent, the proportion of people who can be classified as left-of-centre is exactly the same as it was 12 months earlier, and is still lower than it had been as recently as 2003. The attention paid to bankers' bonuses in the wake of the banking crisis may have aroused much public anger, but it seems it did little to shift the public's underlying attitudes.

Table 6.3 Attitudes towards reducing inequality, 1986–2009[11]

	86	87	89	90	91	93	94	95	96	98	99	00	01	02	03	04	05	06	07	08	09
% agree govt should redistribute income	43	45	51	51	49	48	51	47	44	39	36	39	38	39	42	32	32	34	32	38	36
% left-of-centre	52	55	58	59	54	59	64	61	58	52	50	52	49	53	51	42	44	44	44	48	48

In summary, we have seen that support for government having an active role in reducing material inequality is lower now than in the late 1980s and early 1990s, and – while sympathy for those dependent on welfare benefits has increased a little over the last year – it remains far lower than was the case in earlier decades.

The role of government

Despite the fairly limited changes we have seen in attitudes to welfare and inequality, we might expect to find that the financial crisis has affected attitudes towards the role of government more widely. After all, the recession of 2008–9 saw the government intervene in an unprecedented fashion in the financial system. It had even nationalised some banks, a move that not only contradicted a trend during the last 30 years for government to divest itself of commercial activities but one that would hitherto have been regarded as one that only an 'extreme' socialist government would take. At the same time, the government argued that public spending needed to be maintained, despite falling tax revenues, in order to counteract the impact of the recession the crisis had induced. There was also a change of tone in the pronouncements of Labour ministers, who were now more willing to criticise markets and extol the need for government action to correct their excesses and failures, as demonstrated by the then Prime Minister Gordon Brown's speech at the 2009 Labour conference.[12] So, perhaps, the revelation that the state might properly have a greater role to play in the economy may have caused some to reassess their attitudes towards the proper role of the state.

We begin by looking at attitudes towards nationalisation. In Table 6.4 we show the pattern of responses to a question about state ownership of major public services and industries that had been asked on three previous *British Social Attitudes* surveys in the 1990s:

Major public services and industries ought to be in state ownership

The results suggest that while the idea of state ownership is more popular than might be anticipated from the drift of public policy for much of the last three decades – as many as 41 per cent agree that major services and industries ought to be owned by the state – there is no evidence that support for nationalisation has become markedly higher in the wake of the banking crisis.[13]

Table 6.4 Attitudes towards nationalisation, 1994–2009

	1994	1996	1997	2009
	%	%	%	%
Strongly agree	11	13	10	13
Agree	34	30	28	28
Neither agree nor disagree	27	32	34	35
Disagree	22	19	22	18
Strongly disagree	3	4	3	4
Base	*2929*	*3085*	*1080*	*1017*

Nevertheless, perhaps the recession had an impact on people's attitudes towards the amount spent by government on public services? To assess this, we ask:

> *Suppose the government had to choose between the three options on this card. Which do you think it should choose?*

> *Reduce taxes and spend less on health, education and social benefits*
> *Keep taxes and spending on these services at the same level as now*
> *Increase taxes and spend more on health, education and social benefits*

As Figure 6.3 shows, support for increased taxation and spending has been in decline since 2002, with the public's appetite for more spending seeming gradually to have been satisfied by the substantial increases in actual spending that occurred from 1999 onwards (Curtice, 2010). This trend has not been reversed by the banking crisis. Instead, support for more taxation and spending has fallen by a further five points (to 34 per cent) between 2008 and 2009, and is now lower than it has been at any time since 1983. Of course, it may be that the latest drop is a reflection of concern about the size of government deficit that emerged in the wake of the recession rather than simply a continuation of the trend that was already under way. Either way, it is now apparent why the public did not warm to Labour's argument in the 2010 General Election that the deficit should not be cut too quickly, and that taxes should be used to achieve that aim to a greater extent than was envisaged by the Conservatives.

Figure 6.3 Attitudes towards taxation and spending, 1983–2009.

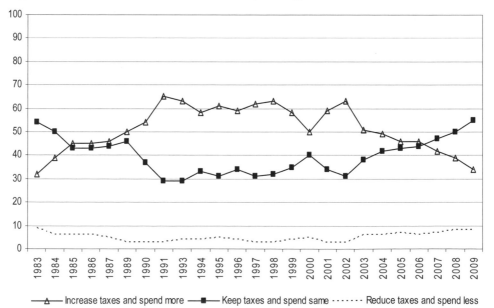

The data on which Figure 6.3 is based can be found in the appendix to this chapter

So it appears that the banking crisis and the recession which followed it has not yet given rise to a reassessment by the public of their attitudes towards the role of government. Despite the furore about bankers' bonuses and the need for the government to nationalise some banks, there is no sign of a renewed enthusiasm for greater government intervention in the economy. However, a pre-existing trend away from a desire for more government spending has continued, perhaps aided by concern about the government deficit.

Banking and credit

We conclude this section by focusing on two issues of immediate and direct relevance to banking. First, we assess the extent of the reputational damage that banks in particular have suffered in the wake of the crisis. Then we examine attitudes towards personal credit. After all, it was not just the banks that were implicated in the banking crisis. It had originated in a willingness of people in the United States to take out mortgages whose repayments they proved unable to maintain. Meanwhile, in the UK personal indebtedness had reached an all-time high, standing at £1,444 billion (£232 billion of which was unsecured debt, including credit cards) in June 2008 (Bank of England, 2008). This meant that the country's banks were particularly vulnerable to bad debts when unemployment started to increase and house prices fell. So we might wonder whether one lesson people might draw from the crisis is that credit should not be used as freely as it has been in the recent past. Certainly the level of indebtedness did start to fall in the wake of the banking crisis, as people opted to pay off some of the debt that they owed (Bank of England, 2010).

It is here that we find our first – but probably our least surprising – example of a sea change in the public mood. Table 6.5 shows the responses to a question that asks people whether they consider various institutions to be well run or not. The question was included on the first ever *British Social Attitudes* survey in 1983 and has been asked on a number of occasions since:

> *Listed below are some of Britain's institutions. From what you know or have heard about each one, can you say whether, on the whole, you think it is well run or not well run?*

Table 6.5 reveals an enormous change in view so far as banks are concerned. In 1983 no less than 90 per cent believed that banks were well run, and their reputation for being well managed was higher than that of a variety of other institutions including the police and the BBC. But now just 19 per cent believe that banks are well run, and their reputation for good management is now even worse than that of the press and trade unions. True, some of that drop was in evidence before the banking crisis; by 1994 only 63 per cent felt that banks were well run, and, perhaps, the banks' reputation had fallen yet further before the banking crisis broke. Even so, this is probably the biggest change in public attitudes ever recorded by the *British Social Attitudes* series, and indicates that

Britain's banking industry now has a poor reputation indeed. On this evidence, it would seem that tighter regulation of the banking industry is one example of greater government intervention that the public would now welcome.

Table 6.5 Perceptions of how well major institutions are run, 1983–2009

	1983	1986	1987	1994	2009	Change 1983– 2009	Change 1994– 2009
% saying institution is well run							
The police	77	74	66	68	62	-15	-6
National Health Service	52	36	35	33	54	+2	+21
BBC	72	70	67	62	49	-23	-13
The press	53	48	39	47	39	-14	-8
Trade unions	29	27	27	47	35	+6	-12
Banks	90	92	91	63	19	-71	-44
Base	*1650*	*1321*	*1212*	*970*	*1017*		

We turn now to examine people's attitudes towards one of the key areas of bank activity – lending money. Table 6.6 looks at responses to three questions about credit and borrowing money that have been asked regularly by *British Social Attitudes* during the course of the last 10 years. Respondents were asked whether they agreed or disagreed that:

> *Credit makes it easier for people to plan their finances*

> *It should be made much harder to borrow money even if this means more people can't get credit*

> *Credit encourages people to spend far more than they can really afford to*

Table 6.6 demonstrates that we are indeed rather more sceptical about credit now than we were at the beginning of the 21st century. For example, 43 per cent now *disagree* that credit makes it easier for people to plan their finances, up nine points on 2001. The other two items in the table exhibit a similar trend. However, it appears that this shift of opinion occurred before the banking crisis. Thus, by 2007, already as many as 61 per cent agreed that it should be harder to borrow money, almost identical to the figure in the most recent survey, and a picture that again is mirrored by the other two items. It seems that the growth in personal indebtedness had already given rise to some concern about the amount of lending by banks to individuals even before the banking crisis hit home, but that the crisis itself has not resulted in that concern being heightened.

Table 6.6 Attitudes towards credit, 2001–9

	2001	2002	2003	2007	2009
% disagree credit makes it easier to plan finances	34	37	34	42	43
% agree should be harder to borrow money	47	50	51	61	60
% strongly agree credit encourages people to spend more than can afford	32	32	36	43	41
Base	*2795*	*2900*	*2649*	*2672*	*2942*

The legacy

Overall, attitudes towards the banking industry apart, we have found little evidence that the banking crisis and the recession which followed it has, in the first instance at least, brought about a dramatic change in the public mood. True, more people now feel insecure about their job than did so before the turmoil began in 2008, while there has been some change in attitudes to welfare, in line with trends during previous recessions. There is, perhaps, also a little more readiness now to spend money on unemployment benefits. However, this is matched by a yet further decline in enthusiasm for government spending in general. Meanwhile, despite the furore about bankers' bonuses and the need for the government to nationalise some banks, there is neither any sign of a renewed enthusiasm for greater government intervention in the economy, nor any indication of an increased desire to do more to reduce inequality. And, although our appetite for credit has been restricted somewhat, this process seemed to begin before the events of 2008/09. On these matters, the underlying values of the British public seem to have been little affected by the crisis at all.

The fallout from the expenses scandal

We turn now to an examination of the impact of the events that dominated the news agenda in 2009; the MPs' expenses scandal. We begin by considering its impact on *political trust*. An apparent breach of trust was, after all, at the heart of the MPs' expenses scandal. Politicians are expected by voters to run the nation's affairs for the good of society as a whole, not to use their privileged position for personal gain. So we might anticipate that trust in politicians has declined as a result of the impressions conveyed by the expenses scandal. Secondly, we examine whether the revelations affected a wider range of *political values and attitudes* that might have more profound implications for the health of the country's politics. Has, for instance, the expenses affair undermined people's sense of 'political efficacy'; that is, the degree to which the political system is able and willing to meet the needs of its citizens. Thirdly, we examine *political engagement and interest*; were people so disenchanted by the scandal that they lost interest in politics and wondered whether it was worthwhile turning out and voting at election time. Finally, we assess whether the fallout from the expenses scandal has stretched beyond the world of politics and affected people's faith not only in politicians but also in their fellow human beings. So we will conclude by examining *social trust* and whether it has declined in the wake of the scandal.

Trust in politics

Politicians are expected by voters to run the nation's affairs for the good of society as a whole, but the practices and behaviours uncovered by the *Daily Telegraph* suggested that many a politician was, in fact, making questionable claims on the taxpayers' purse with an eye to making a personal profit. We thus might anticipate that trust in politicians to act in the country's interests rather than in their own may well have declined as a consequence of the impressions conveyed by the expenses scandal. People might even be moved to wonder whether the country's political system was 'corrupt'.

Political trust is measured by a question that has been asked on a regular basis by *British Social Attitudes* in recent years. Respondents are asked:

> *How much do you trust British governments of any party to place the needs of the nation above the interests of their own political party?*

This question thus taps directly into the issue of whether governments (and by implication politicians) in general can be trusted to put the wider public interest first. At the same time, the expenses scandal also raised questions about whether MPs had always been honest – or at least straightforward – in the expense claims they had submitted (and in their associated dealings with the tax authorities). We might expect this aspect of trust to be tapped by responses to a further question that respondents have been asked on a regular basis in recent years:

> *And how much do you trust politicians of any party in Britain to tell the truth when they are in a tight corner?*

Table 6.7 summarises the pattern of responses to both questions. It shows that trust in politicians has never been particularly high in Britain; in most years, well under a half (and often well under a third) say they trust governments or politicians "just about always" or "most of the time". Moreover trust was clearly in decline long before the MPs' expenses scandal broke. For example, whereas in 1991 as many as one in three said that they trusted governments to put the national interest first "just about always" or "most of the time", by 2006 that figure had fallen to less than one in five (19 per cent). Previous revelations about 'sleaze' that engulfed the 1992–7 Conservative government appear to have caused particular harm. True, trust appears consistently to have recovered in the immediate wake of a general election, but in each case this revival has proved temporary (Bromley and Curtice, 2002). The picture portrayed by the *Daily Telegraph* perhaps occasioned such a strong public reaction because it confirmed the doubts that many people already had about the trustworthiness of their politicians.

Nevertheless, the expenses scandal appears to have helped erode trust yet further. Now no less than two in five say that they "never" trust governments to put the national interest first, six points above the previous all-time high of 34 per cent recorded in 2006 – and around four times as high as the readings that obtained in the late 1980s. Equally, as many as three in five now say they "never" trust politicians to tell the truth, although this is only three points higher than the previous high of 57 per cent in 2006.

These findings might lead one to suggest that a public that has long had its doubts about the trustworthiness of its political class is now on the verge of being straightforwardly cynical in its attitude towards government and politicians.

Table 6.7 Trends in political trust, 1987–2009

	87 (1)	87[+] (2)	91	94	96	97 (1)	97[+] (2)	98	00	01	02	03	05	06	07	09
Trust government	%	%	%	%	%	%	%	%	%	%	%	%	%	%	%	%
Just about always/ most of the time	37	47	33	24	22	25	33	28	16	28	26	18	26	19	29	16
Some of the time	46	43	50	53	53	48	52	52	58	50	47	49	47	46	45	42
Almost never	11	9	14	21	23	23	12	17	24	20	24	31	26	34	23	40
	87 (1)	87[+] (2)	91	94	96	97 (1)	97[+] (2)	98	00	01	02	03	05	06	07	09
Trust politicians	%	%	%	%	%	%	%	%	%	%	%	%	%	%	%	%
Just about always/ most of the time	n/a	n/a	n/a	9	9	8	n/a	9	11	n/a	7	6	8	7	9	6
Some of the time	n/a	n/a	n/a	40	38	40	n/a	43	42	n/a	37	39	39	35	39	39
Almost never	n/a	n/a	n/a	49	49	50	n/a	46	46	n/a	55	54	52	57	49	60
Base	1410	3413	1445	1137	1180	1355	3615	2071	2293	1099	2287	3299	3167	1077	992	1143

n/a = not asked

[+] Source: British Election Study

Political efficacy

The immediate impact of the MPs' expenses scandal on levels of political trust might be considered both unsurprising and of little longer-term consequence. More interesting, perhaps, is whether the revelations affected a wider range of values and attitudes that could have more profound implications for the health of the country's politics. For example, faced with a picture of politicians pursuing personal advantage, perhaps people have come to question what good, if any, Britain's political system can do for the country as a whole? Maybe the affair has undermined their sense of 'political efficacy', the extent to which they feel the political system is able and willing to meet its citizens' needs (Almond and Verba, 1965).

We start by considering the impact of the expenses scandal on the degree to which the public feel that the public good is being subverted by the country's politicians. In 2002 we asked respondents how often they felt Labour "does favours for people or companies who give the party large sums of money", and then went on to ask the same question about the Conservatives. In Labour's case 24 per cent said they felt this happened "very often", while 26 per cent said the same of the Conservatives. Now the figure is 24 per cent in respect for both parties. Here, perhaps, is an indication that the impact of the expenses scandal on public attitudes may have been limited in its scope.

A second indication that this might be the case comes when we look at 'political efficacy'. There are three widely used indicators of this concept, with respondents being asked the extent to which they agree or disagree with each:

Parties are only interested in people's votes, not in their opinions

Generally speaking, those we elect as MPs lose touch with people pretty quickly

It doesn't really matter which party is in power, in the end things go on much the same

The results are shown in Table 6.8, which shows trends in the proportion that "strongly agree" with the proposition in question.[14] As each of these propositions expresses doubts about the ability or willingness of the political system to be responsive to the needs and wishes of the country's citizens, the *higher* this proportion, the *lower* the level of political efficacy.

In many respects past trends in political efficacy have been similar to those we saw for political trust. Levels of efficacy have tended to be lower since 1994 than they were previously. Equally, this has been tempered by a tendency (on occasions at least) for levels of efficacy to be restored temporarily in the immediate wake of a general election. Thus, for example, the proportion who strongly agreed that parties are only interested in votes rose from 16 to 25 per cent between 1991 and 1994, but subsequently fell back in the survey conducted shortly after the 1997 General Election. However, in contrast to political trust, there is no evidence that feelings of efficacy have been eroded further in the wake of the expenses scandal. Thus, for example, 24 per cent now strongly agree that parties are only interested in votes, in line with most readings taken since 1994. Much the same can be said of the other two indicators included in the table.

Table 6.8 Trends in system efficacy, 1987–2009

% strongly agree	87	87[+]	91	94	96	97[+]	98	00	01	02	03	05	09
Parties only interested in votes	15	16	16	25	28	16	21	26	27	29	25	17	24
MPs lose touch quickly	16	n/a	16	25	26	n/a	20	23	25	28	23	16	22
Doesn't matter which party in power	n/a	7	11	16	16	8	17	19	18	22	20	12	21
Base		1410	3826	1445	1137	1180	2906	2071	2293	1099	2287	4432	3167	1143

n/a = not asked
[+]Source: 1987 and 1997 British Election Study

Interest in politics

We turn now to examine whether the expenses scandal has had any apparent impact upon political interest and engagement. Might people have begun to ask whether it is worth their while dealing with, or being interested in, politics and politicians at all? In particular, might people have begun to question whether they should feel any obligation to turn out and vote at election time? A sense of civic duty has been shown to be particularly important in motivating people to make the journey to the polling station (Butt and Curtice, 2010); any erosion of that sense could have deleterious consequences for levels of electoral participation and ultimately the perceived legitimacy of the electoral process.

As Table 6.9 shows, there seems to be little sign that the expenses scandal has eroded people's interest in politics. As we have noted before, the level of such interest has proved remarkably constant in previous years (Butt and Curtice, 2010) and this continues to be the case. At 31 per cent, the proportion of people in our most recent survey who say they have "a great deal" or "quite a lot" of interest in politics is much the same as it has been throughout the period since 1991.

Table 6.9 Trends in interest in politics, 1991–2009

	1991	1994	1997	2000	2003	2005	2007	2009
How much interest in politics	%	%	%	%	%	%	%	%
Great deal/quite a lot	32	32	30	32	30	34	30	31
Some	31	35	33	35	33	34	37	36
Not much/none at all	36	33	37	35	37	32	32	33
Base	*1445*	*2302*	*1355*	*2293*	*4432*	*4268*	*2022*	*1143*

On the other hand, we noted in *The 26th Report* that there had been a notable decline in the proportion of people who feel that they have a duty to vote at election time. To assess this, we ask:

> *Which of these statements comes <u>closest</u> to your view about general elections? In a general election ...*
> *... it's not really worth voting*
> *... people should vote only if they care who wins*
> *... it's everyone's duty to vote*

Table 6.10 indicates that the fall uncovered then by our 2008 survey has largely been maintained; at 58 per cent, the proportion who say that 'it is everyone's duty to vote' is still lower than it has been in any survey before 2008. At the same time, however, it seems that the MPs' expenses scandal has not occasioned any further decline in people's sense of duty to vote; our latest reading is, in fact, two points higher than it was in 2008.

Table 6.10 Trends in civic duty, 1991–2009

	1987[+]	1991	1994	1996	1998	2000	2001	2004	2005	2008	2009
	%	%	%	%	%	%	%	%	%	%	%
Not really worth voting	3	8	9	8	8	11	11	12	12	18	17
Vote if care who wins	21	24	21	26	26	24	23	27	23	23	23
Everyone's duty to vote	76	68	68	64	65	64	65	60	64	56	58
Base	*3413*	*1224*	*970*	*989*	*1654*	*2008*	*2795*	*2609*	*1732*	*990*	*1017*

[+] Source: *British Election Study*

Social trust

So it would appear that while the MPs' expenses scandal did indeed have an immediate impact on the degree to which the British public felt able to trust its politicians, it did not occasion an erosion of some of the deeper values and attitudes that might be thought essential to the health of Britain's political system. In particular it appears not to have brought about a decline in political efficacy, interest in politics or in the feeling that people have a duty to vote. Even so, the scandal might, perhaps, have still had wider implications. Maybe as well as undermining trust in politicians, it has helped undermine people's willingness to trust their fellow citizens in general. It has been argued that a reasonable level of such 'social trust' is essential to the health of society as well as to efficiency and effectiveness of its economy and its politics (Putnam, 2000). But if the lesson that people took from the revelations is that their politicians cannot be trusted, then maybe their faith in their fellow human beings in general has been undermined, too. If so, the revelations may indeed have had important long-term implications for Britain's future.

Our measure of 'social trust' is one that has been used widely in previous research. Respondents are asked:

> *Generally speaking, would you say that most people can be trusted, or that you can't be too careful in dealing with people?*

The more who say that "most people can be trusted", the greater the degree of social trust that would appear to exist in a society.

Table 6.11 shows that there is no sign at all that social trust has been eroded in the wake of the expenses scandal. In fact, at 47 per cent, a higher proportion now think "most people can be trusted" than have done at any point during the last 30 years. Indeed it would seem more generally that the concern that has been expressed in the past about the decline of social trust in the United States in particular (*Putnam, 2000*), is not justified so far as Britain is concerned at all.

Table 6.11 Trends in social trust, 1981–2009

	1981[+]	1990[+]	1997	1998	2000	2002	2005	2006	2007	2008	2009
	%	%	%	%	%	%	%	%	%	%	%
Most people can be trusted	43	42	42	44	45	39	45	41	41	40	47
Can't be too careful	54	55	57	54	54	59	53	57	57	55	51
Base	*1167*	*1484*	*1355*	*2071*	*2293*	*2287*	*3167*	*1077*	*4124*	*2236*	*1143*

[+] Source: *World Values Survey*

Conclusions

The British public has clearly noticed our two crises. The financial crisis has made it feel a little less secure about its jobs and appears to have made it question the effectiveness and efficiency of the nation's banks. And the expenses scandal has served to undermine much of the remaining trust that public had in the probity of politicians. In short, the reputations of those who were thought to be implicated most closely in the two crises took a tumble.

But it seems that neither crisis persuaded people to change their attitudes in any more fundamental fashion. The sight of governments rescuing banks or the stories of bankers' bonuses did not appear to make them question their views about the role that government should play in the marketplace. There has been no renewal of enthusiasm for more active government. Equally, stories about MPs allegedly exploiting the expenses system for personal gain did not increase people's doubts about the efficacy of the country's political system or undermine their willingness to become involved in its political process. People may have been shocked by the two crises, but it seems they see little reason why eventually Britain should not return to business as usual. Of course, it remains to be seen whether it will.

Notes

1. http://www.telegraph.co.uk/news/newstopics/mps-expenses/5330495/MPs-expenses-story-leads-to-biggest-ever-viewing-figures-for-Question-Time.html
2. Although it had primarily been jobs in the private sector rather than those in the public sector that had been lost during the previous 12 months, the decline in the proportion stating that their job was "very secure" was, at six points, almost as big among public sector employees as it was among those working for a private sector organisation (eight points). Those working in the public sector may, of course, have been aware of the cuts that were yet to come as the government attempted to reduce its deficit.
3. We might note that at the same time the proportion who thought that it would be difficult for their employer to replace them has fallen from 44 per cent in 2005 to 37 per cent now.
4. Clearly, if people anticipate a reduction in the number of people employed at their workplace, there is good reason to believe that they are more likely to be concerned about the security of their job. And in practice, in our most recent survey only 16 per cent of those who anticipated a drop in the number of people employed at their workplace said that they felt "very secure" in their job, a little less than half the proportion among those who did not anticipate any reduction.
5. Further evidence also points to this conclusion. Among those who think that they might leave their job over the next 12 months (a group that in most years represents about one in four employees and rarely departs significantly from that figure), 13 per cent now say they think this might happen because they will be made redundant. This is five points above the equivalent figure for 2008, but is still below the 18–20

per cent figure that pertained between 1984 and 1986 or the 18 per cent in 1991 or 17 per cent in 1994.

6. The outrage during the expenses scandal directed at the 'unfair' perks and payments enjoyed by some MPs might also be expected to have some impact on attitudes in this area.

7. These are two items that form part of a scale of attitudes towards welfare, full details of which are to be found in Appendix 1. They are used here to illustrate trends that are similar across all the items in the scale.

8. Even so, the degree to which this has been occasioned by the decline in job security should not be exaggerated. The link between perceptions of job security and, for example, attitudes towards unemployment benefits is only a modest one. While just 19 per cent of those who feel that their job is very secure say that unemployment benefits are too low, the figure only increases to 24 per cent among those who say the job is just "secure" and to 28 per cent among those who say it is neither secure nor insecure (and actually falls to 21 per cent among those who say their job is either insecure or very insecure).

9. We also asked people to agree or disagree with the statement "the government should spend more money on welfare benefits for the poor, even if it leads to higher taxes". Here we found a *decrease* in sympathy between 2008 and 2009, with the proportion agreeing falling from 35 to 27 per cent.

10. The scale runs from a score of 1, meaning that the respondent has given the most socialist or left-wing response to all five items, to 5, indicating that the most laissez-faire or right-wing response has been given on each occasion. We define as left-of-centre those with a score of less than 2.5.

11. Bases for Table 6.3 are as follows:

86	87	89	90	91	93	94	95	96	98	99
1321	2493	2604	2430	2702	1306	2929	3135	3085	2531	2450

00	01	02	03	04	05	06	07	08	09
2980	2795	2900	3621	2609	3559	3748	3578	3990	2942

12. The full text of Gordon Brown's speech can be found at
   http://www2.labour.org.uk/gordon-brown-speech-conference,2009-09-29

13. One possible objection to this analysis is that attitudes towards nationalisation might have become less favourable in the intervening period between 1997 and 2008 (a period for which we have no readings), and then become more favourable as a consequence of the banking crisis.

14. We focus on the proportion that "strongly agree" rather than all those that "agree" because clear majorities have always agreed with these propositions. Consequently, any erosion in political efficacy is primarily reflected in an increase in those saying "strongly agree" rather than in an increase in all those saying "agree".

References

Almond, G. and Verba, S. (1965), *The Civic Culture*, Boston, Mass.: Little, Brown and Company

Bank of England (2008), *Lending to Individuals: June 2008*, available at *http://www.bankofengland.co.uk/statistics/li/2010/jul/lendind.pdf*

Bank of England (2010), *Lending to Individuals: June 2008*, available at *http://www.bankofengland.co.uk/statistics/li/2008/jun/lendind.pdf*

Bromley, C. and Curtice, J. (2002), 'Where have all the voters gone?', in Park, A., Curtice, J., Thomson, K., Jarvis, L. and Bromley, C. (eds.), *British Social Attitudes: the 19th Report*, London: Sage

Butt, S. and Curtice, J. (2010), 'Duty in decline? Trends in attitudes to voting', in Park, A., Curtice, J., Thomson, K., Phillips, M., Clery, E. and Butt, S. (eds.), *British Social Attitudes: the 26th Report*, London: Sage

Gregg, P. and Wadsworth, J. (2010), 'The UK Labour Market and the 2008–2009 Recession', Centre for Economic Performance Occasional Paper No. 25

Putnam, R. (2000), *Bowling Alone: The Collapse and Revival of American Community*, New York: Simon and Schuster

Taylor-Gooby, P. (2004), 'The work centred welfare state', in Park, A., Curtice, J., Thomson, K., Bromley, C. and Phillips, M. (eds.), *British Social Attitudes: the 21st Report*, London: Sage

Acknowledgements

The *National Centre for Social Research* is grateful to the Department for Work and Pensions and the Department for Business, Innovation and Skills for the financial support which enabled us to ask some of the questions reported in this chapter (on welfare and job security respectively). The views expressed are those of the authors alone.

Appendix

The data for Figures 6.1, 6.2 and 6.3 are shown below.

Table A.1 Perceptions of future employment levels in workplace, 1983–2009

	83	84	85	86	87	89	90	91	93	94
	%	%	%	%	%	%	%	%	%	%
Increase in numbers	16	18	22	20	23	25	23	18	19	20
Stay the same	54	51	52	54	52	53	50	54	53	51
Reduce in numbers	29	29	24	23	22	20	25	26	26	27
Base	817	778	857	1532	1381	1462	1307	1236	1144	1447
	95	96	97	98	99	00	01	06	07	09
	%	%	%	%	%	%	%	%	%	%
Increase in numbers	23	24	26	27	27	30	31	26	30	20
Stay the same	54	52	55	53	54	53	51	55	54	54
Reduce in numbers	22	21	18	18	16	15	14	16	14	24
Base	1449	1535	546	1428	1365	1527	1538	1504	1428	1595

Table A.2 Attitudes towards unemployment and welfare benefits, 1983–2009

	83	84	85	86	87	89	90	91	93	94	95	96
% disagree many don't deserve help	n/a	n/a	n/a	n/a	45	45	n/a	47	50	47	43	42
% disagree if benefits less generous, people stand on own feet	n/a	n/a	n/a	n/a	45	46	n/a	50	52	49	44	42
Base	n/a	n/a	n/a	n/a	1281	2604	n/a	2481	2567	2929	3135	3119
% agree unemployment benefits too low	46	49	44	44	51	53	52	54	58	53	51	48
Base	1761	1675	2797	3100	2847	3029	2797	2918	2945	3469	3633	3662
	98	99	00	01	02	03	04	05	06	07	08	09
% disagree many don't deserve help	36	40	37	36	31	30	25	26	32	27	27	32
% disagree if benefits less generous, people stand on own feet	32	34	35	36	30	29	24	25	25	22	20	22
Base	2531	2450	2980	2795	2900	873	2609	2699	2822	2672	3000	967
% agree unemployment benefits too low	29	33	40	37	29	34	23	26	23	26	21	29
Base	3146	3143	3426	3287	3435	3272	3199	3193	3240	3094	3358	1139

n/a = not asked

Table A.3 Attitudes towards taxation and spending, 1983–2009

	83	84	85	86	87	89	90	91	93	94	95	96	97
	%	%	%	%	%	%	%	%	%	%	%	%	%
Reduce taxes/spend less	9	6	6	6	5	3	3	3	4	4	5	4	3
Keep taxes/ spend same	54	50	43	43	44	46	37	29	29	33	31	34	31
Increase taxes/spend more	32	39	45	45	46	50	54	65	63	58	61	59	62
Base	1761	1675	1804	3100	2847	3029	2797	2918	2945	3469	3633	3662	1355

	98	99	00	01	02	03	04	05	06	07	08	09
	%	%	%	%	%	%	%	%	%	%	%	%
Reduce taxes/spend less	3	4	5	3	3	6	6	7	6	7	8	8
Keep taxes/ spend same	32	35	40	34	31	38	42	43	44	47	50	55
Increase taxes/spend more	63	58	50	59	63	51	49	46	46	42	39	34
Base	3146	3143	2292	3287	3435	3272	2146	2166	3240	3094	2229	1139

7 Resentment or contentment? Attitudes towards the Union 10 years on

Rachel Ormston and John Curtice[*]

The establishment in 1999 of devolved parliaments in Scotland and Wales was one of the most important changes to the constitutional arrangements of the United Kingdom since the Act of Union in 1707. The move followed three decades of fierce debate about its wisdom. Advocates of devolution argued it would strengthen the Union. By allowing for the expression of distinctive national identities and policy preferences within the framework of the United Kingdom, devolution would dampen demands for Scottish and Welsh independence (Mackintosh, 1998; Bogdanor, 1999; Aughey, 2001). However, critics predicted that devolution would be the start of a 'slippery slope' to the break up of the United Kingdom. They believed it would fuel demands for ever more powers and, ultimately, for independence in Scotland and Wales, while making England resentful of the advantages apparently bestowed on the rest of the United Kingdom (Dalyell, 1977; Thatcher 1998).[1]

A decade on, political developments in Scotland appear to have confirmed the first of these fears. In 2007, the Scottish National Party (SNP) acquired power for the first time ever, albeit only as a minority government, after coming first in that year's devolved Scottish election. The SNP's raison d'être is to secure Scotland's independence from the rest of the UK. Its 2007 manifesto included a pledge to hold a referendum in 2010 on whether the devolved Scottish government should open independence negotiations with the UK government, in the expectation that after experiencing three years of nationalist government the Scottish public would be persuaded to vote in favour of such negotiations. It seemed that devolution was indeed proving to be a stepping stone towards independence after all.

On the other hand, there has been apparently little impetus behind attempts to suggest how England should respond to the apparent 'unfairness' of being left out of the devolution settlement (Hazell, 2006). None of the major political

---

[*] Rachel Ormston is a Research Director at *the Scottish Centre for Social Research* (ScotCen), part of *NatCen*, and Co-Director of the *Scottish Social Attitudes* survey. John Curtice is Research Consultant at *ScotCen* and Professor of Politics at Strathclyde University.

parties has come out in favour of an English parliament, let alone the dissolution of the Union. Although the UK Labour government that first came to power in 1997 promoted the idea of elected regional assemblies throughout England, that possibility ground to a halt when a proposal to create such an assembly in the North East of England was decisively rejected by voters in a referendum in November 2004 (Sandford, 2009). Meanwhile, although the Conservative Party has argued for some time that, following devolution, only English MPs should be able to vote on laws that would only apply to England (Conservative Party, 2000), its most recent proposal on the subject suggested that this rule only apply to the committee and report stages of such bills (Conservative Democracy Task Force, 2008). Meanwhile the coalition government that the party has now formed with the Liberal Democrats is committed to doing no more than establishing yet another commission on the issue (Cabinet Office, 2010). Contrary to the fears of devolution's critics, England, it would appear, has been surprisingly quiescent.

But it is unwise to presume that public opinion on an issue can be discerned from the outcome of an election, however momentous, or from the direction of elite-level initiatives and debate. People base their votes on a variety of issues and considerations, while elites may ignore or misread public opinion. In this chapter we look directly at trends since the advent of devolution in 1999 in attitudes towards Scotland's constitutional position and the implications of the current settlement for England. Was the SNP's electoral success in 2007 the product of increasing dissatisfaction with the Union and a growing demand for independence in Scotland? And has public opinion in England really failed to react to the developments of the last decade or so?

The answers to both these questions have acquired new importance in the light of the result of the 2010 UK general election. The senior partner in the UK coalition government, the Conservative Party, was left once again with just one MP in Scotland, and barely registered any increase in its share of the vote north of the border. This inevitably raises questions about whether the party has a mandate to govern Scotland. At the same time, the Conservatives have a clear overall majority of English MPs, so if only English MPs could vote on English laws, the party would have no need at all for the votes of their Liberal Democrat partners to secure the passage of English legislation. This new political configuration thus appears to have increased the potential for arguments about the legitimacy of the current constitutional arrangements.

To this has been added the potential for tension and conflict between Scotland and England created by the fallout from the financial crisis of 2008 and the consequent economic recession and ballooning government deficit. For the first time since the advent of devolution, the UK government is committed to making real reductions in public expenditure. Under the Barnett formula, which determines the amount of money that the UK government gives the Scottish government to spend, any reductions in the level of spending in England on matters that, in Scotland, are the responsibility of the devolved institutions are automatically reflected in reductions to the overall Scottish budget. So the devolved Scottish government will find itself required to cut spending north of the border as a result of decisions made by the UK government in London. Meanwhile, critics of the current devolution arrangements, such as Guy Lodge of the Institute for Public Policy Research, have argued that this period of public spending austerity is likely to generate increased resentment in England about the fact (which predates devolution) that the level of public spending per head is persistently higher in Scotland than in England (see also McLean *et al.*, 2008). Commenting on a decision by the UK government to allow Scotland to defer an initial set of spending cuts from 2010/11 to 2011/12, he argues:

> Holding off cuts to the block grant until 2011/12 might help David Cameron to win friends in Scotland, Wales and Northern Ireland, but it risks a backlash from England – particularly those poorer areas which already look jealously at the funding those parts of the UK receive. (IPPR Press Release, 28th May 2010)

At the same time, the debate about devolution has also moved on. Following the SNP's success in the 2007 Scottish Parliament election, the Conservative, Labour and Liberal Democrat parties in the Scottish Parliament and at Westminster jointly established a commission under the chairmanship of Sir Kenneth Calman to review the devolution settlement and make recommendations that would:

> ... enable the Scottish Parliament to serve the people of Scotland better, improve the financial accountability of the Scottish Parliament, and continue to secure the position of Scotland within the United Kingdom. (Commission on Scottish Devolution, 2009)

The key proposal to emerge from the commission was that, instead of being wholly funded by a block grant from Westminster, around one third of the revenues required by the devolved Scottish institutions should be provided by the revenues from some of the taxes, including a portion of income tax, raised within Scotland. All three parties that backed the commission accepted its report in principle and committed themselves to its implementation in their 2010 election manifestos. The UK Conservative/Liberal Democrat coalition government is similarly committed, although the coalition agreement is silent on how the size of the block grant that would still fund two-thirds or so of devolved expenditure in Scotland should be determined in future (Cabinet Office, 2010).

The Calman proposals are intriguing politically. On the one hand, they can be presented as a way of increasing the financial powers and autonomy of the devolved Scottish institutions. Indeed, lacking the votes it needs in the Scottish Parliament to be able to hold its promised referendum on independence,[2] even the minority SNP government seems to have come to accept that it may have to limit its ambitions in the short term to securing an increase in the financial powers of the Parliament (Johnson, 2010; Linklater and MacLeod, 2010; Scottish Government, 2010). On the other hand, the proposals can also be regarded as a way of making the Scottish Parliament more fiscally 'responsible'. Part of its funding at least would depend on money raised from taxpayers in Scotland rather than a 'subsidy' from their counterparts south of the border. So Calman might appeal not only to those north of the border who would like a more powerful parliament in Edinburgh, but also to those south of the border concerned about the current financial arrangements. This chapter aims to assess whether this is indeed the case.

To do so, we look first backwards and then forwards. First, we assess trends in attitudes towards the constitutional relationship between England and Scotland in the wake of the creation of the Scottish Parliament. We consider whether public opinion in those two countries has come together or grown apart in their attitudes towards the governance of the UK. This gives us some understanding of how far the existing relationship between the two countries may be capable of withstanding the new strains that recent developments appear to have put on it. At the same time we examine whether the implementation of the proposals made by the Calman Commission is likely to weaken or strengthen that relationship.

To undertake these tasks the chapter uses data not only from *British Social Attitudes* but also its sister survey, *Scottish Social Attitudes*. Although *British Social Attitudes* covers Scotland, too few interviews are conducted north of the border (315 in 2009) to allow detailed analysis of public attitudes there. Since 1999 *Scottish Social Attitudes* has filled that gap by interviewing around 1,500 people each year in Scotland using a similar methodology to *British Social Attitudes*, and including some questions that are identical (or functionally equivalent) to those on the British survey.[3] We begin our analysis, however, by examining how England views the financial and constitutional position of its neighbour north of the border, revisiting and updating some of the themes discussed in *The 25th Report* (Curtice, 2009). We then move on to consider public opinion in Scotland on much the same issues using data from *Scottish Social Attitudes*. Finally, we consider whether Calman or any similar set of proposals may indeed be able to help address public concerns – north and south of the border – within the framework of the Union.

The view from England: resentment or indifference?

As discussed above, one of the original major fears of devolution's Unionist opponents was that it would provoke an 'English backlash'. That fear has subsequently been exacerbated because of some of the decisions made by the devolved institutions in Scotland and Wales. Their populations have benefited from the introduction of policies such as free personal care, free prescriptions and the abolition of university tuition fees, whereas people in England still have to pay for these services. As a result, it seems that the higher levels of public spending per head enjoyed by Scotland and Wales have made it possible for the devolved institutions to introduce benefits that are denied to people in England, even though the funding for those benefits comes from taxes paid by people throughout the UK. So funding is certainly one aspect of the current devolution settlement that might be expected to have become an increasing source of resentment among people in England.

As discussed in *The 25th Report* (Curtice, 2009), when commercial opinion polls ask people in England how they feel about public spending in Scotland, they typically preface the question by telling respondents that public spending per head in Scotland is much higher than that in England. As such, it is unsurprising that such polls generally find Scotland's share is viewed by a majority as unfair.[4] What is left unclear by this approach is whether it taps *pre-existing* resentment among people in England, or whether the question wording itself provokes such a reaction. If people in England are unaware of the details of Scotland's share of public financing, they may well be unconcerned about it. To avoid this difficulty, *British Social Attitudes* simply asks people whether they think Scotland gets more or less than its fair share, without advising them of the current position. Our question reads:

> *Would you say that compared with other parts of the United Kingdom, Scotland gets **pretty much** its fair share of government spending, **more** than its fair share, or **less** than its fair share of government spending?*

Using this approach we find that only a minority believe that Scotland gets more than its fair share (see Table 7.1). However, that minority does appear to be a growing one. In 2000, just 21 per cent said that Scotland received either much more or a little more than its fair share. But by 2008, this figure had almost doubled, to 41 per cent – a level at which it more or less remains in 2009. Meanwhile the proportion who feel that Scotland gets *less* than its fair share has fallen during the same period from 11 per cent in 2000 to just four per cent now, while the proportion who believe that Scotland gets 'pretty much its fair share' has also dropped from 42 per cent to 30 per cent.

Table 7.1 Attitudes in <u>England</u> towards Scotland's financial position in the Union, 2000–2009

How much government spending Scotland receives, compared with rest of UK	2000	2001	2002	2003	2007	2008	2009
	%	%	%	%	%	%	%
Much more than its fair share	8	9	9	9	16	21	18
A little more than its fair share	13	15	15	13	16	20	22
Pretty much its fair share	42	44	44	45	38	33	30
A little less than its fair share	10	8	8	8	6	3	4
Much less than its fair share	1	1	1	1	1	*	*
Don't know	25	23	22	25	22	23	25
Base	*1928*	*2761*	*2897*	*1917*	*859*	*982*	*980*

Base: respondents living in England

So fears of growing English resentment over Scotland's apparently privileged financial position in the Union do appear to have some basis in public attitudes.

But has this resentment actually resulted in a substantial English 'backlash'? Such a backlash could manifest itself in at least two different ways. The first, and more extreme, form that such a backlash could take would be for England to withdraw its support for the maintenance of the Union with Scotland. Clearly if such a backlash were to occur among the largest partner in the United Kingdom, it would pose a serious threat to the Union's continued existence. However, it is also possible that people in England might simply decide that they would like the apparent advantages that they see Scotland gaining from devolution for themselves. In this case, the backlash would take the form of growing support for some kind of devolution for England.

Taking the more 'extreme' potential English backlash first, there is, in fact, no evidence of any growth in support during the last decade for Scotland to become independent (Table 7.2). Since the establishment of devolution in 1999, consistently only around one in five people in England have felt that Scotland should be independent from the rest of the UK. Meanwhile, according to the most recent available reading (taken in 2007) just under half (47 per cent) of people in England support Scotland having its own parliament, but remaining part of the UK. And of these, most believe that the Scottish Parliament should have some tax-raising powers – a point to which we return later. However, it is worth noting that the proportion of people in England choosing devolution as their preferred option for the government of Scotland did fall from 57 per cent in 1999 to 47 per cent in 2007. At the same time, the proportion saying they did not know how Scotland should be governed rose from eight per cent to 15 per cent. This may be an indication of growing indifference or uncertainty in England about the best way of governing Scotland.

Table 7.2 Attitudes in <u>England</u> to how Scotland should be governed, 1997–2007

	1997[+]	1999	2000	2001	2002	2003	2007
How Scotland should be governed	%	%	%	%	%	%	%
Become **independent**, separate from UK and EU, or separate from UK but part of EU	14	21	19	19	19	17	19
Remain part of UK, with own elected parliament, which has **some** taxation powers	38	44	44	53	41	50	36
Remain part of the UK, with its own elected parliament, which has **no** taxation powers	17	13	8	7	11	8	12
Remain part of UK, **without** an elected parliament	23	14	17	11	15	13	18
Don't know	8	8	11	10	14	11	15
Base	2536	902	1928	2761	1924	1917	859

Base: respondents living in England
[+]Source: British Election Study

If there is no evidence that people in England have become increasingly likely to want Scotland to leave the Union, is there any to suggest growing support for English devolution? Two different forms of devolution have been proposed for England. The Campaign for an English Parliament argues that England as a whole should have its own parliament, with similar powers to those enjoyed in Scotland and Wales. Others (including, as noted earlier, at one point the Labour Party) have argued for elected regional assemblies with responsibility for administering some public services and promoting economic growth in their part of the country. *British Social Attitudes* has asked people to choose between one of these two options, or maintenance of the *status quo*, on a number of occasions since 1999. Specifically, respondents have been asked:

With all of the changes going on in the way the different parts of Great Britain are run, which of the following do you think would be best for England ...

... for England to be governed as it is now, with laws made by the UK Parliament

... for each region of England to have its own assembly that runs services like health

or, for England as a whole to have its own new parliament?

As shown in Table 7.3, the *status quo* – England being governed by the UK Parliament – has consistently been the most popular option among the English public. However, it is notable that support for this proposition has fallen to below half for the first time, compared with 62 per cent a decade earlier. At the same time, support for the idea of England having its own parliament has increased recently, from 17 per cent in 2007 to 29 per cent by 2009. Support for regional assemblies, on the other hand, appears to have fallen away since the defeat of the proposals for a North East Regional Assembly in 2004.

Table 7.3 Attitudes in <u>England</u> to how England should be governed, 1999–2009

	99	00	01	02	03[5]	04	05	06	07	08	09
How England should be governed	%	%	%	%	%	%	%	%	%	%	%
As it is now, with laws made by the UK parliament	62	54	57	56	50	53	54	54	57	51	49
Each region of England to have own assembly that runs services like health	15	18	23	20	26	21	20	18	14	15	15
England to have its own new parliament with law-making powers	18	19	16	17	18	21	18	21	17	26	29
Base		*2718*	*1928*	*2761*	*2897*	*3709*	*2684*	*1794*	*928*	*859*	*982*	*980*

Base: respondents living in England

So there are some signs that, in recent years in England, both discontent about Scotland's share of public spending and support for the idea of an English parliament have increased. But are these two developments linked in any way? There is some tentative evidence that they might be (Table 7.4). In the early years of devolution there did not appear to be much relationship between people's views of Scotland's share of the public finances and support for an English parliament. Thus there was no reason to anticipate that any increase in concern about Scotland's share of public spending would translate into increased support for an English parliament. However, more recently those who think that Scotland gets more than its fair share – and especially those who say that it gets *much* more – have been more likely to say they would prefer England to have its own parliament. In both 2008 and 2009 two-fifths (41 per cent) of those who believe Scotland gets much more than its fair share say they would like England to have its own parliament, compared with only around a quarter or so of those who say either that Scotland gets pretty much its fair share or that Scotland gets less than its fair share. Although the change is not quite statistically significant at conventional levels, it does look as though a link between resentment about the amount of money Scotland has to spend and support for an English parliament may have begun to emerge, and that increasing concern about the former may have helped fuel the apparently growing demand for the latter.[6]

Table 7.4 Support in <u>England</u> for an English parliament, by views of Scotland's share of government spending, 2000–2009

	% think England should have own parliament with law-making powers							
	2000	*Base*	**2001**	*Base*	**2008**	*Base*	**2009**	*Base*
Government spending Scotland receives, compared with rest of UK								
Much more than its fair share	26	*159*	22	*254*	41	*213*	41	*187*
A little more than its fair share	25	*241*	19	*400*	29	*198*	34	*214*
Pretty much its fair share	18	*799*	15	*1211*	22	*313*	25	*295*
A little/much less than its fair share	25	*213*	18	*237*	33	*29*	26	*31*
Don't know	15	*508*	12	*659*	18	*226*	21	*252*
All	19	*1928*	16	*2761*	26	*982*	29	*980*

Base: respondents living in England

So, despite the apparent lack of impetus behind the relevant elite-level debate in England, we have uncovered some evidence of an English 'backlash'. In more recent years at least, there has been growing discontent about Scotland's share of public spending and increased interest in an English parliament. True, both outlooks are still only shared by a minority, and there seems to be little appetite for ending the Union or even denying Scotland the devolution it now enjoys. Nevertheless, it appears that, from an English perspective at least, there may now be a need to pay some attention to the financial relationship between England and Scotland if tension between the two countries is not to grow.

The view from Scotland: growing discontent?

But what of the position in Scotland? Was the success of the SNP in the 2007 Scottish election an indication of a growing restiveness north of the border, too? And even if that were not the case, has the experience of having a nationalist government in power helped, as the SNP hoped it would, to increase support for independence thereafter?

Surprising though it might seem, there is little evidence to support such speculation. Far from indicating increasing support for Scottish independence, data from *Scottish Social Attitudes* suggest that the SNP's victory in 2007 actually coincided, if anything, with a low point in support for Scotland leaving the Union (Table 7.5). In 2007, just 24 per cent of people in Scotland said they would prefer Scotland to be independent – the lowest proportion recorded by *Scottish Social Attitudes* since 1997.[7] Meanwhile, although this figure has since increased slightly to 28 per cent, the increase is insufficient to support the contention that the experience of having an SNP government in Edinburgh has helped to increase support above previously attained levels. Rather, the overall picture since the advent of devolution is one of little or no change in levels of support for independence in Scotland – consistently somewhere between a quarter and a third have expressed a preference for Scotland to leave the Union, but never much more than that. A majority of people in Scotland appear content with remaining part of the UK, but with a Scottish parliament – around a half to two-thirds have chosen this as their preferred option in each year since 1999. And, since the 1997 referendum at least, the vast majority of these have wanted that parliament to have tax-raising powers.

Table 7.5 Attitudes in <u>Scotland</u> to how Scotland should be governed, 1997–2009

	1997 May[+]	1997 Sept.[++]	1999[+++]	2000	2001	2002
How Scotland should be governed	%	%	%	%	%	%
Independent, separate from UK and EU, or separate from UK but part of EU	27	37	27	30	27	30
Part of UK, with own parliament with **some** taxation powers	21	32	50	47	54	44
Part of UK, with own parliament with **no** taxation powers	28	9	8	8	6	8
Part of UK, without an elected parliament	11	17	10	12	9	13
Don't know	7	4	5	3	4	6
Base	*882*	*676*	*1482*	*1663*	*1605*	*1665*

	2003	2004	2005	2006	2007	2009
How Scotland should be governed	%	%	%	%	%	%
Independent, separate from UK and EU, or separate from UK but part of EU	26	32	35	30	24	28
Part of UK, with own parliament with **some** taxation powers	48	40	38	47	54	49
Part of UK, with own parliament with **no** taxation powers	7	5	6	7	8	7
Part of UK, without an elected parliament	13	17	14	9	9	8
Don't know	6	5	8	7	5	7
Base	*1508*	*1637*	*1549*	*1594*	*1508*	*1482*

[+] Source: 1997 May Scottish Election Study
[++] Source: 1997 Sept. Referendum Study[9]
[+++] Source: 1999–2009 *Scottish Social Attitudes* survey

Still, even if the electoral success of the SNP did not indicate a growing demand that Scotland should become independent, it might still have signified growing discontent with the way in which Scotland is treated within the Union. Or perhaps the sight and sound of nationalist ministers willing to dispute with the UK government in public when they feel that Scotland is being disadvantaged has subsequently helped to fuel such discontent? There is, in fact, little evidence to support these two suppositions either. Rather, if anything, in the last few years, Scotland has appeared somewhat more content with its place in the Union than it was previously.

First, people in Scotland appear to have shifted away from thinking that their country loses out in the distribution of public spending, and towards believing that it gets at least its fair share (Table 7.6). In 2000, no less than 59 per cent felt Scotland received less than its fair share of public spending. By 2009, this figure has fallen to 38 per cent. During the same period, the proportion who felt Scotland secured either its fair share or even more than its fair share increased from 37 per cent to 53 per cent.

Table 7.6 Attitudes in <u>Scotland</u> towards the financial relationship between England and Scotland, 2000–2009

	2000	2001	2003	2005	2007	2009
Government spending Scotland receives, compared with rest of UK	%	%	%	%	%	%
Much more than its fair share	2	2	2	3	3	2
A little more than its fair share	8	8	8	7	13	11
Pretty much its fair share	27	36	34	32	37	39
A little less than its fair share	35	32	35	32	25	29
Much less than its fair share	23	15	13	17	11	8
Don't know	4	6	7	8	11	10
Base	*1663*	*1605*	*1508*	*1549*	*1508*	*1482*

Source: *Scottish Social Attitudes*

Second, compared with a decade ago, people in Scotland are now also apparently less likely to feel that *England* benefits more economically from the Union than Scotland (Table 7.7). *Scottish Social Attitudes* respondents were asked:

> *On the whole, do you think that England's economy benefits more from having Scotland in the UK, or that Scotland's economy benefits more from being part of the UK, or is it about equal?*

In 2000, 42 per cent of people in Scotland believed England's economy benefited more, but by 2007 this figure had fallen to 27 per cent and it remains no more than 28 per cent now. As a result people are nowadays only slightly more likely to think that England benefits more than they are to feel that Scotland does. Again it appears that, far from reflecting increased dissatisfaction with the operation of the Union, the SNP's first term in government has coincided with a period of relative contentment with Scotland's economic position within the UK.

Table 7.7 Perceptions in <u>Scotland</u> of whose economy benefits more from Scotland being part of the UK, 2000–2009

	2000	2001	2003	2005	2007	2009
Whose economy benefits more from having Scotland in the UK	%	%	%	%	%	%
England	42	38	30	36	27	28
Scotland	16	18	24	21	25	24
Both equally	36	39	40	34	39	40
Base	*1663*	*1605*	*1508*	*1549*	*1508*	*1482*

Source: *Scottish Social Attitudes*

On non-economic aspects of the Union, too, there is evidence that the 2007 election, in fact, coincided with increased contentment with Scotland's position. After an initial wave of optimism, between 2004 and 2006 more people felt that devolution was making no difference to Scotland's voice in the UK than felt it was strengthening that voice. But in the weeks and months immediately after the SNP's success in 2007, no less than 61 per cent felt that devolution was giving their country a stronger voice. Although this figure has since fallen back somewhat to 52 per cent, perceptions of the impact of devolution are still more favourable now than they were at any time between 2004 and 2006.

Table 7.8 Perceptions in <u>Scotland</u> of impact of having a Scottish parliament on Scotland's voice in the UK, 2000–2009

	2000[+]	2001	2002	2003	2004	2005	2006	2007	2009
Impact of having a Scottish parliament on Scotland's voice in the UK	%	%	%	%	%	%	%	%	%
Stronger voice	52	52	39	49	35	41	43	61	52
Weaker voice	6	6	6	7	7	6	6	4	5
Making no difference	39	40	52	41	55	50	49	32	40
Base	*1663*	*1605*	*1665*	*1508*	*1637*	*1549*	*1594*	*1508*	*1482*

Source: *Scottish Social Attitudes*
[+] In 2000, respondents were asked whether having a Scottish parliament *is going to give* Scotland a stronger or weaker voice in the UK. Thereafter they were asked whether having a Scottish parliament *is giving* Scotland a stronger or weaker voice

Why might the advent of a nationalist government in Edinburgh have coincided with rather greater satisfaction with the Union? One, ironic, possibility is that having a government in Edinburgh that (in contrast to the Labour–Liberal Democrat administration that preceded it) unashamedly claims to put Scotland's interests first – and is willing to argue Scotland's case in public even if it provokes disagreement with the UK government in London – means that people in Scotland are now more likely to feel that devolution is helping to ensure that their country's distinctive interests and identity are being adequately defended within the framework of the United Kingdom. The SNP may have hoped that experience of nationalist government would help persuade people in Scotland of the merits of independence, but it might instead have helped persuade them that devolution can be made to work effectively to their country's benefit after all (see also Curtice, 2008).

Given this increased contentment with the Union, it is, perhaps, surprising that support for independence has not fallen further. After all, as Table 7.9 demonstrates, in both 2001 and 2009, support for independence is lower among those who feel that Scotland does well financially out of the Union. For example, in 2009 only around one in five of those who think Scotland gets pretty much or more than its fair share of UK government spending favoured independence, less than half the equivalent proportion among those who feel that Scotland secured less than its fair share. So given that more people now feel that Scotland does reasonably well out of the Union, the overall level of support for independence should have fallen. The fact that, in practice, it has remained largely unchanged is largely accounted for by a particularly sharp increase in support for independence among those who still feel that Scotland loses out from its membership of the Union. For example, 50 per cent of those who feel that England benefits more from the Union now support independence, compared with 40 per cent in 2001.[10] Perhaps those who feel that Scotland loses out financially from the Union now consist rather more of those whose commitment to independence is such that they are never likely to be persuaded that their country does not lose out from its continued membership of the UK.

Table 7.9 Support in <u>Scotland</u> for independence, by perceptions of the financial operation of the Union, 2001 and 2009

	2001		2009	
	% support independence	Base	% support independence	Base
All	27	1605	28	1482
Whose economy benefits more from having Scotland in UK				
England	40	625	50	411
About equal	23	616	25	595
Scotland	9	277	12	347
Government spending Scotland receives, compared with rest of UK				
More than fair	16	150	19	203
Pretty much fair	21	591	20	576
Less than fair	36	763	42	565

Source: *Scottish Social Attitudes*

So it seems that in Scotland, in contrast to the position in England, it is the hopes of the advocates of devolution rather than the fears of its critics that appear the closer to being realised. People north of the border are now rather more likely to feel that their country is benefiting from its membership of the Union and maybe, even, that the advent of devolution has helped bring this about. Despite the SNP's success in 2007, there is no evidence of a growing appetite for independence.

But although recent trends in Scotland may look very different from those in England there are, in fact, some important similarities in the outlook of the two countries. Both appear to agree that some form of devolution with tax-raising powers is the best way of governing Scotland. Meanwhile, public opinion in the two countries has shifted in the same direction in so far as the issue of Scotland's share of public spending is concerned – Scotland is now less likely to feel that it secures less than its fair share while England is apparently beginning to wonder whether Scotland has more than its fair share. We have also uncovered evidence on both sides of the border of an association between perceptions of the financial consequences of the Union and constitutional preferences. So perhaps changing how Scotland is funded by giving her Parliament more responsibility for raising its own revenues might indeed strike an important chord with public opinion in both England and Scotland. It is to attitudes towards this subject in particular that we now turn.

Addressing the financial questions

Both *British Social Attitudes* and *Scottish Social Attitudes* included in their 2009 survey a question designed to tap people's attitudes towards the principle that services provided in Scotland should be paid for out of taxes raised in Scotland. It asks respondents how strongly they agree or disagree that:

> *Now that Scotland has its own parliament, it should pay for its services out of taxes collected in Scotland*

Although support for this principle appears to be stronger in England than in Scotland, a majority in both countries agree (Table 7.10). In England, 82 per cent do so, in Scotland, 57 per cent. Although the proposals put forward by Calman are less radical than the position implied by our statement – they would only result in one third or so of devolved spending being funded directly out of taxes raised in Scotland, not all of it – it would appear that they are in sympathy with the broad direction of public opinion on both sides of the border.

Table 7.10 Attitudes towards Scotland paying for services out of taxes collected in Scotland, by country, 2009

Scotland should pay for its services out of taxes collected in Scotland	England	Scotland[+]
	%	%
Strongly agree	36	8
Agree	46	49
Neither agree nor disagree	10	18
Disagree	6	18
Strongly disagree	*	4
Base	980	1482

+ Source: *Scottish Social Attitudes*

Indeed, it seems that support for the principle has grown in both parts of the UK since the advent of devolution (Table 7.11). In 2001, 73 per cent of people in England agreed that Scottish services should be paid for from Scottish taxes; now that figure stands at 82 per cent. Over the same period support for the idea in Scotland has increased from 51 per cent to 57 per cent. The climate for introducing such a mechanism is apparently even more propitious now than when devolution was first established.

Table 7.11 Agreement with view that Scotland should pay for services out of taxes collected in Scotland, by country, 2001–2009

	% agree Scotland should pay for its services out of taxes collected in Scotland			
	2001	2003	2007	2009
Country				
England	73	74	75	82
Base	2761	1917	859	980
Scotland+	51	51	57	57
Base	1605	1508	1508	1482

+ Source: *Scottish Social Attitudes*

However, our line of questioning on this issue may be thought to have its limitations. Methodological research on surveys has demonstrated that respondents have a tendency to agree rather than disagree with whatever propositions are put to them. This might be particularly true of a statement such as this, which, perhaps, appears all too self-evidently reasonable (Schuman and Presser, 1996). Moreover, our proposition does not invite people to compare the merits of funding services in Scotland out of taxes raised in Scotland with those of the current system of funding via a block grant. To address the possibility that our style of questioning exaggerates the level of support for the principle of funding Scottish services out of Scottish taxes, the 2009 *Scottish Social Attitudes* also asked its respondents the following question:

> *Thinking about public services in Scotland, such as health and education, that are nowadays the responsibility of the Scottish government. How do you think these services in Scotland should be paid for ...*
>
> *... out of a sum of money decided by the UK government and funded out of taxes collected across the UK, or*
>
> *... out of taxes decided and collected by the Scottish government in Scotland?*

Over half (53 per cent) say services in Scotland should be paid for by taxes decided and collected in Scotland (only slightly below the 57 per cent who agree with our earlier statement) while just two in five (40 per cent) said they prefer the block grant. Similarly, when respondents in Scotland were asked yet a further question about who they thought should make most of the important decisions for Scotland about tax, nearly six in ten (59 per cent) said it should be the Scottish Parliament, and just 33 per cent the UK government.[11] Thus, however the issue is addressed, consistently somewhere between a half and six in ten people in Scotland say they would like Scotland's services to be paid for out of taxes controlled and raised in Scotland. Our initial measure may well be reasonably reliable after all.

   Still, this does not mean necessarily that people support the idea as a matter of principle. Perhaps the motivation of people in Scotland is a relatively base and contingent one – they believe they would pay less tax as a result. This, though, does not appear to be the case. *Scottish Social Attitudes* respondents were asked what they thought would happen to the level of taxes in Scotland if, instead of being decided by the UK government, they were to be decided by the Scottish Parliament – would they be higher, lower or would it make no difference? Overall, most people in Scotland (60 per cent) believe that taxes would be higher if they were set in Scotland – including 18 per cent who think they would be a lot higher. Only seven per cent think they would be lower.[12] Meanwhile, among those who believe that taxes would be a "little higher" if they were raised in Edinburgh, 61 per cent nonetheless agree that Scotland's public services *should* be paid for out of taxes set and collected in Scotland (Table 7.12). Only among those who believe that taxes would increase "a lot" if responsibility shifted north is support for Scotland raising its own taxes markedly lower (39 per cent).

Table 7.12 Agreement in <u>Scotland</u> that Scotland should pay for services out of taxes collected in Scotland, by beliefs about impact of Scottish Parliament setting taxes on taxation levels, 2009

	What would happen to Scottish taxes if decided by the Scottish Parliament			
	A lot higher	A little higher	No difference	A lot/a little lower[+]
Scotland should pay for its services out of taxes collected in Scotland	%	%	%	%
Agree	39	61	67	66
Neither agree nor disagree	14	18	19	18
Disagree	45	20	11	16
Base	*289*	*604*	*369*	*99*

Source: *Scottish Social Attitudes*
[+] "A lot lower" and "a little lower" were coded separately, but as the numbers falling into each category were small they have been combined here

So it appears that moving towards a system whereby some of the services in Scotland for which the devolved Scottish Parliament is responsible, are funded out of taxes decided and raised there *would* be in tune with public opinion on both sides of the border. Still, this does not necessarily mean that the motivations for supporting the proposal are the same in both countries. As we noted earlier, in England, the idea might be seen as a means of imposing a necessary fiscal responsibility and discipline upon a part of the UK that currently enjoys a higher level of government spending per head. In Scotland, in contrast, it might be regarded as a way of increasing the country's freedom and autonomy to make its own decisions about the appropriate level of public spending.

There is some evidence that suggests the motivations on the two sides of the border *are* somewhat different. In Table 7.13 we show separately for England and Scotland the level of support for funding Scottish services out of Scottish taxes, broken down by perceptions of Scotland's share of public spending. In England those who feel that Scotland secures more than its fair share of public spending are a little more likely to believe that Scottish services should be paid for out of Scottish taxes. Nine in ten (91 per cent) of those who think Scotland gets more than its fair share of UK government spending agree that Scotland should raise its own taxes, compared with 81 per cent of those who think Scotland gets pretty much its fair share. In Scotland, in contrast, it is those who think that Scotland receives *less* than its fair share who are keenest on the idea. However, in both cases the association is only a weak one and the proposition has majority support among all the groups identified in Table 7.13.

Table 7.13 Agreement that Scotland should pay for services out of taxes collected in Scotland, by views of Scotland's share of government spending, by country, 2009

	% agree Scotland should pay for its services out of taxes collected in Scotland			
	England	*Base*	Scotland[+]	*Base*
Scotland's share of government spending	%		%	
More than fair	91	*401*	57	*203*
Pretty much fair	81	*295*	54	*576*
Less than fair	75	*31*	63	*565*

[+] Source: *Scottish Social Attitudes*

There is a sharper difference between England and Scotland if we look at the link between attitudes towards paying for Scottish services out of Scottish taxes and attitudes towards how Scotland should be governed. As Table 7.14 shows, among those in Scotland who support independence, no less than 77 per cent support Scotland raising its own taxes and paying for its own services. But this figure falls to 53 per cent among those who support having a Scottish parliament within the Union, and just 32 per cent among those who would prefer not to have a Scottish parliament at all. Among people in England, however, the relationship between attitudes towards how much political autonomy Scotland should have and how its services should be paid for is less straightforward. Although, as in Scotland, those who think Scotland should leave the Union are most likely to favour Scotland paying for its own services, those who think that Scotland ought not to have its own parliament at all are also relatively favourable towards the idea. This suggests that, in England, at least some of those who say that Scotland should pay for its services out of its own taxes are, in fact, simply expressing a degree of resentment about Scottish devolution. But even so, it should be borne in mind that this is a relatively small group. For the most part, it would seem that making the Scottish Parliament responsible for funding the services it provides is backed on both sides of the border because people regard it as a more appropriate way of implementing a system of devolution.

Table 7.14 Agreement that Scotland should pay for services out of taxes collected in Scotland, by attitudes to governing of Scotland, by country

	% agree Scotland should pay for its services out of taxes collected in Scotland			
	England (2007)	Base	Scotland (2009)[+]	Base
How Scotland should be governed				
Independent, separate from UK and EU, or separate from UK but part of EU	92	*159*	77	*404*
Part of UK, with own parliament with **some/no** taxation powers	72	*407*	53	*845*
Part of UK, without an elected parliament	84	*159*	32	*129*

[+] Source: *Scottish Social Attitudes*

Conclusions: a stable constitutional future?

In this chapter, we have seen that impressions drawn from political developments and elite debates about Scotland's position in the Union are not necessarily reflected in patterns of public opinion. In England, although debates about redressing some of the alleged unfairness of the devolution settlement have apparently failed to catch fire, it appears that public discontent about Scotland's share of public spending has been mounting. Although this development has not led to any increase in the proportion who would like to see Scotland leave the Union, it may in part have helped stimulate support for the idea of an English parliament. In Scotland, meanwhile, far from signalling growing discontent with Scotland's position in the Union, the SNP's electoral success in 2007 appears to have coincided with a low point in support for independence, and with a reduction in discontent about Scotland's position within the Union.

It is, then, England and not Scotland that has become less happy about the current state of the Union. As a result there would appear to be a need to address a perceived financial inequity between Scotland and England in order to stem an incipient 'English backlash'. But at the same time, it appears it might be possible to introduce measures that would help achieve this while working with the grain of public opinion on both sides of the border. People in Scotland are more willing than they once were to accept that Scotland does at least get its fair share of government spending. Meanwhile, there appears be consistent and, perhaps even growing support – in both England and Scotland – for the idea that public services in Scotland should be paid for out of taxes raised in Scotland, rather than almost wholly out of a UK-funded and determined block grant.

Perhaps what is more uncertain is whether the Calman proposals or anything similar that might eventually be introduced by the UK government will prove sufficient to satisfy public opinion in either England or Scotland. After all, the

Calman proposals represent a compromise between retaining the block grant and giving the Scottish Parliament the freedom to set its own budget and the responsibility to raise its own revenues. Certainly the SNP's initial response to Calman was that it was a 'messy fudge' (Scottish Government, 15th June 2009). So although implementing Calman might help ensure the arrangements for governing Scotland are closer to the public mood, we might still find that such a development proves too little either to meet the disquiet increasingly felt by some in England or to fulfil the aspirations that many still have for devolution in Scotland.

Notes

1. Dalyell (1977) also famously coined what Enoch Powell dubbed 'the West Lothian question', in which he queried why an MP from West Lothian in Scotland should be able to vote on matters affecting the NHS, education, and so on in England, when an MP from West Bromwich in England had no voting rights with respect to similar matters in Scotland.
2. The SNP have just 47 seats in the 129 seat chamber. Apart from two Green MSPs the remaining members of the parliament remain opposed to holding a referendum.
3. For further technical details of the 2009 *Scottish Social Attitudes* survey, see Annex B of Ormston (2010).
4. For example, a YouGov poll conducted for The Sunday Times between 16th and 17th April   2010 asked its respondents, 'Scotland currently receives 20% more public spending per head of population than England. Do you think Scotland gets more than its fair share of government spending, pretty much its fair share given Scotland's large land area and the costs that arise from this, or less than its fair share.' As many as 59 per cent said more than its fair share in response to this prompt.
5. In 2004–2006 the second option read "that makes decisions about the region's economy, planning and housing". The 2003 survey carried both versions of this option and demonstrated that the difference of wording did not make a material difference to the pattern of response. The figures quoted for 2003 are those for the two versions combined.
6. We fitted a log-linear model as follows. Data for 2000 and 2001 and those for 2008 and 2009 were combined. Respondents who said that Scotland secured anything less than much more than its fair share of public spending were combined into a single category, while respondents who favoured regional assemblies or did not know which system of government they preferred for England were omitted from the analysis. We then fitted all the main effects for year, attitudes towards Scotland's share of spending and preferred form of government for England, together with all the interaction effects between each pair. The three-way interaction was not fitted. The residual chi-square from this model was 3.6, which with one degree of freedom has a p value of .06. Alternative ways of modelling the data produced much the same result.

7. Rather than exploiting a rising tide of support for independence, the SNP's electoral success was based primarily on persuading more of those who *already* backed independence or at least a more powerful devolved parliament to support the party than had done in the past (Curtice *et al.*, 2009).

8. Scottish Election Studies were conducted as part of a series of British Election Studies in 1974, 1979, 1992 and 1997. In each case, they took place in the immediate aftermath of the relevant UK General Election. Samples were chosen using a random selection procedure modified by stratification and clustering. In 1997 882 interviews were achieved , a response rate of 62 per cent. For further detail, see Brown *et al.* (1998).

9. The Scottish Referendum Survey was undertaken in September and October 1997 by *NatCen*, with funding from the ESRC. It began immediately after the referendum on devolution on 11th September 1997. The sample design was similar to that used for *Scottish Social Attitudes* – a stratified, clustered random sample drawn from the Postcode Address File and weighted to correct for differential selection probabilities. There were 676 face-to-face interviews conducted, with a response rate of 68 per cent.

10. The intensification of the relationship between perceptions of whose economy does best out of the Union and support for independence is statistically significant. We conducted the following log-linear analysis. First, data for 2001 and 2003 were combined as were data for 2007 and 2009. Perceptions of whose economy does best from the Union were collapsed into England *versus* any other answer, while constitutional preferences were collapsed into independence *versus* any other answer. To these data we then fitted a model that contained all possible terms, except the three-way interaction between perceptions of whose economy benefits more from the Union, support for independence and year. The residual chi-square for this model was 4.1, which with one degree of freedom has a p value of .044. Note, however, that a similar analysis of the relationship between perceptions of whose economy benefits most from the Union and support for independence does not demonstrate that the apparent (but weaker) strengthening of the relationship between those two variables over time is statistically significant.

11. A further four per cent thought local councils should make most decisions about tax, while one per cent felt it should be the European Union and four per cent said they did not know who should make such decisions.

12. Twenty-six per cent thought taxes would remain the same if they were decided in Scotland and seven per cent did not know what would happen.

References

Aughey, A. (2001), *Nationalism, Devolution and the Challenge to the United Kingdom State*, London: Pluto Press

Bogdanor, V. (1999), *Devolution in the United Kingdom*, Oxford: Oxford University Press

Brown, A., McCrone, D., Paterson, L., Surridge, P. (1998), *The Scottish Electorate: the 1997 election and beyond*, London: Macmillan

Cabinet Office (2010), *The Coalition: Our Programme for Government*, London: Cabinet Office available at http://www.cabinetoffice.gov.uk/media/409088/pfg_coalition.pdf

Commission on Scottish Devolution (2009), *Serving Scotland Better: Scotland and the United Kingdom in the 21st Century*, Edinburgh: Commission on Scottish Devolution, available at http://www.commissiononscottishdevolution.org.uk/

Conservative Democracy Task Force (2008), *Answering the Question: Devolution the West Lothian Question and the Future of the Union*, London: Conservative Party

Conservative Party (2000), *Strengthening Parliament: Report of the Commission to Strengthen Parliament*, London: Conservative Party

Curtice, J. (2008), 'How FIrm are the Foundations? Public Attitudes towards the Union in 2007', in Devine, T. (ed.), *Scotland and the Union 1707–2007*, Edinburgh: Edinburgh University Press

Curtice, J. (2009), 'Is there an English backlash? Reactions to devolution', in Park, A., Curtice, J., Thomson, K., Phillips, M. and Clery, E. (eds.), *British Social Attitudes: the 25th Report*, London: Sage

Curtice, J., McCrone, D., McEwen, N., Marsh, M. and Ormston, R. (2009), *The 2007 Scottish Elections: Revolution or Evolution?*, Edinburgh: Edinburgh University Press

Dalyell, Tan (1977), *Devolution: the end of Britain?*, London: Jonathan Cape

Hazell, R. (ed.) (2006), *The English Question*, Manchester: Manchester University Press.

IPPR (28th May 2010), 'Press release: Real tests for relationship between Cameron government and devolved administrations lie ahead', available at http://www.ippr.org/pressreleases/?id=4009

Johnson, S. (2010), 'Alex Salmond "drops independence for the timebeing", *Daily Telegraph*, 29th May

Linklater, M. and MacLeod, A. (2010), 'Salmond: tax powers can save Scotland', *The Times*, 25th June

Mackintosh, J. (1998), 'A Parliament for Scotland', reprinted in Paterson, L. (ed.), *A Diverse Assembly: The Debate on the Scottish Parliament*, Edinburgh: Edinburgh University Press

McLean, I., Lodge, G., Schmuecker, K. (2008), *Fair Shares? Barnett and the politics of public expenditure*, IPPR, available at http://www.ippr.org/ipprnorth/publicationsandreports/publication.asp?id=619

Ormston, R. (2010), *Scottish Social Attitudes survey 2009: Core module – Attitudes to government, the economy and public services in Scotland*, Edinburgh: Scottish Government Social Research, available at http://www.scotland.gov.uk/Publications/2010/03/15102525/0

Sandford, M. (ed.) (2009), *The Northern Veto*, Manchester: Manchester University Press

Schuman, H. and Presser, S. (1996), *Questions and Answers in Attitude Surveys*, Thousand Oaks, Calif., Sage

Scottish Government (15th June 2009), 'Calman Commission', news release, available at http://www.scotland.gov.uk/News/Releases/2009/06/15151304

Scottish Government (2010), *Scotland's Future: Draft Referendum (Scotland) Bill Consultation Paper*, Edinburgh: Scottish Government, available at http://www.scotland.gov.uk/Publications/2010/02/22120157/1

8 Age identity and conflict: myths and realities

Rory Fitzgerald, Eric Harrison and Frank Steinmaier[*]

Age has been described as the "neglected dimension of stratification" (Bradley, 1996: 145). This area of social science was, for a hundred years, shaped in terms of the three dimensions of inequality identified by Max Weber – "class, status and party" (Gerth and Mills, 1970). From the 1970s onwards, this triumvirate has been supplemented, with gender and ethnicity both gaining increasing recognition as potential sources of both individual identity and material inequality. More generally, the influence of postmodernism has broadened the range of inequalities still further, reducing the primacy of traditional identities like social class. The trend in social theorising has moved away from seeking to identify overarching patterns of social explanation towards acknowledging multiple sources of identity, many of them distinctive to the contemporary era.

To some extent, an appreciation of the importance of age prc-dates these recent theoretical developments. It is a well-established sociological principle that people's perceptions of, and attitudes towards, the world around them will vary according to their age. This may reflect the importance of the life-course; for example, the belief that people become more socially or politically conservative in their views as they get older. Alternatively, it might reflect generational or cohort influences; for example, the fact that younger people are more liberal or environmentally conscious than their elders, and will remain so as they get older. Meanwhile, quantitative and qualitative work has demonstrated the social and cultural distinctiveness of particular age groups, though most attention has been focused on each end of the scale – on the elderly and on 'youth' (Arber and Ginn 1991, Miles 2000).

The debate has recently taken a new twist in Britain following a series of books and articles focusing directly on overt conflict between generations over

[*] Rory Fitzgerald (Deputy Director) and Eric Harrison (Senior Research Fellow) are both based at the Centre for Comparative Social Surveys (CCSS) at City University London. CCSS houses the European Social Survey. Frank Steinmaier was a visiting Research Fellow at City University in the summer of 2010

both ideas and resources. This is most cogently summarised in David Willetts's *The Pinch* (2010) which claims that the 'Baby Boomer' generation born in the years after World War Two has enjoyed an unprecedented period of opportunity, mobility and affluence. In doing so it has broken the 'generational contract', mortgaged the future of today's youth and left them to endure a legacy of stagnation and debt. Arguments about inter-generational equity have been in circulation for many years (for a useful summary see Attias-Donfut and Arber, 2000), but acquired an extra salience in 2010 as the first Boomers reached retirement age at a time when the future of pension provision is under review and Britain faces up to widespread cuts in public expenditure and an extended period of austerity.

Age identity may well be an important factor in shaping any generational conflict over the distribution of resources. Indeed, the likelihood of such collective action taking place will be strongly shaped by the nature of age identity in Britain. Age identity does not simply denote views and/or behaviours in common, but an awareness of these similarities, a feeling of solidarity towards others in the same position (and by implication a potential antagonism towards those who are different), and a willingness to act on the basis of these experiences. Bradley operationalises this distinction in terms of three *levels* of social identity:

a) *passive* social identities are derived from 'sets of lived relationships' (such as class, gender and ethnicity) but are not acted upon;

b) *active* social identities are ones which individuals are both conscious of and which move them to act on their basis. The formation and promotion of an active identity can be a defensive response to the actions or perceptions of others, for instance pejorative labelling or overt discrimination;

c) identities are *politicised* when they become the primary frame of self-reference for those individuals and provide a more consistent basis for action than is the case with active identities. Politicised identities imply a far greater degree of collective organisation and action. (Bradley 1996: 25–6)

Consequently, the likelihood of there being generational conflict and collective action should be at its highest when identities are politicised and at its lowest when they are passive.

In order to understand the nature and role of identity, social scientists have to acknowledge that subjective identity and objective position are not necessarily the same thing. For example, someone in a professional occupation, who would be described as 'middle class' by any social scientist, may themselves choose to call themselves 'working class', perhaps because of their family background or their perception of what it is to be a worker. Two individuals with the same ethnic background and identical migration trajectory might tick different boxes on the census form because their experiences of life in Britain have caused them to develop a different consciousness. For the data analyst these are acts of technical 'misclassification'; for the sociologist interested in self-identity the perception of the respondent is paramount.

Of equal importance is the strength of adherence to an identity group. It is one thing to be able to allocate oneself (accurately or not) to a particular category, or to wish to be ascribed a label that one finds agreeable. It is quite another to develop fully an empathy with others in that group and to be prepared to act in concert with them. The individual needs to be able to recognise 'people like me' and to have some conception of who, and what, they are. As Weeks remarks:

> Identity is about belonging, about what you have in common with some people and what differentiates you from others. (1990: 88)

While politicians and pundits often speculate about generational conflict, there has been much less empirical focus on the importance of age identity. This chapter seeks to address this by exploring age identity in Britain today, and assessing its implications as regards the extent to which potential clashes over resources and ideas might become real generational battles. We begin by examining the degree of congruence between the age group with which people identify and their own actual age, and then assess the strength of their affiliation with others in the same age group. We then address the question of how far 'age' really is a social force in its own right – a "generation in actuality" to borrow from Mannheim (1952) – rather than just an analytic category. To do this, we examine the degree to which age group identification predicts social attitudes and the extent to which those in different age groups feel they are subject to discrimination on the basis of their age. Finally, in the third section, we examine a further question – not of whether different age groups think differently, *but what they think of each other*.

The chapter uses data from the 2005 *British Social Attitudes* survey, which included an extensive set of questions about different social identities (Heath *et al.*, 2007). We also use data from the European Social Survey Round 4 (ESS 2008/9[1]), which included a detailed set of questions both on age identity and ageism, in order to measure ageing-related perceptions, relationships and stereotypes surrounding age (Abrams, 2007).

Age identification in practice

In everyday life it is routine practice to be asked for one's date of birth or to place oneself in one of a series of categories, each one defined by an apparently arbitrary age range. Those requesting the information usually do so because they believe the boundaries they set constitute significant social markers relating to preferences and behaviour. They are right more often than not. But to what extent does a person's chronological age affect their age identity? And how strongly do people identify with people within the same age group? It is to these questions that we now turn.

Identifying your age group

We begin by considering the age groups with which people identify. As with most socio-demographic measures, the design and phrasing of the question is crucial in shaping the quality of the responses. In contrast to some other subjective identities, there is no particular agreement on the best way of measuring age identity; not surprisingly, the two surveys of interest to us use different questions. The 2005 *British Social Attitudes* survey asks:

> *Irrespective of how old you actually are, do you **usually** think of yourself as being in any of the categories on this card, or are none of these right for you?*
>
> *A middle aged person*
> *An older person*
> *A young person*
> *A thirty-something person*
> *None of these are right for me*

Table 8.1 shows the results broken down by people's actual age. Overall, the vast majority (85 per cent) were able to choose one of the identities, with this apparently being easiest for the youngest and oldest groups. So, while only 10 per cent of people aged 70 and above did not choose an age identity, the same applied to over a quarter of those in their forties. The most popular category chosen was "young" (selected by 28 per cent); the least popular was "older" (13 per cent). Nearly half (44 per cent) chose to describe themselves as either "middle aged" or "thirty-something".

It is clear from Table 8.1 that respondents resolutely resist the onset of social ageing. A little under a third of those in their thirties refused the "thirty-something" description and opted instead to choose "young" (while only three per cent described themselves as "middle aged"). Among older respondents the proportion choosing "young" remains surprisingly high – applying to 14 per cent of people in their forties and 11 per cent of those in their fifties. Even a small minority in their sixties (five per cent) and aged 70+ and above (four per cent) choose to describe themselves as young. The majority of respondents rejected the "older" category until they were 70 or over: most in their sixties (47 per cent) still opted for "middle aged", as did a quarter (27 per cent) of those aged 70 and over. Clearly, many respondents appear to 'misclassify' their subjective identity in relation to their objective status.

Table 8.1 Self-assigned age group, by actual age group, 2005

Self-assigned age group	Actual age group						
	18–29	30–39	40–49	50–59	60–69	70+	All
	%	%	%	%	%	%	%
Middle aged	2	3	30	51	47	27	25
Older	3	1	1	7	24	57	13
Young	85	31	14	11	5	4	28
Thirty something	3	58	27	14	5	2	20
None of these*	8	7	27	18	19	10	15
Base	302	380	405	360	306	349	2102

The group 'None of these' includes 18 respondents who self-assigned themselves to more than one category

The ESS takes a different approach to measuring age identity, and asks:

> *Which box best describes the age group you see yourself as belonging to? If you see yourself as very young, pick the first box. If you see yourself as very old, pick the last box. Otherwise pick one of the boxes in between.*

Respondents were asked to pick a box from a card with nine possible options laid out horizontally. The first three boxes (A, B and C) were described as "young", the next three (D, E and F) as "middle" and the final three (G, H and J) as "old". (The exact layout of the showcard can be found in the appendix to this chapter.)

Table 8.2 shows the results, again broken down by actual age. The most popular category was "middle aged", chosen by just over six in ten people. A fifth (21 per cent) said they were "young", while 17 per cent choose to describe themselves as "old".

Three categories are particularly popular: C (the oldest "young" category) and D and E (the two younger "middle" categories); these account for around half of all respondents aged between 18 and 59. Nearly half of those aged below 30 (49 per cent) chose the highest "young" category (C), while just over half in their thirties (55 per cent) chose the youngest category (D) in the "middle" group. Most striking, perhaps, is that around half of those in their forties (49 per cent) and fifties (52 per cent) chose the same category (E) – the mid-point of the "middle" category on the scale. Perhaps this reflects a desire to be perceived as precisely in mid-life, aware that 'young' is no longer an option but not ready yet to accept being labelled 'old'. Among those aged 70 and above, it is notable that only a small minority (14 per cent) choose the highest "old" label (J).

There are a number of key differences between these results and those obtained by the *British Social Attitudes* survey.[2] The most obvious reflects the inclusion of a "thirty something" category in the latter study. But, even when these responses are added to those choosing to describe themselves as "middle aged", the ESS question still finds a higher proportion of people who describe themselves as middle aged (62 *versus* 45 per cent). However, once "thirty something" becomes a less viable category, the differences between the survey findings narrow somewhat. For instance, 27 per cent of *British Social Attitudes* respondents and 25 per cent of ESS respondents aged 70+ defined themselves as 'middle/middle aged'. Most importantly, however, both studies find very clear evidence that people of the same age do not necessarily identify with the same age group. That a quarter (24 per cent) of 18–29 year olds in Britain choose to identify themselves as "middle aged" in the ESS is as surprising as the 14 per cent of people in their fifties who identify as "thirty-something" in the *British Social Attitudes* data. Equally importantly, it is very clear that many people choose to identify with an age group that is 'younger' than that to which they might be assigned objectively.

Table 8.2 Self-assigned age group, by actual age group, 2008/9

| | \multicolumn{7}{c}{Actual age group} | | | | | | |
Self-assigned age group	18–29 %	30–39 %	40–49 %	50–59 %	60–69 %	70+ %	All %
All "young"	**75**	**25**	**9**	**4**	**3**	**3**	**21**
A	3	1	1	1	-	1	1
B	23	2	1	1	1	-	5
C	49	22	7	2	1	2	15
All "middle"	**24**	**74**	**90**	**85**	**59**	**25**	**62**
D	20	55	33	10	4	2	23
E	3	18	49	52	27	11	28
F	1	1	8	23	28	12	11
All "old"	**-**	**-**	**2**	**10**	**39**	**73**	**17**
G	-	-	2	8	32	28	10
H	-	-	-	2	6	31	5
J	-	-	-	-	1	14	2
Base	*330*	*382*	*437*	*340*	*323*	*370*	*2182*

Source: European Social Survey 2008/9

The strength of age identity

The evidence presented so far shows that most people acknowledge an age identity when asked. This is not a very demanding test of issue salience. In order for an identity to move from the 'passive' to the 'active' level, individuals need to have developed some consciousness, not just of fitting into a category, but of solidarity with others like them.

To assess this, the 2005 *British Social Attitudes* survey followed up the question about age group identity (as shown in Table 8.1) by asking respondents how much they felt they had in common with others in their chosen age group. So, for instance, someone who had described themselves as "young" was asked:

> *How much do you feel you have in common with young people in general, compared with other people?*
> *A lot more in common with them than with other people*
> *A little more in common with them than with other people*
> *No more in common with them than with other people*

As Table 8.3 shows, half of respondents (50 per cent) reported feeling that they had "a lot" or "a little" more in common with people in the same age group than they did with other people. In fact, of the six different identities we asked about, age identity emerged as being the most 'bonding', closely followed by gender (47 per cent) and ethnic group (46 per cent). By comparison, only a third (32 per cent) felt they had more in common with people who identified with the same political party than with others, while 37 per cent felt they had more in common with those from the same social class than with others. Overall, religious (and non-religious) affiliation had the lowest strength of identity, with just over a quarter (27 per cent) feeling that they had more in common with people from the same religious background than with other people, although the figure is notably higher among those who attend religious services regularly (Heath *et al.*, 2007).

Table 8.3 also shows some interesting differences between those who assign themselves to particular age categories and their other group identifications. Of all the age identities, those who describe themselves as young are the most likely (66 per cent) to feel they have more in common with other people with the same identity. Indeed, they are more likely to feel a bond on the basis of age than on the basis of any of the other identities shown in Table 8.3. Feelings of commonality on age grounds are lower among those with older age identities; the lowest being found among those in the "older" group, 53 per cent of whom feel they have more in common with others in this group than with different age groups. And, unlike the "young", those with older age identities are likely to feel similar 'bonds' with other groups; among the "middle aged" for instance, while 55 per cent feel they have more in common with middle aged people than with others, 53 per cent feel they have more in common with people from the same ethnic group than they do with those from a different ethnic background.

Table 8.3 Perception of whether has "a lot" or "a little" more in common with social groups, by self-assigned age group, 2005

	Self-assigned age group				
	Young	Thirty-something	Middle aged	Older	All
% more in common with group	%	%	%	%	%
Age group	66	57	55	53	50
Gender	52	54	47	39	47
Ethnic group	39	49	53	50	46
Social class	31	40	44	39	37
Party identifiers	31	30	33	40	32
Religion	31	28	27	30	27
Base	*484*	*412*	*566*	*309*	*2102*

Percentages add to more than 100 since respondents could mention up to 6 groups
Groups were asked about at separate questions

Table 8.4 examines the strength with which respondents identify with each of the age groups. The young (35 per cent) are the most likely to say they have a lot more in common with other self-assigning youngsters while the 'thirty somethings' are the least likely to say this (28 per cent). Those describing themselves as middle aged (45 per cent) and older (47 per cent) are the most likely to say they have no more in common with those in their age group.

Table 8.4 Perception of how much has in common with own age group, by self-assigned age group, 2005

	Self-assigned age group				
	Young	Thirty-something	Middle aged	Older	All
How much has in common with age group, compared with other people	%	%	%	%	%
A lot more	35	28	30	24	30
A little more	31	29	35	29	29
No more	34	43	45	47	41
Base	*486*	*422*	*566*	*309*	*1783*

Further analysis of responses to these questions shows that the distinctiveness of the young does not reflect their having an over-developed tendency to form attachments to identity groups compared with others – in short, being 'joiners'.

The 2008/9 ESS adopted a different approach to this issue, and asked whether people had a weak or strong sense of belonging to the age group they had chosen, using a scale from 0 ("very weak sense of belonging") to 10 ("very strong sense of belonging"). (The exact layout of the showcard can be found in the appendix to this chapter.) The results are shown in Table 8.5, which reports the mean scores for each of our self-assigned age identities, with a higher score indicating a stronger sense of belonging.

As with the earlier *British Social Attitudes* findings, this shows that those who describe themselves as "young" have the strongest sense of belonging (6.76, compared with 6.29 for all). This is particularly true of the youngest of our "young" groups (A), who show the strongest sense of attachment to their age group (8.33). However, unlike the *British Social Attitudes* findings, the oldest age group (J) also has a high attachment to their age group (7.96), suggesting that the more nuanced ESS question has picked up something masked by the less subtle *British Social Attitudes* question.

Table 8.5 Mean strength of belonging to an age group (11-point scale), by self-assigned age group, 2008/9

	Mean	Base
Self-assigned age group		
All "young"	6.76	401
A	8.33	23
B	7.13	91
C	6.51	290
All "middle"	6.08	1319
D	5.96	485
E	6.13	605
F	6.18	254
All "old"	6.48	435
G	5.91	249
H	6.99	147
J	7.96	57
All	6.29	2156

Source: European Social Survey 2008/9

Does age identity drive attitudes?

If age group identities are to be regarded as significant in social analysis, then we would expect an expressed affiliation with a particular group to be linked to and help explain a range of distinctive attitudes, in the way that class or party identification does. Previous work on the *British Social Attitudes* survey suggests that different age groups have distinctive socio-political outlooks (e.g. Heath and Park, 1997), so we turn now to examine whether membership of a 'self-assigned' age group might show the same effects. To do this, we focused on the relationship between the four age identities offered to respondents on the 2005 *British Social Attitudes* survey and the extent to which they display 'authoritarian' or 'libertarian' values on issues such as freedom of expression, censorship and the need for 'traditional' British values. These are measured by a set of questions which together make up a widely used libertarian–authoritarian scale (more details of which can be found in the appendix to this report). Table 8.6 shows that those who self-assign as young (3.52) have the lowest and most 'libertarian' score on this scale while the old have the highest and thus least 'libertarian' score (3.99).

Table 8.6: Mean score on the libertarian–authoritarian scale, by self-assigned age group, 2005

	Mean score	Base
Self-assigned age group		
Young	3.52	*387*
Thirty something	3.74	*355*
Middle aged	3.86	*476*
Older	3.99	*240*

We next used regression analysis to examine the relationship between libertarian–authoritarian attitudes and age identities while taking into account key socio-demographic characteristics (age, sex and education), identification with other identity groups (class and religion) and the strength of any identification. The full results can be found in Table A.1 in the appendix to this chapter; the key finding for our purposes is that those who consider themselves to be a "younger person" are significantly more libertarian in their views than those who do not identify with any of the age identity groups. This relationship exists even when 'real' age is taken into account, so is not merely a reflection of the well-known link between attitudes and age itself. So, someone in their 20s who defines themselves as a "younger person" will have significantly more libertarian attitudes than someone of the same age who does not choose to identify with any of the age identity groups. This association could run in either direction – those with libertarian views may associate their own values with those of 'youth' and therefore feel empathy with that group. Alternatively, this general empathy might lead them to adopt younger people's values. None of the other three age identities significantly differed from this 'no age identity' group. This suggests that it is only the young who are perceived as having a single coherent set of values – as a generation ages it perhaps loses its sense of unity and people's views and lives bifurcate. Overall, our analysis showed that the more familiar sociological characteristics of (actual) age, sex and education, along with traditional identities such as class and religion, are better predictors of attitudes on this measure than self-ascribed age group.

Discrimination and age identity

Our initial analysis indicates that, although the idea of being in an age group – and having a sense of common feeling with others within that group – is widely accepted in Britain, it does not seem to 'matter' very much in the sense of being related to people's attitudes and values. A tentative judgement on the basis of this limited evidence is that 'age identity' is only salient to the extent that such groupings are clear and obvious to respondents and therefore relatively easy to identify with. It is, perhaps, age itself and the experiences it brings along with it, rather than some underlying consciousness about being part of a generation, that drives attitudes. However, an important dimension of Bradley's 'active' social identity is a defensive response to the negative perception of others (Bradley 1996). There might therefore be a relationship correlation between the experience of discrimination and age group identification, an issue to which we now turn.

The 2008/9 ESS used several questions to tap potential discrimination. Respondents were asked how often in the past year someone had shown "prejudice against them or treated them unfairly because of their age", how often they were "shown a lack of respect" and 'how often they were treated badly, e.g. being insulted". Answers ranged from "never" to "very often".

Table 8.5 shows the proportions of people in different age groups who report any age discrimination in the last year. The key finding is that the youngest group, those aged 18–29, are the most likely to have encountered each of these three forms of age discrimination. Just over half (55 per cent) say they have experienced unfair treatment or prejudice because of their age in the last year, compared with around a quarter (24 per cent) of 30–39 year olds, and a fifth (20 per cent) or less of those aged 60–69. And just over two-thirds of those aged 18–29 (68 per cent) say that over the last year they felt a lack of respect as a result of their age, over twice the proportion found among those in their sixties (33 per cent).

Table 8.7 Age discrimination experienced in last year, by actual age group, 2008/9

	Actual age group						
	18–29	30–39	40–49	50–59	60–69	70 plus	All
In past year …	%	%	%	%	%	%	%
… treated with prejudice because of age	55	24	24	26	20	16	28
… felt lack of respect because of age	68	41	33	34	33	28	40
… treated badly because of age	38	19	18	19	17	14	21
Base	*331*	*384*	*440*	*343*	*327*	*374*	*2199*

Source: European Social Survey 2008/9

This relationship between perceptions of discrimination and age is also apparent when we consider self-assigned age group. Just under half (49 per cent) of those who describe themselves as "young" say they have been treated with prejudice because of their age in the last year, compared with just under a quarter of those who see themselves as "middle" (23 per cent) or "old" (24 per cent).

A key question is whether the relationship with self-assigned identity simply reflects the relationship identified above between real age and discrimination (Table 8.7) or whether it plays a more independent role. Table 8.8 examines these relationships for the item on "treatment with prejudice because of age". This variable was selected because it showed some of the largest differences by actual age. Note that some caution is required in interpreting the results due to small sample sizes.

Among the 18–29 and 30–39 year olds, those who self-assign as young are somewhat more likely to say they have been discriminated against because of their age than those who describe themselves as "middle". In other words feeling young is associated with a greater likelihood of perceived age prejudice than feeling middle aged. Among those aged 40–69, those associating with the middle category were less likely to report being subject to age discrimination than those who describe themselves as young and old. For example, those aged 50–59 who describe themselves as young are almost twice as likely to report age discrimination (54 per cent) as those who assign as middle (23 per cent). Among those aged 70+, those who self-assign as old are the least likely to say they have suffered from discrimination.

Table 8.8 Experience of being treated with prejudice in last year because of age, by self-assigned age group, 2008/9

	Actual age group								
	18–29			30–39			40–49		
	Young	Middle	Old	Young	Middle	Old	Young	Middle	Old
	%	%	%	%	%	%	%	%	%
Treated with prejudice because of age in past year	57	51	-	27	22	-	43	22	38
Base	246	84	-	98	284	-	34	395	8

	Actual age group								
	50–59			60–69			70 plus		
	Young	Middle	Old	Young	Middle	Old	Young	Middle	Old
	%	%	%	%	%	%	%	%	%
Treated with prejudice because of age in past year	54	23	44	32	13	32	38	19	15
Base	11	293	36	5	194	124	9	84	277

Source: European Social Survey 2008/9

Perhaps the 56 year old who feels young is discriminated against because they behave like a youngster rather than adopting the conventions of middle age. It would be interesting to examine such issues further in the future. However, it is not possible from this analysis to conclude that certain types of self-assigned age identity cause people to feel greater discrimination. For instance, the data may still hide patterns within each of the cohorts. For example, those in the young self-assigned age category may be more likely to be from the younger end of that cohort in terms of their actual age. Nevertheless this table suggests that age identity acts independently of actual age, affecting how some people perceive themselves and how they themselves are treated by others.

In summary it is obvious that young people – whether defined by actual age or self-assigned age identity – report suffering from age discrimination more often than middle-aged and older people. Both middle-aged and older people are, comparatively, rarely affected by these types of age discrimination; something that runs counter to the argument that it is primarily old people who suffer from a lack of respect in modern Britain.[3] This is an issue to which we will return later in this chapter.

Attitudes to the young and to the old

While the experience of discrimination might cause one's age group identification to strengthen, this is not the same as arguing that it produces an identity which is antagonistic and directly oppositional in nature, as predicted by Willets in *The Pinch* (2010). For this to occur it has to be clear to an identity group just who it is in conflict with and why. To put it another way, as with the case of class, gender and religion, it is as important to define the 'other' as well as the self.

We explore this using some of the many questions about ageism included on ESS 2008/9 (Abrams *et al.*, 2007). Our focus here is on a set of questions which were designed to tap into the overall positivity and negativity of respondents towards those in their 20s and those over 70, these being potentially very salient to our interest in inter-generational conflict.

We begin by looking at overall attitudes towards those in their 20s and the over 70s. The survey asked:

> *Using this card, tell me overall how negative or positive you feel towards people in their 20s? Please tell me on a score of 0 to 10, where 0 means extremely negative and 10 means extremely positive*

The same question was then asked about "people over 70". As the first row in Table 8.9 shows, respondents in Britain were mildly positive about both groups, with both achieving mean scores in the top half of the scale. However, those in their 70s obtained a higher score (7.4) than those in their 20s (6.18). This is not, perhaps, surprising, given the frequent attention paid by the media and others to various shortcomings among young people (although it does contradict an equally popular media view that there is a lack of respect for the elderly).

The remaining rows show the mean scores given by people in our three age identity groups. The three groups do not differ much in their views about those over 70, but those who describe themselves as "old" are notably less positive about those in their 20s than are the "young" age identity group.

Table 8.9 Mean score "how negative or positive feel about people in their 20s/over 70", by self-assigned age group, 2008/9

Self-assigned age group	Views about those ...			
	... in their 20s		... the over 70s	
		Base		*Base*
Young	6.62	*404*	7.31	*404*
Middle	6.09	*1344*	7.42	*1344*
Old	5.97	*453*	7.45	*453*
All	6.18	*2201*	7.40	*2201*

Twenty-five respondents (one per cent) volunteered that they had no sense of belonging to their age group. They have been excluded from Table 8.9
Source: European Social Survey 2008/9

Next we asked more detailed questions about the role these age groups play in relation to different aspects of British life. We began by asking:

Please tell me whether you think most people in their 20s/most people over 70 have a good or bad effect on Britain's customs and way of life? Choose your answer from this card where 0 means an extremely bad effect and 10 means an extremely good effect

Overall, Table 8.10 shows that people attribute far more credit to those over 70 (who get a mean score of 7.45) than they do to people in their 20s (who get a mean score of only 5.28). This gap between people's perceptions of these two groups is notably bigger than it was when we asked for people's overall views of people in these two age groups. As with people's overall views about these age groups, all our self-assigned age groups felt more positively about those over 70 than they did about those in their 20s. This is true even among those who define themselves as "young" but, as the last column shows, is most pronounced of all among the self-assigned "old".

Table 8.10 Mean score "people in 20s /over 70s have a good or bad effect on Britain's customs and way of life", by self-assigned age group, 2008/9

	View about those ...				
	... in their 20s		... the over 70s		Difference (over 70)-(20s)
Self-assigned age group		*Base*		*Base*	
Young	5.78	*404*	6.96	*404*	+1.18
Middle	5.06	*1344*	7.31	*1344*	+2.25
Old	5.33	*453*	8.46	*453*	+3.13
All	5.28	*2201*	7.45	*2201*	+2.17

Twenty-five respondents (one per cent) volunteered that they had no sense of belonging to their age group. They have been excluded from Table 8.10
Source: European Social Survey 2008/9

Finally, we asked about the impact of these two age groups on the British economy:

All things considered, do you think people in their 20s/people over 70 contribute very little or a great deal economically to Britain these days? Please use this card where 0 means they contribute very little economically to Britain and 10 means they contribute a great deal.

As Table 8.11 shows, the perceived differences between the two age groups of interest are relatively small and, for the first time, people in their 20s are seen slightly more positively than those over 70. However, as the last column shows, this more positive view is only really evident among those who describe themselves as "young". Considering the fact that most of those over 70 will generally be economically inactive, it is surprising that more people do not recognise the economic contribution made by those in their 20s, and this, perhaps, reflects the less positive views generally held about people in their 20s.

Table 8.11: Mean score "people in their 20s / over 70s contribute very little / a great deal economically to Britain" by self-assigned age group, 2008/9

	View about those ...				
	... in their 20s		... the over 70s		Difference (over 70)-(20s)
Self-assigned age group		Base		Base	
Young	5.69	404	4.42	404	-1.27
Middle	5.34	1344	4.98	1344	-0.36
Old	5.30	453	5.25	453	-0.05
All	5.41	2201	4.91	2201	-0.5

Twenty-five respondents (one per cent) volunteered that they had no sense of belonging to their age group. They have been excluded from Table 8.11
Source: European Social Survey 2008/9

The differences that we have found between the perceptions of different self-assigned age groups do not, it appears, simply reflect "real" age. A regression analysis was performed looking at how positive or negative people feel overall about those in their 20s and 70s (the full results can be found in Table A.2 and Table A3 in the appendix to this chapter). Even when real age is taken into account, self-assigned age group still had an independent effect on respondents' attitudes to both groups. What is equally interesting is that the strength of self-assigned identity was also a significant predictor with those who associate more strongly with their self-assigned age group also displaying more positive attitudes towards those in their 20s and 70s. In other words, a stronger age identity makes you more positive about those in other age groups. This suggests that at least at the present time age identity is, perhaps, an unlikely agent for inter-generational conflict.

Conclusions

At the start of this chapter we referred to three levels of identity outlined by Bradley – namely passive, active and politicised. Using *British Social Attitudes* and ESS data for Britain we can confirm that age forms the basis at least for passive identity, in the sense that respondents can recognise themselves as members of an age group. However, many identify only very weakly and a substantial minority (15 per cent of *British Social Attitudes* survey respondents in 2005) do not identify with any age group at all.

For most in Britain, however, age group has more active connotations. *British Social Attitudes* data from 2005 has shown that, along with gender and ethnicity, age is one of the most important bases on which respondents will express feelings of commonality with others in their selected identity group. In this sense self-assigned age identity does constitute a '... positive element in an individual's self-identification' (Bradley, 1996: 25). There is also some support for the view that one section of respondents – those who see themselves as 'younger' – feel more discriminated against on the grounds of their age than do older age-identifiers.

Despite the potential for identity formation in response to negative treatment, there is little evidence of this being translated into a strong and stable shared outlook on society, or of it forming the basis for conflict or collective action. Self-assigned age group as a whole appears to be a less reliable predictor of libertarian–authoritarian values than class, gender or education, though the exception is those who describe themselves as 'younger'. Negative sentiments towards the young by the old in Britain do not seem to be reciprocated by the young. Of particular note, perhaps, is the suggestion from the data that those who identify most strongly with a self-assigned age group description are more likely to feel positively about those in other age groups.

Age is probably no longer the 'neglected dimension of stratification'. Equally, as a source of identity it has quite different properties to other dimensions. Unlike gender, it is not fixed for life. Unlike religion, it cannot be chosen. And unlike class, it cannot be inherited or passed on. A person's age identity has a narrative progression to it unlike most others. At any time there is clearly an element of choice in age identification, but the numerical reality of ageing means that the menu from which to choose is limited by the stage in the life-course, and the dishes change and finally diminish in number over time. It is the experience of being different ages, and the experiences that accompany those life-stages, that override subjective perceptions of one's age group.

The use of two surveys with different approaches to the measurement of age identification demonstrates some of the difficulties in measuring such an unusual dimension of social stratification. One barrier to the development of age-conscious identities is the lack of widely accepted labels with which respondents can identify, especially the further away from the beginning and end of life one is. Further development work in this area would be useful. While current levels of age identification do not currently support the predictions of generational warfare set out by Willetts and others, the signs of discontent are there. The data in this chapter show a well-developed sense of discrimination among the young which might serve as a catalyst for resentment in the longer term. While attitudes to those in old age do seem benign, the conflicts of the future may be between today's young and their parents' generation. Current claims that, to quote Neil Boorman (2010), "it's all their fault", could lead to the formation of a defensive identity among the baby boomer generation. As home ownership becomes less accessible to the young, the ending of the retirement age poses challenges for youth employment, and the costs of higher education become punitive, it remains quite plausible that the fault lines of age could become increasingly well defined. The current financial austerity might even serve to deepen these fault lines especially if they are accompanied by a stronger discourse of age inequality and an accompanying set of policy demands from different groups. In these circumstances the 'myth of generational conflict' might still take on a new reality.

Notes

1. ESS Round 4: European Social Survey Round 4 Data (2008/9). Data file edition 3.0. Norwegian Social Science Data Services, Norway – Data Archive and distributor of ESS data. The European Social Survey (ESS) provides nationally representative probability samples of all residents aged 15 and over in more than 20 countries, and covers a wide range of social and political topics. Five rounds have been carried out to date, the data used in this chapter being from Round 4 which was conducted between September 2008 and January 2009. Unlike the *British Social Attitudes* survey, ESS collects data for the whole of the United Kingdom, including Northern Ireland, but we have excluded cases from Northern Ireland from the analyses included here. Further details about the ESS can be found at: www.europeansocialsurvey.org

2. In particular, ESS did not explicitly offer respondents the opportunity to decline to self-assign to an age group/category ("none of these"), reducing the number of people who did not give a response. It also had a less verbalised answer option, and did not use the phrase "middle class" (opting instead for "middle"). Perhaps the most notable difference, however, relates to the inclusion in the *British Social Attitudes* question of the term "thirty-something". Originally the title of a US drama about a group of urban professional baby boomers, it has now adopted a more neutral descriptive meaning stripped of some of its middle-class connotations (Bonner and du Gay, 1992). However, there are no equivalent words in the dictionary for those in their forties and fifties and so including this in the list of answer options will have affected the proportion of people giving "young" and "middle aged" categories. Indeed, 74 per cent of people in their thirties choose 'middle aged' when asked the ESS question, compared with just three per cent of those in the same age group when asked the *British Social Attitudes* version.

3. For example, see http://www.dailymail.co.uk/news/article-1262976/Grandparents-ignored-values-disappearing-warns-government-families-advisor.html

References

Abrams, D., Lima. L. and Coudin, G. (2007), *Experiences and Expressions of Ageism*, ESS Module Application, available at www.europeansocialsurvey.org

Arber, S., and Ginn, J., (1991), *Gender and later life*, London: Sage

Attias-Donfut, C. and Arber, S. (2000), 'Equity and solidarity across the generations', in Arber, S. and Attias-Donfut, C. (eds.) *The Myth of Generational Conflict*, London: Routledge/ESA, pp. 1–21

Boorman, N. (2010), *It's All Their Fault: A Manifesto*, London: The Friday Project Limited

Bonner, F. and Du Gay, P. (1992), 'Representing the Enterprising Self: Thirtysomething and Contemporary Consumer Culture', *Theory, Culture & Society,* **9**: 67–92

Bradley, H. (1996), *Fractured Identities: Changing Patterns of Inequality*, Cambridge: Polity Press

Gerth, H. and Mills, C. (1970), *From Max Weber: Essays in Sociology*, London: Routledge, pp. 180–94

Heath, A., Martin, J. and Elgenius, G. (2007), 'Who do we think we are? The decline of traditional social identities', in Park, A., Curtice, J., Thomson, K., Phillips, M. and Johnson, M. (eds.), *British Social Attitudes, the 23rd report*, London: Sage, pp. 1–34

Heath, A. F. and Park, A. (1997), 'Thatcher's children?' in Jowell, R., Curtice, J., Park, A., Brook, L., Thomson, K. and Bryson, C. (eds.), *British Social Attitudes: the 14th Report*, Aldershot: Ashgate, pp 1-22

Miles, S. (2000), *Youth Lifestyles in a Changing World*, Buckingham: Open University Press

Mannheim, K. (1952), 'The Problem of Generations', in Mannheim, K., *Essays on the Sociology of Knowledge*, London: Routledge

Weeks, J. (1990) 'The Value of Difference', in Rutherford, J. (ed.), *Identity*, London: Lawrence and Wishart, pp. 88–100

Willetts, D. (2010), *The Pinch: How the baby boomers took their children's future – and why they should give it back*, London: Atlantic Books

Acknowledgements

The European Social Survey is funded jointly by the European Commission (FP5–FP7), the European Science Foundation and academic funding bodies in participating countries (The ESRC in the UK). This chapter is also based on questions from an ESRC-funded project 'Are traditional identities in decline?' (Grant RES–154–25–0006), which was part of the ESRC's Identities Programme.

Appendix

Showcards

The showcards used for the questions reported in Tables 8.2 and 8.5 are shown
below.

ESS Age group showcard

-------YOUNG-------			-------MIDDLE-------			--------OLD---------		
☐	☐	☐	☐	☐	☐	☐	☐	☐
A	B	C	D	E	F	G	H	J

ESS Sense of belonging showcard

Very weak sense of belonging										Very strong sense of belonging
0	1	2	3	4	5	6	7	8	9	10

Multivariate analysis

The multivariate analysis technique used is linear regression, about which more details can be found in Appendix I of this report. Three regression analyses are presented below in Tables A.1, A.2 and A.3. The dependent variable for Table A.1 is the score on the libertarian–authoritarian index. The dependent variable for Table A.2 is the score given between 0 and 10 when asked to rate "how negative or positive you feel towards people over 70". The dependent variable for Table A.3 is the score given between 0 and 10 when asked to rate "how negative or positive you feel towards people in their 20s". For categorical variables, the reference category is shown in brackets after the category heading.

Table A.1 Regression results for libertarian–authoritarian index (*British Social Attitudes*, 2005)

	Coefficient	Standard error	p value
Age of respondent in years	**.005	.001	.000
Sex of respondent (male)	**-.078	.030	.009
Education (First or postgraduate degree)	**-.519	.052	.000
Higher education, A level	**-.136	.044	.002
O level, CSE	-.045	.043	.297
Self-assigned age group (Middle age)	.014	.028	.624
Older person	.042	.041	.307
Younger person	**-.117	.035	.001
Thirty something	.059	.031	.055
Feeling in common with people of same age group	.020	.030	.516
Belonging to middle class	*-.069	.033	.037
Feeling closer to one's class	**.089	.031	.004
Religion	**.136	.034	.000
Feeling in common with people of same religion	.014	.040	.720
Intercept	**3.589	.082	.000
R²	.186		
Base	*1604*		

* = significant at 95% level
** = significant at 99% level

Table A.2 OLS Regression Positive/Negative feeling towards those over 70 (ESS data for 2008/9: Great Britain, 18+)

	Coefficient	Standard error	p value
Sex of respondent (male)	**-.273	.071	.000
Age of respondent (20s)	**-.437	.165	.008
30s	*-.284	.141	.044
40s	-.024	.123	.845
60s	-.078	.132	.554
70s	-.158	.159	.323
80s	-.047	.201	.814
Self-assigned age group (Group A)	**1.202	.359	.001
Group B	-.017	.212	.936
Group C	-.050	.146	.730
Group D	-.056	.112	.616
Group F	-.242	.128	.058
Group G	.123	.144	.395
Group H	-.018	.183	.921
Group J	*-.601	.270	.026
Strength of belonging to age group	**.075	.014	.000
Constant	**7.241	.134	.000
R²	0.037		
Base	2199		

* = significant at 95% level
** = significant at 99% level

Table A.3 OLS Regression Positive/Negative feeling towards those in their 20s (ESS data for 2008/9: Great Britain, 18+)

	Coefficient	Standard error	p value
Sex of respondent (male)	*-.199	.087	.023
Age of respondent (20s)	-.127	.203	.533
30s	-.204	.174	.241
40s	.052	.152	.734
60s	-.050	.163	.758
70s	.068	.197	.729
80s	.041	.247	.869
Self-assigned age group (Group A)	-.104	.442	.814
Group B	*.631	.261	.016
Group C	**.556	.180	.002
Group D	.130	.138	.347
Group F	-.203	.158	.198
Group G	.109	.178	.538
Group H	-.266	.226	.240
Group J	**-.891	.335	.008
Strength of belonging to age group	**.067	.017	.000
Constant	**5.757	.165	.000
R²	0.027		
Base	*2199*		

* = significant at 95% level
** = significant at 99% level

9 Post-war British public opinion: is there a political centre?

*John Bartle, Sebastian Dellepiane Avellaneda
and James A. Stimson**

Politics is a mechanism for solving disagreement. Political attitudes and opinions are, therefore, what make democratic politics tick: they motivate people to join political parties, provide direction to government policy and, where they are intense or all pull in one direction, they cause people to switch from one party to another and alter election outcomes. The *British Social Attitudes* survey series represents one of the most valuable sources of evidence about changing political attitudes in Britain; from its foundation in 1983 right through to the present day, it has demonstrated a commendable – and quite atypical – commitment to repeated measurement of attitudes towards controversial issues using precisely the same question format and wording. *British Social Attitudes* has measured views about issues ranging from tax and spending, through to welfare, environmental policy and much else besides. Unusually among the major studies it has a particularly rich set of items touching on issues of personal freedom (censorship, the legalisation of drugs, sexuality, etc.) and moral issues (euthanasia, adultery, etc.). As a consequence it provides information about changing opinions across many of the issues that have arisen in the last 27 years. The cumulative evidence in these datasets provides a particularly informative indicator of the political 'mood'. British social science would certainly be much poorer without it.

Yet for all its commitment to repeated measurement and breadth even *British Social Attitudes* has its limitations. The most obvious (and the most trivial or important depending on your point of view) is that it can tell us nothing about British attitudes prior to its founding. It was, for example, not around to document the rise of Thatcherism and it alone cannot explain why the electorate held the attitudes they did in 1983 when the survey series began. Nor was it there to document opinions in the consensus years of the 1950s when political

* John Bartle is a senior lecturer in the Department of Government at the University of Essex; Sebastian Dellepiane Avellaneda is a research fellow at University College Dublin. James A. Stimson is Raymond Dawson Professor of Political Science at the University of North Carolina at Chapel Hill.

disagreements were reputed to be narrow. To be sure, one can speculate what story *British Social Attitudes* would have told if it had been established in the 1950s but we can never actually know. True, Gallup was carrying out opinion polls in the 1950s and asked a range of questions about issues that were relevant at the time: attitudes towards a proposed commercial television company funded by advertising (what became ITV), the need for controls on industry, the nationalisation of the steel industry, the testing of the H-bomb, and so on. But none of these questions were of much relevance by the 1980s, let alone 2010. The political debate had moved on.

The fact that *British Social Attitudes* was not around in the 1950s is unfortunate because there are good grounds for believing that attitudes evolve over very long periods of time (Stimson, 1991, 2004; Wlezien, 1995; Soroka and Wlezien, 2009). At first glance, however, there seems to be no way of linking the Gallup and *British Social Attitudes* data; they speak of a different time and use a different language. This is the challenge we address in this chapter. We will show how data about different issues from different survey series can be used to draw inferences about changes in political attitudes and their underlying dimensions in the long haul from 1950 to 2009. And, furthermore, we will show that it is possible to use all the available data from all the available sources to measure something of great importance: 'the political centre'. In order to make full use of all this evidence, however, we will need to depart from the standard individual level approach that analyses snapshots of attitudes at a particular time and instead focus on the dynamics of aggregate attitudes.

Methodology: a matter of perspective

Micro- and macro-level approaches

To date most studies of political behaviour have focused squarely on individuals: their party loyalties, attitudes and evaluations. This micro-level mode of analysis has tried to understand the relationship between social characteristics and attitudes and between attitudes and behaviour (Bartle, 1998). It has also sought to establish how people 'think' about politics and how these thoughts influence behaviour. More particularly it has tried to identify patterns and draw inferences about the dimensions underlying those attitudes (Goren, 2008a, 2008b; Jacoby, 2008).

The micro-level approach remains the dominant mode of analysis. It does, however, have its limitations. Most individual level data is collected in cross-sectional snapshot surveys, which interview individuals at a single point in time. Consequently, it is very difficult to explore how individuals acquire their views and identify the causal relationship between different characteristics. It is also now widely accepted that attitudes are measured with considerable error (Achen, 1975; Ansolabehere *et al.*, 2008). These problems have been addressed by the wider use of data from panel studies, which interview the same people at different points in time. These help reduce measurement error and allow analysts to gain a better understanding of the characteristics that underpin people's attitudes and behaviour. Efforts have also been made to develop scales that aggregate several items to reduce measurement error (Heath *et al.*, 1994). Yet it is still far from clear whether such evidence can be used to infer the causal order among characteristics. And it is a wholly different order of difficulty to examine how people 'think' about politics (Kuklinski, 2002). Attempts to operationalise spatial models of voting behaviour have, for example, been plagued with problems since reported party positions may reflect the voters' understanding of the parties' positions, projections of their own positions or rationalisations of their behaviour.

Other studies have set aside the detailed information contained in individual level surveys and instead aggregated across individuals. The resulting evidence is then arranged in a time-series (Erikson *et al.*, 2002; Soroka and Wlezien, 2009). Data are not used to infer how people 'think' about politics.[1] Instead, econometric techniques are used in order to unravel the dynamic relationships between variables. Previous studies have, for example, showed that the level of partisanship varies with both economic circumstances and presidential approval (MacKuen *et al.*, 1989). Other research has combined evidence about party positions from the Comparative Manifestos Project and the location of the average voter to test spatial models of voting behaviour.[2] These have demonstrated that proximity to the median voter is a powerful influence on presidential outcomes in the US (Erikson *et al.*, 2002).

The macro-level perspective allows analysts to assess the existence of any feedback within a system of equations. This is important because party competition takes place within a system where a response by one actor produces a response by another and so on. This process of mutual adjustment is important in the case of attitudes and opinions because they are likely to respond to policy (Wlezien, 1995). Attitudes at time t are caused by government activity at time t_{-1} and in turn cause vote shares at time t. This in turn causes government activity at time t_{+1} and so on (Erikson *et al.*, 2002; Soroka and Wlezien, 2009).

Summary of macro-level research to date

Our own research has squarely adopted a macro-analytic perspective and has focused on the measurement, causes and consequences of political attitudes and opinions. We have aggregated data across individuals and across issues. And furthermore, we have aggregated across survey organisations that use different sampling methods (quota and random sample) and survey modes (face to face, self-completion, telephone and internet). Both these steps are necessary to arrive at an estimate of political opinions and the mean value of this series, which we have labelled 'the political centre' (Bartle et al., forthcoming).

This research has proved moderately successful. We have demonstrated – at least to the satisfaction of some friends, some colleagues and some journal reviewers – that the estimated series seems to be a passably good indicator of what many people would take to be the political centre. The dynamic properties of the estimated centre correspond to standard understandings of post-war opinion. The centre also responds to government activity in theoretically prescribed ways and has a discernible relationship with election outcomes.

Although our research has stimulated some interest it has attracted criticisms that may undermine the validity of our measure. We address two of these here. The first relates to aggregation across issues. It has been suggested that our approach has (falsely) assumed a unidimensional structure of attitudes and opinions. No one, of course, ever likes to be thought of as 'one dimensional' and we show below this objection is based on a misunderstanding. We take this opportunity to provide new estimates of the centre based on an expanded database and we estimate a second dimension and examine its content. In principle the method can be extended to estimate a third, fourth and even fifth dimension. It turns out, however, that it is not necessary to go beyond the second dimension.

The second criticism relates to aggregation across data sources. This focuses on our apparent dependence on a few major studies such as Gallup in the earlier period and *British Social Attitudes* in the present day. It is assumed that any study that contributes a large number of items and, in particular, that produces long time-series will heavily influence our inferences, since our method of inferring the underlying dimensions makes use of evidence about changes in attitudes. In the earlier period we are indeed dependent on Gallup because there is no other data source until 1963 when the British Election Study and NOP were established.[3] Accordingly, we cannot assess the effect of our reliance on Gallup on our estimates until 1963. We can, however, examine our reliance on *British Social Attitudes* because we have many other sources in the later period.

The rest of this chapter is structured as follows. We first briefly review the theoretical literature on dimensionality in order to establish why it matters and why so many people have strong prior beliefs on the issue. We then examine dimensionality using our macro-level data. We finally examine whether our estimates of the political centre are, in any way, over-dependent on the *British Social Attitudes* survey series.

Dimensionality in theory

The number of issues that is generated in any political system is virtually limitless (Bartle et al., 2009). They range from relatively abstract issues such as the desirability of freedom and equality, through to enduring debates about public policy such as the need for regulation of the market economy or the availability of abortion, right through to contemporaneous debates about how to regulate the banks or whether to allow abortion in certain circumstances. Despite this complexity, however, there are two good reasons why individual attitudes and opinions might be 'constrained' or underpinned by non-observable dimensions (or ways of organising opinions and attitudes) (Converse, 1964). The first is that some beliefs at least logically imply others. This is most obvious where they are constrained by some accounting identity, such that income = expenditure. We might suppose, for example, that some people at least might balance their views about taxation with those about spending. It has, of course, long been realised that people do not devote much time to politics. They do not engage in the sort of internalised Socratic dialogue that is required to identify and remove inconsistencies. Thus, some (possibly many) individuals can prefer *both* higher spending and lower taxes.[4] This combination of views makes perfect sense to the individual. There is, moreover, often no necessary relationship between attitudes; in some alternate reality it is possible to imagine that anti-abortion attitudes might be bundled together with pro-government spending attitudes. Indeed, many opinions may 'go together' given greater elaboration (Scarbrough, 1984).

There is a second reason for believing that attitudes may be underpinned by some unobservable dimension. Human beings are social creatures: they interact with each other and acquire attitudes and opinions from others (Converse, 1964). The process of learning what goes with what is, therefore, a social process: a matter of discovering what is generally *thought* to go with what (Lupia and McCubbins, 1998). It is in this nexus between individual and group that clues about the dimensionality of attitudes is to be found.

Many analysts have strong prior beliefs about the dimensionality of public opinion. Some maintain that opinions are inherently multidimensional (McLean, 2004; Nagel, 2004; Robertson, 2004). Most standard representations of British public opinion, for example, take it for granted that political opinions are underpinned by at least two dimensions: a left–right issue relating to equality, collectivism and government activity and a liberal–authoritarian dimension relating to freedom of thought and conscience, freedom of association and freedom to pursue one's own course in life (Heath *et al.*, 1994). These dimensions are generally held to be orthogonal to (uncorrelated with) each other, and the occurrence of left-authoritarians and right-liberals thus appears to cast doubts on the existence of a single dimension to public opinion. Fortunately, *British Social Attitudes* has a very large number of items that might touch on the liberal–authoritarian dimension if it exists. Nevertheless, it is important to note that those who advocate 'multi'-dimensionality do not suggest that there are a very large number of dimensions. There is, furthermore, little agreement about the content of those dimensions. Some have, for example, speculated that Europe (Evans, 1998) and post-materialism (Inglehart, 1977; Dalton, 2008) might be emerging as distinct dimensions.

The prior belief in the multidimensionality of public opinion appears to be based on the assumption that politics is inherently complicated and that there are just too many conflicts between groups (labour *versus* capital, core *versus* periphery, urban *versus* rural, Catholic *versus* Protestant, and so on) to be able to simplify opinions as a position on a single dimension or by a single statistic.

There is another reason for believing that politics is multidimensional: politicians – particularly those who are currently out of power – have an incentive to introduce new issues that cannot be incorporated on existing dimensions. Political entrepreneurs may use political rhetoric and heresthetic manoeuvres to open up new dimensions that break coalitions and parties (Riker, 1982; Mackie, 2003).

This multidimensional view is apparently supported by factor analyses of cross-sectional data, which tends to suggest that several factors underpin public opinion. Nothing in this paper will challenge that proposition (Goren, 2008a, 2008b; Jacoby, 2008). There are, however, some equally good reasons for believing that attitudes can be represented as a single dimension over time. The main reason for this is that voters do not choose between issues, they choose between parties. We know that plurality electoral systems tend to produce two parties. The modern British party system was founded on a simple conflict between those on the left who wanted to extend government activity and those on the right who opposed it. The left position greatly appealed to the interests of the newly enfranchised working class and parts of the middle class so all parties had to take positions on this issue or risk annihilation. In principle many other group conflicts could produce differences that would cut across this dimension but the parties have historically adopted positions that reduced dimensionality (McLean, 2002). The party system formed around this disagreement before the emergence of many politicised social differences or cleavages. Thus, when new issues emerge that cut across the existing dimension we might expect that politicians and voters who find themselves out of alignment either resort themselves into the right parties or change their views (Carmines and Stimson, 1990). Political entrepreneurs might try to create new dimensions but these are largely folded into the existing left–right dimension. The content of this dimension will therefore vary over time in order to reflect this bundling up of issues by the parties. This gives the dimension its durability.

This review of the literature helps us to understand why many people have such strong prior beliefs about dimensionality, but it does nothing to resolve the issue. There is little by way of 'strong theory' that makes a compelling prediction about how many dimensions there are, though there are many hunches and speculations. The dimensionality of attitudes is an *empirical* matter at both the individual and aggregate level. And we would be unsurprised, moreover, if the number of dimensions that are required to describe the data differ at these levels.

Dimensionality in practice: the macro-level perspective

We begin by outlining the data that we have available and then move on to show how we infer average attitudes ('the political centre') and assess the number of dimensions underlying those attitudes.

Data

The method we use depends on the availability of data on people's attitudes. Our database is made up of the overall responses to survey questions relating to very many issues. These simply record the percentage taking 'sides'; selecting a 'left' or 'right' option, 'supporting' or 'opposing' specific proposals and 'agreeing' or 'disagreeing' with statements. We exclude those questions that refer to a named party or politician because such cues make it difficult to untangle a person's opinion on an issue from their attitude to these partisan objects.

Some items are asked repeatedly. One item on whether trade unions are a good thing, for example, was administered by Gallup in 40 separate years (and sometimes more than once a year) between 1952 and 1997. Another question, about whether the government should bring industry and unions together to agree wages and prices, was administered by Gallup just twice in 1957 and 1962. This adds little to what is known about changes in opinions. However, all evidence is valuable and we include both these types of item in our database.

Table 9.1 summarises the sources and extent of data that we have been able to gather to date. The database is not complete because we have yet to track down and input all the data. The task of recording all the attitudes in our database is rather like painting the Forth Rail Bridge. Nevertheless, it already contains more evidence about people's attitudes than has ever been gathered before: 4,241 readings for 700 individual questions. Although we have data from 1938 onwards, our analyses begin in 1950 because data are thin in the 1930s and 1940s. Many of the sources are particular survey series (more details of which can be found in the appendix to this chapter); others are the regular opinion polls run by many of Britain's market research companies.

Our measure is based on observing changes in the distribution of attitudes over time. Thus, the attitudes database includes only *identical* questions asked in at least two separate years. Since even minor variations in question wording, question order, filter style and response categories can produce different responses, we treat such differences as creating non-comparable items (Schumann and Presser, 1996). As we have noted, *British Social Attitudes* has a quite atypical commitment to measuring change and this makes that source particularly valuable for our purposes; it accounts for 34 per cent of the readings included in the database. In some cases we do tolerate very minor variations in question wording, especially for the 1950s from which data are in short supply. We also generally treat different modes (face to face, telephone, self-completion questionnaires, etc.) as producing non-comparable items.

Responses to the questions were coded as 'left' or 'right'. This was a fairly simple task, the most important exception being the issue of Britain's membership of the European Union, which was initially supported by the right in the 1970s and opposed by many on the left. By the late 1980s and 1990s, however, positions had changed with the right opposing further integration and the left tending to support it. Given detailed knowledge of the European issue, it is tempting to impose the assumption that the 'polarities' reversed at some specific date. But pinpointing the exact date would be hazardous. Rather than do this we (tentatively) code pro-European responses as left and anti-European responses as right. It should, however, be noted that even if we made a mistake in coding, the algorithm that we use would still be able to use the information as long as we are consistent. In addition to 'left' and 'right' responses, we also included a 'neutral' code. The latter were discarded from the analysis and an index of attitudes calculated.[5]

Table 9.1 Sources of data, 1938–2009

	Questions	Readings		Year range	Time span (years)
	N	N	%		
British Election Panel Study	6	42	1.0	1992–1997	5
British Election Study	86	302	7.2	1963–2006	43
British Election Survey Continuous Monitoring Surveys	2	42	1.0	2008–2009	2
British Household Panel Study	37	211	5.0	1991–2009	18
British Social Attitudes	278	1693	40.1	1983–2009	26
European Social Survey	9	34	0.8	2003–2008	6
Eurobarometer	3	90	2.1	1973–2009	36
Gallup polling	194	1258	29.8	1938–2001	49
ICM polling	15	159	3.8	1990–2007	17
MFS polling	1	18	0.4	1999–2002	3
MORI polling	40	279	6.6	1972–2009	37
NOP polling	12	49	1.2	1964–1984	20
Populus polling	2	6	0.1	2003–2008	5
World Values Survey	6	9	0.2	1981–2003	22
YouGov polling	9	29	0.7	2002–2008	6
Total	700	4221	100.0		

Further details of these studies can be found in the appendix to this chapter

Method

We use the dyad ratio algorithm to extract our estimates of political attitudes and opinions. This method is inspired by the following quotation:

> People in and around government sense a national mood … The idea goes by different names. … But common to all is the notion that … this national mood changes from one time to another in discernible ways … (Kingdon, 1984: 153)

If policy makers can sense this mood, it seems plausible to suggest that this is also picked up in citizens' responses to survey questions on a diverse range of issues. This proposition is supported by theories of survey response, which suggest that responses to any question are a function of underlying attitudes, non-random error (the result of question wording and the response categories offered respondents) and truly random error (Zaller and Feldman, 1992). The algorithm used here reduces error by focusing on changes in responses to identical questions and then aggregating across all issues. Shifting the focus from absolute values to change over time reduces non-random error because question wording and response categories are identical; any changes must be the result of real changing attitudes. Aggregating across both individual respondents and individual survey items, moreover, greatly reduces random error.

The dyad ratio algorithm applies these principles by expressing items as ratios of values at other time points. This produces a common metric across items. Since the expected value of this ratio is 1.0 they can be averaged across items to produce a measure of the aggregate attitudes. The algorithm starts with all the items at the latest time point t and then moves on to repeat this step using t-1 as a base for comparison. It proceeds iteratively, exploiting all the available information about a particular time point and averaging scores to produce an estimate of underlying attitudes. The items are then weighted in proportion to their validity (relationship with the estimated series) and the estimates are smoothed to mitigate the influence of sampling error (see Stimson, 1991 and Bartle *et al.*, forthcoming for further details.)

The principles underlying the algorithm are simple but the amount of number crunching, given the large number of items that are to hand, is quite mind-boggling. The technology is justified, however, by the fact that it produces an annual estimate of the political centre; something that is otherwise not measurable. Somewhat less importantly, it also produces a way of comparing responses to questions about the H-bomb in 1954 with a question about tax and spending in 2010 and a way of comparing responses to questions about the creation of ITV in 1955 with a question about welfare in 1987, since we can assess their relationships with the political centre.

The first dimension

If standard accounts of party competition are correct, we might expect to find two dimensions (Webb, 2000). And, if some accounts are also to be believed, we should expect to find a left–right dimension that should cycle back and forth depending on policy and a liberal–authoritarian dimension that tracks in a steadily liberal direction reflecting gradual social changes such as the dying out of cohorts socialised in a more 'conservative' age and the impact of increasing education levels (Ross and Sacker, 2010). This is not, however, what we find.

Figure 9.1 displays the first two dimensions extracted by the algorithm. The higher the score, the more 'left' the series is. Both series appear to move up and down over time and have similar patterns though their precise inflection points differ.[6] There is little indication in either series of a general upward trend of the sort that one might expect if one of the series were picking out a latent liberal–authoritarian dimension that was becoming more liberal across time.

Figure 9.1 The first two dimensions of attitudes, 1950–2009

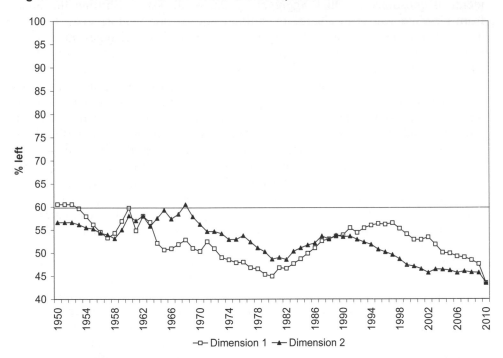

The key to interpreting the content of a latent dimension is examining the survey items which are most highly associated with it. We capture that in 'loadings' (Pearson product moment correlations); these show the correlation between survey items treated as time-series and the estimated latent dimension. The survey items that are most closely and regularly associated with a latent dimension tell us what the dimension is and what it means. To display the loadings we make some dramatic selections, as we have many separate series that contribute to the estimates and many items have too few available cases for the correlations to be meaningful. Accordingly, we employ two selection criteria:

- Whether the series is available for 10 or more years.

- Whether the correlation is larger than 0.60 on at least one of the dimensions.

Table 9.2 Loadings for the first and second dimensions

Abbreviated question wording	Survey/ Poll	N	1st Dim	2nd Dim
Trade unions have too much power in Britain today	MORI	17	0.97	0.02
Trade unions becoming too powerful	Gallup	22	0.97	0.00
Reduce or increase taxes and spending	Gallup	20	0.92	0.04
Gap between incomes too big	BSA	22	0.90	0.00
Nuclear power plants safe	Gallup	10	0.90	0.05
Trade unions extreme	MORI	14	0.90	0.00
Reduce or increase taxes and spending	BSA	24	0.85	0.07
Trade unions are a good thing	Gallup	40	0.85	0.10
People stand on own feet without welfare	BSA	18	0.82	0.30
Support union closed shop	Gallup	11	0.81	0.23
Many people don't deserve social security	BSA	18	0.81	0.29
Abolish monarchy	MORI	12	0.81	0.29
Trade unions are essential to protect workers	MORI	15	0.78	-0.18
People could get a job if they wanted	BSA	18	0.76	0.37
One law for the rich and one for the poor	BSA	22	0.76	-0.01
Management try to get the better of workers	BSA	21	0.74	-0.11
Building roads creates more traffic	BSA	13	0.74	0.16
Membership of EU a good thing	Eurob	33	0.74	0.25
Post-materialist values	Eurob	22	0.72	0.05
EU is a good thing	Gallup	24	0.71	0.24
Business has too much power	BES+	10	0.71	-0.39
Equal opportunities for women gone too far	BES+	10	0.70	0.12
Government should redistribute	BES+	22	0.68	0.35
Trade unions have too much power	BES+	18	0.64	-0.45
Vote in European referendum	MORI	17	0.64	-0.45
Abortion if couple cannot afford child	BSA	13	0.64	0.00
Spend more on benefits for poor	BSA	17	0.63	0.52
Long-term policy towards Europe	BSA	15	0.62	0.37
Whether there is a class struggle	Gallup	14	0.62	-0.37
NHS only available to low incomes	Gallup	17	0.61	0.05
Ordinary people do not get fair share of wealth	BSA	19	0.60	-0.08
Government spending on pensions	Gallup	20	0.60	-0.30
Level of benefits too high	BSA	24	0.48	0.67
Welfare makes people less likely to look after self	BSA	14	0.31	0.65
People receiving welfare made to feel second class	BSA	14	0.47	0.76
Many people who claim welfare make false claims	BSA	17	-0.17	0.87
Abortion if risk of defect	BSA	10	-0.30	0.74

Full survey names can be found in the appendix to this chapter.

+ Indicates also from *British Social Attitudes*.

Table 9.2 contains the items that contribute the most valid variance to the estimates. Column four displays the factor loadings for the first dimension. The highest loadings are for those items relating to trade unions, tax and spending, income inequality and welfare. What these items have in common is disagreement about the scope of government activity; the core of the broad left-right battle that underpins British party competition. The prominence of trade unions, accounted for by seven of the highest loading items, should not come as a surprise; they are one of three main disagreements between left and right in post-war Britain (Crewe *et al.*, 1977).

However, other questions also load heavily on this dimension, including two items on abortion, as well as items on the monarchy, Britain's membership of the European Union, nuclear power and the existence of a class struggle. Post-materialism, an emphasis on autonomy and self-expression over economic and physical security, is also highly correlated with this first dimension. This suggests that neither Europe nor post-materialism are distinct dimensions within British public opinion. Although in theory both *could* be distinct dimensions, in practice they are not; both appear to have been folded into the left–right dimension, just as theories of issue evolution suggest.

The second dimension

The two extracted series displayed in Figure 9.1 track each other closely and correlate quite highly (Pearson's R = 0.47). The second series is, however, generally less smooth than the first. It peaks somewhat later than the first series in the 1960s and begins declining before the first series in the early 1990s. One clue as to the significance of the second dimension is provided by the summary statistics for the two series. These show that the first dimension explains the variance of nearly half (46 per cent) of the items we examined, while the second is far less powerful and accounts for just six per cent. The remaining 48 per cent of variance is either unexplained or the result of item specific-movement.

The loadings for the second dimension in column five of Table 9.2 are far less easy to interpret than the first. Only five of the items that were asked more than 10 times load on the second series at more than 0.6. Four of these broadly refer to welfare while one relates to abortion. It is tempting to suggest that the second series represents a distinct welfare dimension. Such a finding would, after all, hardly be surprising given ambivalent attitudes towards the welfare state. Popular political commentary is full of concern that those who 'play by the rules' and work hard are denied access to welfare while incorrigible 'scroungers' obtain a great deal. A glance at the first column, however, shows that several similar items load highly on the first dimension. Widening the range of questions to include those with loadings between 0.6 and 0.5 on the second dimension (still asked in at least 10 separate years) gives few further clues about content. This adds a further abortion item and a statement that young people do not have enough respect for traditional values. Neither is much help in labelling the dimension. And looking at those items with more than 10 readings but loadings below 0.5 sheds no light. All in all, we are inclined to conclude that the second extracted series is not a 'proper' dimension at all; it is made up of stand-alone issues and those that have not yet been fully folded into the left–right dimension.

The dimensionality of post-war opinion

What does this add to our understanding of the dimensions that underpin political attitudes and opinions within modern Britain? Two key points emerge. First, we would maintain that the evidence provided by our macro perspective suggests that post-war British political opinion is pretty much one dimensional. The second dimension – such as it is – seems to be a residual made up of those items that are independent of the left–right dimension and those that are in the process of being incorporated. Even if we label the second dimension a 'dimension' proper it is clear that it accounts for relatively little variance and it is not orthogonal to the first dimension. But our evidence should not be taken as reading that every single issue loads on the first dimension. Some issues are quite distinct in the sense that their trends point in a different direction; some can be identified from *British Social Attitudes* data (Curtice, 2010). It does, however, provide some support for our decision to label the mean of the first dimension 'the political centre'. And it casts doubt on the widespread practice of representing British party competition in terms of both a left-right and a cross-cutting liberal–authoritarian dimension.

Second, even if our conclusions were not correct we would plead alternatively that party competition could be usefully treated 'as if' it were one dimensional. This argument is supported by analyses of party programmes, which suggest that party positions can be adequately summarised by a position on a single left–right scale (Budge *et al.*, 2001). Treating opinion in this way enables us to locate both parties and voters on the same scale and test the spatial model of voting behaviour without relying on dubious reports of perceptions of party position (Erikson *et al.*, 2002). To be sure, every assumption is a distortion or a 'lie' but the assumption of unidimensionality seems to be *both* a good approximation and very useful (Fiorina, 1975: 138; Budge, 2006).

What the first dimension tells us about post-war opinion?

In our previous research we have interpreted the first dimension as concerning attitudes towards government activity and have (tentatively) suggested that this corresponds to what most people think of as 'left–right' (Bartle *et al.*, forthcoming). Accordingly, we interpret the drift downwards between 1950 and 1979 as a shift to the right of the sort that has been documented in previous studies (Crewe *et al.*, 1977: Heath *et al.*, 1985, Heath *et al.*, 1997).[7] Equally, we interpret the drift upwards between 1979 and 1997 as indicating a move back to the left. This finding is again hardly original (Crewe and Searing, 1988; Heath *et al.*, 1997). We interpret the reverse after 1997 as a further shift back to the right (and pretty sharp it is, too). This development has received little attention (though see Curtice, 2010). This is surprising; according to our estimates, the electorate were nearly as 'right-wing' in 2009 as 1979, the year that Mrs Thatcher came to office. And it should be noted that if we were to extend our estimates to 2010, when some evidence is available from MORI and YouGov – but not *British Social Attitudes* – we find that attitudes were even further to the right in 2010 than 1979. This is a striking observation.[8] It suggests that the public are now less supportive of 'big government' than at any time since the late 1970s. If correct this may well go some way to explaining why Labour lost over six points at the 2010 election.

The overall pattern suggested by the first dimension has a degree of face validity and conforms to some fairly standard accounts of post-war (Marr, 2007). It also broadly fits what one might expect if the electorate were responding 'thermostatically' to government activity and moving in the opposite direction to policy (Wlezien, 1995; Soroka and Wlezien, 2009; Bartle et al., forthcoming). One naïve operationalisation of policy suggests that governments always pursue ideological goals: that Labour governments expand government activity while Conservative governments reduce government activity. The problem with this operationalisation of policy is that the Conservative government of the 1950s and 1960s generally accepted the post-war settlement and went along with the 'consensus' about 'bigger' if not 'big' government. Thus the years 1950–1979 were a period of generally expanding government activity and many ordinary people found that they were drawn into the income tax system. It hardly seems surprising that the electorate responded by moving to the right. The period 1979–1997 saw attempts by the Thatcher/Major government to reverse the 'ratchet effect' of socialism as well as large increases in unemployment. Again it hardly seems surprising in these circumstances that the electorate drifted leftwards. The state subsequently grew rapidly under New Labour, particularly after 2000, and this appears similarly to be accompanied by a drift back to the right. Detailed econometric analyses suggest that the electorate moves to the left when unemployment increases (when people want government to act) and move to the right as public expenditure and taxes increase (Bartle et al., forthcoming). Political attitudes thus, broadly speaking, conform to the thermostatic prediction (Wlezien, 1995).

Dependence on British Social Attitudes

Earlier we outlined one criticism of our work; that we are too dependent on the *British Social Attitudes* series, and that this calls into question the robustness of our findings. *British Social Attitudes* data are, without a doubt, very important to our database, as illustrated by Table 9.1. The series currently contributes 278 separate questions asked a total of 1,693 separate times (a figure that will no doubt rise in future). This means that *British Social Attitudes* contributes 40 per cent of all questions and readings to the database. In recent years, moreover, the dominance of this source has become striking, partly reflecting a tendency by commercial pollsters to focus primarily on assessments of parties and leaders rather than political opinions and attitudes more generally. Despite 2005 being an election year (meaning that British Election Survey data are also available), *British Social Attitudes* contributed 45 per cent of our readings. In 2007, it contributed fully 66 per cent of data.

So clearly our approach can be vulnerable to the claim that we are over-dependent upon the results of the *British Social Attitudes* survey.[9] The study in question happens to be a paragon of quality in survey research, so such dependence may not be such a bad thing. But the claims we make for the movements in British public opinion would be stronger still if we can claim that we are picking up parallel tracks produced by the reported data of multiple survey organisations. So we turn now to examine the degree of dependence of our findings on the *British Social Attitudes* series, and ask whether or not we would produce roughly the same estimate of attitudes if data from this source did not contribute so much. We address two questions. Firstly, how different are attitudes estimated only from *British Social Attitudes* data than ones which also reflect large numbers of (mainly commercial) survey organisations? And, secondly, how different would our estimates be without the *British Social Attitudes* data?

In Figure 9.2 we show four differing estimates of the concept of 'the political centre' that make use of (1) all data for the period 1950–2009, (2) all data, 1983–2009, (3) BSA only data, 1983–2009 and (4) no BSA data, 1983–2009. The question is: are these measures tapping one concept or four?

We focus on the period between 1983 and 2009 and begin by asking whether the global view of attitudes that one would gather from restricting analyses to *British Social Attitudes* data does or does not reflect the wider mix of surveyed British public opinion. The evidence of Figure 9.2 is that the centre identified by using only *British Social Attitudes* data is very similar to that estimated from all our sources of data. (Compare the 'BSA only' to the 'all surveys 1983–2009' line.) It is clear that there are not massive differences between an academic survey such as *British Social Attitudes* and the world of commercial polling organisations; the picture one gets of British public opinion is the same in both. (Compare the 'BSA only' line with the 'No BSA' line.) It is one public seen through two lenses, not two publics. Nothing would have changed in our interpretations if we had restricted ourselves to using only *British Social Attitudes* data for the period where they are available.

Lastly, we can ask what effect is to be seen by excluding *British Social Attitudes* from our global estimates. Here the effect is slightly greater. (Compare the 'No BSA' line with the 'All surveys' line.) An estimate of the centre that excludes *British Social Attitudes* data from the analysis is slightly more to the left (which doesn't matter very much) and shows one notable difference, a movement to the left between 2008 and 2009, when all other evidence points to a movement to the right that year.

Figure 9.2 The moving centre of British political attitudes, four estimates, 1983–2009

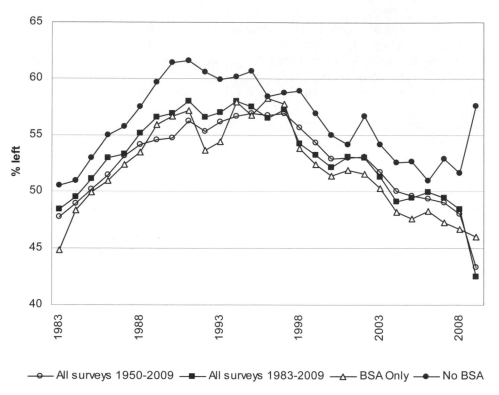

—○— All surveys 1950-2009　—■— All surveys 1983-2009　—△— BSA Only　—●— No BSA

The basic interpretation of the patterns in Figure 9.2 is that inclusion or exclusion of *British Social Attitudes* data does not fundamentally affect our estimates of the centre. We are dependent on *British Social Attitudes* data, that is, but not over-dependent.

Of course, our interest is in estimating the political centre for almost the full span of the post-war era. If we repeat Figure 9.2 for the full 1950–2009 span of our analysis we find that the series estimated without use of *British Social Attitudes* data is essentially identical to the one estimated with them.[10] Because we prefer an estimate based on more data to one based on less, we prefer to include *British Social Attitudes* data. Clearly we do not have to do so.

This confirms that the trends over time we have identified depend little on which survey organisation has produced the data and over what period of time. Further analysis also confirms that the survey source used has few implications for the underlying dimensions we have identified; whether we include or exclude *British Social Attitudes* data, the overall pattern remains very similar.

Conclusions

Our goal is to estimate the political centre of Britain as it moves over time. That presumes that such a thing really exists, that it is more than a hypothesis, more than an analytic convenience. In this chapter we have some evidence to bring to bear on the question. We have shown that British political attitudes look pretty much unidimensional and that the decision of whether or not to employ the important data from *British Social Attitudes* is a decision with small consequences for our estimates. That may seem a limited demonstration. But think about what a survey series entails. It is a different mix of topics, a different mix of topic areas, a different set of questions, a different set of question wordings, and a different sampling method. And, varying all these things, we still estimate the same centre and we still see the same year to year movements.

Commercial survey organisations tend to set their agenda by the news. They pose questions about topics that are relatively hot, things thought to influence the coming election.[11] *British Social Attitudes*, in contrast, is committed to continuity of questions, which necessarily means posing questions that are not page one material at the time. Even still, the centre that we estimate from commercial polls is very much the same one that we find with *British Social Attitudes* questions. This, we think, is remarkable. And it is testimony that the survey enterprise taps into something real.

We haven't proven that the centre is real. But we have demonstrated that reasonable variations on estimation strategies tend to recover the same centre and the same year to year movements in it. If that is not a basis for confidence, it is at least grounds for hope.

Notes

1. If pressed on the point some macro-level analysts will suggest that since they are not psychologists they cannot be expected to know how people think about politics. If pressed still further they might also hazard that psychologists don't know how people think either.
2. The Manifestos Project has analysed the general election manifestos of parliamentary parties across over 50 countries across the world, in many cases covering the entire post-war period (Budge *et al.*, 2001).
3. This may change. We hope to track down data in various places, including Mark Abrams private papers at Churchill College Cambridge. Abrams was the founder of RSL, a market research company, and did private polling for the Labour Party.
4. We set aside the complicating issue of borrowing for the moment.

5.
$$\text{Index of Preferences} = \frac{\sum_{i=1}^{N}(\text{Left Preferences})}{\sum_{i=1}^{N}(\text{Left and Right Preferences})}$$

6. The two series correlate quite highly with a Pearson's r of 0.47.
7. The series 1951–1964 gives the impression that there are a series of U-shaped movements in this period. This is the result of the low number of cases and the consequent higher standard errors. If we were to put a confidence interval around the estimates it would greatly strengthen our interpretation of the period 1950–79 as one of rightward drift. See Bartle *et al.*, (forthcoming), figure 1.
8. However, we do not place too much emphasis on this finding. It is based on just a few bits of evidence and does not incorporate other data gathered nearer to the election and not yet input into our database.
9. The Dyad Ratios algorithm, which is the heart of our estimation strategy, weights its various component series by how numerous they are and by the number of studies (years in this case) for which the exact same question is posed. *British Social Attitudes* contributes more series to our estimates than any other source and those series extend for long periods of time (indeed, only one question asked by Gallup spans a longer period). Since the relationship multiplies two factors (numbers, time length) and the *British Social Attitudes* data are (thankfully) high on both, that does suggest the possibility of a super-dependence of our estimates on the results of one survey organisation.
10. If we compare estimates for the full span estimated with *British Social Attitudes* (and other) data to those estimated without using *British Social Attitudes* data we find they are correlated at 0.98. This exercise also shows that the anomalous rise in left sentiment (from Figure 2) in 2009 does not occur when the estimate is based on the full dataset, either with or without *British Social Attitudes*.
11. But we shouldn't overstate the case. The commercial organisations most recently have a decent record of asking the same questions year after year.

References

Achen, C.H. (1975), 'Mass political attitudes and survey response', *American Political Science Review*, **69**: 1218–1231

Ansolabehere, S., Rodden, J. and Snyder J.M. (2008), 'The strength of issues: Using multiple measures to gauge preference stability, ideological constraint and issue voting', *American Political Science Review*, **102**: 215–232

Bartle, J. (1998), 'Left–right matters, but does social class? Causal models for the 1992 general election', *British Journal of Political Science*, **28**: 501–529

Bartle, J., Dellepiane, S. and Stimson, J. A. (2009), *The dimensionality of British political opinion, 1950–2009*, Paper presented at 5th general conference European Consortium for Political Research, Potsdam, Germany, September

Bartle, J., Dellepiane, S. and Stimson, J.A. (forthcoming), 'The moving centre: Policy in Britain, 1950–2005', *British Journal of Political Science* (forthcoming)

Budge, I. (2006), 'Identifying dimensions and locating parties', in Katz, R.S. and Croty, W. (eds.), *Handbook of Party Politics*, Beverley Hills: Sage

Budge, I., Klingemann, H.D., Volkens, A., Bara, J. and Tanenbaum, E. (2001), *Mapping political: Estimates for parties, electors and governments, 1945–1998*, Oxford: Oxford University Press

Carmines, E.G. and Stimson, J.A. (1990), *Issue evolution: Race and the transformation of American politics*, Princeton, NJ: Princeton University Press

Converse, P.E. (1964), *Ideology and discontent*, London: Free Press of Glencoe

Crewe, I., Sarlvik, B. and Alt, J. (1977), 'Partisan dealignment in Britain 1964–197', *British Journal of Political Science*, **7**: 129–190

Crewe, I. and Searing, D. (1988), 'Ideological change in the British Conservative party', *American Journal of Political Science*, **82**: 361–384.

Curtice, J. (2010), 'Thermostats or weathervane? Public reaction to spending and redistribution under New Labour', in Park, A., Curtice, J., Thompson, K., Philips, M., Clery, E. and Butt, S. (eds.), *British Social Attitudes: the 26th Report*, London: Sage

Dalton, R.J. (2008), *Citizen politics: Public opinion and political parties in advanced industrial democracies*, 5th edition, Washington: CQ Press

Erikson R.S., MacKuen, M.B. and Stimson, J.A. (2002), *The macro polity*, Cambridge: Cambridge University Press

Evans, G. (1998), 'Euroscepticism and Conservative electoral support: How an asset became a liability', *British Journal of Political Science*, **28**: 573–590

Fiorina, M.P. (1975), 'Formal models in political science', *American Journal of Political Science*, **19**: 133–159

Goren, P. (2008a), 'The two faces of government spending', *Political Research Quarterly*, **6**: 147–157

Goren, P. (2008b), 'Dimensionality redux: A reply to professor Jacoby', *Political Research Quarterly*, **61**: 162–164

Heath, A., Evans, G. and Martin, J. (1994) 'The measurement of core beliefs and values: The development of balanced socialist/laissez faire and libertarian/authoritarian scales', *British Journal of Political Science*, **24**: 115 –132

Heath, A., Jowell, R. and Curtice, J. (1985), How Britain Votes, Oxford: Pergamon

Heath, A., Jowell, R. and Curtice, J. (1997), *The rise of New Labour: Party policies and voter choices*, Oxford: Oxford University Press

Inglehart, R. (1977), *The silent revolution: Changing values and political styles among western publics*, Princeton: Princeton University Press

Jacoby, W.G. (2008), 'Comment: The dimensionality of public attitudes to government spending', *Political Research Quarterly*, **61**: 158–161

Kingdon, J.W. (1984), *Agendas, alternatives and public policy*, Boston: Little, Brown

Kuklinski, J.H (ed.) (2002), *Thinking about political psychology*, Cambridge: Cambridge University Press

Lupia, A. and McCubbins, M.D. (1998), *The democratic dilemma: Can citizens learn what they need to know?*, Cambridge: Cambridge University Press

Mackie, G. (2003), *Democracy defended*, Cambridge: Cambridge University Press

..

MacKuen, M.B., Erikson, R.S. and Stimson, J.A. (1989), 'Macropartisanship', *American Political Science Review*, **83**: 1125–1142

Marr, A. (2007), *The making of modern Britain*, Basingstoke: Macmillan

McLean, I. (2002), *Rational choice and British politics: An analysis of rhetoric and manipulation from Peel to Blair*, Oxford: Oxford University Press

McLean, I. (2004), 'On the dimensionality of party ideologies' in Bara, J. and Weale, A. (eds.), *Democratic politics and party competition*, London: Routledge

Nagel, J. (2004), 'Occam no, Archimedes yes', in Bara, J. and Weale, A. (eds.), *Democratic politics and party competition*, London: Routledge

Riker, W. (1982), *Liberalism against populism: A confrontation between the theory of democracy and the theory of social choice*, Prospect Heights, Ill.: W. H. Freeman & Co Ltd

Robertson, D. (2004), 'On the dimensionality of political space and its inhabitants' in Bara, J. and Weale, A. (eds.), *Democratic politics and party competition*, London: Routledge

Ross. A. and Sacker, A. (2010), 'Understanding the dynamics of attitude change', in Park, A., Curtice, J., Thomson, K., Phillips, M., Clery, E. and Butt, S. (eds.), *British Social Attitudes: the 26th report*, London: Sage

Scarbrough, E. (1984), *Political ideology and voting behaviour: An exploratory study*, Oxford: Clarendon Press

Schumann, H. and Presser, S. (1996), *Questions and answers in attitude surveys: Experiments on question form, wording and context*, Thousand Oaks, Calif.: Sage

Soroka, S. and Wlezien, C. (2009), *Degrees of democracy: Politics, public opinion, and policy*, Cambridge: Cambridge University Press

Stimson, J. A. (1991), *Public opinion in America: Moods, cycles and swings*, Boulder, Calif.: Westview Press

Stimson, J.A. (2004), *Tides of Consent: How public opinion shapes American politics*, Cambridge: Cambridge University Press

Webb, P. (2000), *The Modern British Party System*, London: Sage

Wlezien, C. (1995), 'The public as thermostat: Dynamics of for spending', *American Journal of Political Science*, **39**: 981–1000

Zaller, J.R. and Feldman, S. (1992), 'A simple theory of survey response: Answering questions versus revealing', *American Journal of Political Science*, **36**: 579–616

Acknowledgements

This research was supported by the Economic and Social Research Council under award number: 000-22-2053.

Appendix

In addition to *British Social Attitudes* data, the other sources of data included in our attitudes database include:

- The British Election Survey (BES): a survey series carried out after (and often before) British general elections. Linked to the monthly BES Continuous Monitoring Survey, carried out via the internet.

- The British Election Panel Study (BEPS): a study that followed a group of respondents to the 1992 British Election Survey and interviewed them at regular intervals until 1997.

- The British Household Panel Study (BHPS): an ongoing study that follows a sample of households, first interviewed in 1991.

- European Social Survey (ESS): a biennial cross-European survey series which began in 2002.

- Eurobarometer (Eurob): a series of surveys performed on behalf of the European Commission since 1973.

- World Values Survey (WVS): cross-national survey series which began in 1981.

- Plus polling data carried out by the organisations named in Table 9.1.

10 Exploring Labour's legacy

The Labour government that came to power in 1997 was very different from its predecessors. Rebranded as 'New Labour' when Tony Blair became leader in 1994, the party had opted to convey a more moderate image designed to enhance its appeal to more 'aspirant' and middle-class voters. In that vein, it entered office with a commitment not to increase the basic rate of income tax and, for the first two years of its tenure, to stick to the (restrained) public spending plans of the previous Conservative government. At the same time, although it had some ambitious targets for reducing childhood poverty and was committed to introducing a minimum wage, members of the new government seemed reluctant to talk about the need for greater equality, let alone advocate the case for 'redistribution'. If greater equality was to be achieved under New Labour, it was to be secured primarily through getting more people off welfare and into paid work, assisted by a more 'flexible' labour market, rather than through redistributing income via the tax and benefit systems.

But if the new government seemed to have travelled a long way away from its socialist roots so far as its attitude towards economic issues was concerned, it had a distinctively radical edge when it came to its approach to Britain's constitution. Devolution was to be introduced in Scotland and Wales, hereditary peers removed from the House of Lords, and significant new laws on freedom of information and human rights introduced, developments that between them would constitute the biggest set of changes to the British constitution since the early part of the 20th century. And although it may not have been the original motivation for these changes, Labour hoped that, together with introducing greater transparency in the funding of political parties, these measures would also help restore trust in politics and the political system, following the damage caused by the allegations of 'sleaze' during the final years of the previous Conservative administration.

Inevitably, perhaps, not everything turned out as originally intended. In particular, after largely upholding its commitment to keep initially to the spending plans of the previous government, thereafter Labour presided over a considerable expansion in public spending, financed in part by an increase in the rate of a close cousin of income tax, national insurance. But as well as spending more money on public services, Labour also became increasingly concerned about the need to 'reform' those services in order to make them both more efficient and more responsive to the needs and wishes of service users. In part this was to be achieved through the use of quasi-market mechanisms, mechanisms of which the party had as recently as 1997 been suspicious.

How did the public react to 13 years of a rather different kind of Labour rule? Did people become more satisfied with their public services? What happened to their perceptions of, and views, about inequality, redistribution and the operation of the labour market? And did reform of Britain's constitutions help the public feel more positive about the way in which Britain is governed? The chapters in this book provide us with a considerable body of evidence with which to address these questions. Here our conclusion draws on that evidence to summarise the legacy left by Labour when it comes to the country's social and political attitudes.

Tax and public services

Given the scale of the additional resources that were invested in public services, together with the considerable effort Labour invested in trying to 'reform' those services, one might anticipate that the public feel that Britain's core public services are better now than they were a decade or more ago. For the most part Labour seems to have succeeded in this respect – at least in England to which the UK government's writ in respect of services such as health and education has been confined since the advent of devolution.

In Chapter 4, Appleby and Robertson show that, following an unsteady start in the government's early years, satisfaction with the health service overall has increased substantially and consistently since 2001, and is now at a higher level than at any time since the *British Social Attitudes* series started in 1983. True, Labour has had more impact on satisfaction with some parts of the health service than it has with others. In the case of the dental service, for example, the declining levels of satisfaction evident during the 1980s have continued, doubtless because of the persistent shortage of NHS dentists in many parts of the country. In contrast, satisfaction increased most of all in relation to outpatient services, which were the focus of much of the party's efforts to reduce the waiting times that attracted so much criticism in the 1990s. Indeed, Appleby and Robertson suggest that the reduction of waiting times has been one of the key reasons for the increased levels of satisfaction we have seen with the health service overall. This attention to waiting times certainly seems to have been more important than the distinctive policy that was to characterise Labour's approach towards the health service in England in later years, that of providing patients with greater 'choice' in how they access hospital services.

In the field of school education, too, it seems that people feel that things have got better. In Chapter 3, Clery and Low show that there have been noticeable increases during the lifetime of the Labour government in the proportion who think that secondary schools do a good job of teaching the three Rs and bringing out pupils' natural abilities. At the same time, Clery and Low also indicate that the public appear to concur with Labour's decision to place greater emphasis on developing a wider range of practical and life skills, rather than just focusing on traditional academic ones. All in all it would seem that Labour has had some considerable success in persuading people that the two key public services they care most about – health and education – have been improved.

But there is a sting in the tail. Just as public concern about the state of the country's public services has eased, so the focus of the their attention has shifted back to the amount of tax they have to pay to finance those services. In the 1990s *British Social Attitudes* results showed that increasing proportions of the public took the view that more money needed to be spent on public services, and that they were willing to pay more in tax to fund that growth – a finding that New Labour explicitly rejected in its stance on taxation and spending at the time of the 1997 General Election. But once Labour *did* decide to increase spending, support for increased 'tax and spend' started to fall away and it is now lower than at any time since 1983. Doubtless the new government will consider it fortunate that the public mood has moved in that direction as the administration struggles to rein back public expenditure in the wake of the large hole that has developed in the public finances. But it is notable that even now only a small minority wish to explicitly say they actually want spending levels to *fall*; the majority would rather they remained as they are. If the decline in public spending over the next few years has an adverse impact on the perceived quality of public services, we should not be surprised if the public mood swings back once again. This, after all, is what happened during the 1980s. The public mood on tax and spend appears to be an ever moving target that no government of any political persuasion can ultimately hope to satisfy.

Inequality and redistribution

Inequality comes in different guises. One aspect is that those engaged in some occupations are paid far more than those employed in others, while those of working age without a job and reliant on benefits are likely to be the worst off of all. Another is that those from less fortunate backgrounds are less likely than those from more advantaged ones to end up in a middle-class job. Both these aspects of inequality have been addressed in this volume.

As Chapter 2 discusses, there is some dispute about whether levels of social mobility have fallen or not in recent years. In any event, any action to increase social mobility is only likely to bear fruit some years after the government responsible for that action has left office. But Heath *et al.* demonstrate that while Labour have been in office there has been some decline in the proportion who feel they are in a higher status job than the one occupied by their father. The lesson for government may be that fostering the feeling that there has been large-scale upward social mobility is simply an impossible objective for any government to achieve. For as the authors note, as more and more people have come to be employed in middle class occupations, the relative status of some of those occupations may well decline. The son of a carpenter who himself becomes a bank clerk may nowadays be less likely to feel that they have travelled a long way socially than someone who followed that same trajectory 20 or 30 years ago. The more the hopes that working class parents may have for their children are actually realised, the less likely it is that those children will feel they have conquered the inequalities created by their class background.

In contrast to social mobility, income inequality would appear capable of being reduced over a relatively short timescale. And unlike social status, income is not necessarily relative in character. However, Labour proved unable to reverse the sharp increase in income inequality that had occurred during the 1980s (see also the National Equality Panel, 2010). Indeed, in Chapter 2, Heath *et al.* demonstrate that the public recognise the fact that actual income differentials widened over the last decade, even though their perceptions of what income differentials are legitimate have not changed. At the same time, in Chapter 5, Bryson and Forth report that the introduction of the minimum wage has not been accompanied by increased satisfaction with their wages among the lowest paid.

Given these findings we might expect there to have been high, even growing, public concern about income inequality during Labour's time in office. As Rowlingson *et al.* show in Chapter 1, as many as three-quarters now think that differences in income are too large. But this figure is no higher now than it was prior to Labour's arrival in office, so there is no sign here of an increase in concern about unequal incomes. Indeed Bryson and Forth find that, at just under a half, the proportion who feel that too high a gap exists between the highest and the lowest paid at their workplace actually fell during Labour's time in power. At the same time, Rowlingson *et al.* also demonstrate that people are markedly less likely to be concerned about inequality if they think that people are 'in need' as a consequence of their own actions, while others accept inequality because they feel differences in income are necessary for the country's prosperity as a whole.

So it seems there has been surprisingly little outcry about the continuing high levels of income inequality that persisted under Labour. Perhaps this is because Labour's relative reluctance to talk about equality and redistribution left its mark on public opinion. Indeed, as Chapter 6 shows (and further evidence in Chapter 1 confirms) support for redistribution fell markedly between 1994, the year that the New Labour brand was born, and 1999, two years into Labour's term in office. Labour's emphasis on work rather than welfare also appears to have encouraged people to adopt a less sympathetic stance towards welfare benefits, even though feelings of job insecurity are more widespread than in the 1980s. True, more recently these trends have largely stopped, if not indeed reversed a little. But even so, Labour appears to have bequeathed a country that is less concerned to see its government take action to reduce inequality. In fact, according to Bartle *et al.* in Chapter 9, public opinion in Britain is generally further to the 'right' than it was when the party first came to power in the 1990s.

Politics

Of all of Labour's constitutional changes, devolution to Scotland and Wales was perhaps the most radical of all. It was certainly one whose potential consequences had been debated fiercely before Labour came to power. In practice it seems that both sides of the argument may have exaggerated their case. As Chapter 7 shows, on both sides of the Anglo-Scottish border, the advent of devolution seems neither to have helped reinforce support for the maintenance of the Union between England and Scotland nor served to undermine it. A substantial minority – but no more than a minority – of people in Scotland would like to leave the United Kingdom. And most people in England would like Scotland to stay, while accepting that Scotland might want a distinctive degree of self-rule. However, the financial arrangements surrounding devolution, particularly those relating to the perceived financial inequity between England and Scotland, appear to be devolution's unfinished business, something that the public on both sides of the border would like to see addressed.

But what of Labour's wider aspirations for the relationship between politicians and the public? What happened to its ambition to restore trust in politics? Here there must be a sense of disappointment. As Curtice and Park show in Chapter 6, even before the MPs' expenses scandal hit the headlines in 2009, trust in governments and politicians was typically even lower during Labour's time in office than it had been in the 1990s in the wake of the 'sleaze' allegations that dogged the last Conservative government. And, although levels of political efficacy – the extent to which people feel the political system is willing or able to meet their needs – seem unaffected by the expenses scandal, they, too, are lower now than they were in the 1980s and early 1990s. Perhaps not least of the reasons for this development was that introducing greater transparency in the funding of politics resulted in the creation of complex rules of which parties and politicians could easily fall foul, thereby undermining rather than enhancing their reputation for probity (Public Administration Select Committee, 2007). Tighter regulation is, it seems, no guarantee of enhanced trust.

Meanwhile, during Labour's time in office a new gulf has opened up between politicians and the people. Shortly after Labour come to power, turnout in local and European elections hit all-time lows, a development that presaged a precipitate drop in turnout in the 2001 General Election. Although these initial falls in turnout may have largely been caused by short-term political circumstances, they appear to have left a longer-term legacy – a decline in the proportion of people who feel that they have a duty to vote, and thus have the motivation to go to the polling station irrespective of the degree of excitement and interest that might surround any particular election. Consequently, as Labour finally fell from power in 2010 in what was widely thought to be one of the more exciting British elections of the post-war era, only 65 per cent turned out to vote, still below the 70 per cent level that before 1997 had long been regarded as the minimum to which general election turnout could possibly fall. Labour may have rewritten many parts of the constitution, but it has left power with the central institution of British democracy – elections – looking more fragile than ever before.

Conclusions

There is it seems something of a paradox about how the public have reacted to 13 years of New Labour rule. Labour's biggest success seems to have come in the area – public services – for which its initial plans in 1997 had seemed rather unambitious, but where it subsequently invested considerable money and effort. Britain's health service and schools are widely thought to be in a better state now than they were 13 years ago. What, of course, remains in question is whether that legacy will prove to be a lasting one now that public spending is having to be reined in.

In contrast, perhaps one of Labour's biggest failures has been in the area where it had initially promised to be most radical. Labour's rewriting of the constitution may not have given rise to any kind of political crisis, but it has apparently done little to strengthen the bonds of trust and participation between the citizen and the state. Instead, voters distrust politicians even more than they did before, and are less likely to feel an obligation to vote – one way or the other – when election time does come around. It is thus perhaps not surprising that further constitutional reform, including to the electoral process itself, also features on the agenda of the new Conservative/Liberal Democrat coalition government. Whether it will prove any more successful in restoring the links between voters and politicians remains to be seen.

But, perhaps, what might worry Labour above all about its legacy is that Britain now looks rather less like a social democratic country than it did 13 years ago. Inequality was not reduced while Labour was in power – and in some respects appeared to increase. Yet support for measures to reduce inequality, including the use of welfare benefits, is noticeably lower now than it was when Mrs Thatcher was in power. Perhaps if inequality rises further under the new government, the British public will reactively shift back to the 'left' once again. But there must also be a suspicion that in moving Labour towards the centre, New Labour helped move the public in the same direction, too – and that moving people back again towards the goal of the more equal society that many in the Labour Party espouse might prove an elusive goal.

References

National Equality Panel (2010), *An Anatomy of Economic Inequality in the UK: report of the National Equality Panel*, London: Government Equalities Office
Public Administration Select Committee (2007), *Ethics and Standards: The Regulation of Conduct in Public Life: Fourth Report of Session 2006-7*, London: The Stationery Office

Appendix I
Technical details of the survey

In 2009, the sample for the *British Social Attitudes* survey was split into three sections: versions A, B and C, each made up a third of the sample. Depending on the number of versions in which it was included, each 'module' of questions was thus asked either of the full sample (3,421 respondents) or of a random third, or two-thirds of the sample. The structure of the questionnaire can be found at www.natcen.ac.uk/bsaquestionnaires

Sample design

The *British Social Attitudes* survey is designed to yield a representative sample of adults aged 18 or over. Since 1993, the sampling frame for the survey has been the Postcode Address File (PAF), a list of addresses (or postal delivery points) compiled by the Post Office.[1]

For practical reasons, the sample is confined to those living in private households. People living in institutions (though not in private households at such institutions) are excluded, as are households whose addresses were not on the PAF.

The sampling method involved a multi-stage design, with three separate stages of selection.

Selection of sectors

At the first stage, postcode sectors were selected systematically from a list of all postal sectors in Great Britain. Before selection, any sectors with fewer than 500 addresses were identified and grouped together with an adjacent sector; in Scotland all sectors north of the Caledonian Canal were excluded (because of the prohibitive costs of interviewing there). Sectors were then stratified on the basis of:

- 37 sub-regions;
- population density with variable banding used, in order to create three equal-sized strata per sub-region; and
- ranking by percentage of homes that were owner-occupied.

Two hundred and twenty-six postcode sectors were selected, with probability proportional to the number of addresses in each sector.

Selection of addresses

Thirty addresses were selected in each of the 226 sectors or groups of sectors. The issued sample was therefore 226 x 30 = 6,780 addresses, selected by starting from a random point on the list of addresses for each sector, and choosing each address at a fixed interval. The fixed interval was calculated for each sector in order to generate the correct number of addresses.

The Multiple-Occupancy Indicator (MOI) available through PAF was used when selecting addresses in Scotland. The MOI shows the number of accommodation spaces sharing one address. Thus, if the MOI indicates more than one accommodation space at a given address, the chances of the given address being selected from the list of addresses would increase so that it matched the total number of accommodation spaces. The MOI is largely irrelevant in England and Wales, as separate dwelling units (DU) generally appear as separate entries on PAF. In Scotland, tenements with many flats tend to appear as one entry on PAF. However, even in Scotland, the vast majority (98.7%) of MOIs had a value of one. The remainder were incorporated into the weighting procedures (described below).

Selection of individuals

Interviewers called at each address selected from PAF and listed all those eligible for inclusion in the *British Social Attitudes* sample – that is, all persons currently aged 18 or over and resident at the selected address. The interviewer then selected one respondent using a computer-generated random selection procedure. Where there were two or more DUs at the selected address, interviewers first had to select one DU using the same random procedure. They then followed the same procedure to select a person for interview within the selected DU.

Weighting

The weights for the *British Social Attitudes* survey correct for the unequal selection of addresses, DUs and individuals and for biases caused by differential non-response. The different stages of the weighting scheme are outlined in detail below.

Selection weights

Selection weights are required because not all the units covered in the survey had the same probability of selection. The weighting reflects the relative selection probabilities of the individual at the three main stages of selection: address, DU and individual. First, because addresses in Scotland were selected using the MOI, weights were needed to compensate for the greater probability of an address with an MOI of more than one being selected, compared to an address with an MOI of one. (This stage was omitted for the English and Welsh data.) Secondly, data were weighted to compensate for the fact that a DU at an address that contained a large number of DUs was less likely to be selected for inclusion in the survey than a DU at an address that contained fewer DUs. (We use this procedure because in most cases where the MOI is greater than one, the two stages will cancel each other out, resulting in more efficient weights.) Thirdly, data were weighted to compensate for the lower selection probabilities of adults living in large households, compared with those in small households.

At each stage the selection weights were trimmed to avoid a small number of very high or very low weights in the sample; such weights would inflate standard errors, reducing the precision of the survey estimates and causing the weighted sample to be less efficient. Less than one per cent of the sample was trimmed at each stage.

Non-response model

It is known that certain subgroups in the population are more likely to respond to surveys than others. These groups can end up over-represented in the sample, which can bias the survey estimates. Where information is available about non-responding households, the response behaviour of the sample members can be modelled and the results used to generate a non-response weight. This non-response weight is intended to reduce bias in the sample resulting from differential response to the survey.

The data were modelled using logistic regression, with the dependent variable indicating whether or not the selected individual responded to the survey. Ineligible households[2] were not included in the non-response modelling. A number of area-level and interviewer observation variables were used to model response. Not all the variables examined were retained for the final model: variables not strongly related to a household's propensity to respond were dropped from the analysis.

The variables found to be related to response were; Government Office Region (GOR), dwelling type, population density of the postcode sector, relative condition of the address and whether there were entry barriers to the selected address. The model shows that response increases if there are no barriers to entry (for instance, if there are no locked gates around the address and no entry phone) and if the general condition of the address is good. Response is also higher for addresses in the North East, North West, and East Midlands, but lower for semi-detached and terraced houses. The full model is given in Table A.1.

Table A.1 The final non-response model

Variable	B	S.E.	Wald	df	Sig.	Odds
Govt Office Region			54.07	10	0.00	
North East	0.41	0.12	12.44	1	0.00	1.51
North West	0.29	0.09	9.58	1	0.00	1.33
Yorks. and Humber	-0.13	0.10	1.73	1	0.19	0.88
East Midlands	0.35	0.10	11.51	1	0.00	1.43
West Midlands	0.14	0.10	2.06	1	0.15	1.15
East of England	0.03	0.09	0.08	1	0.77	1.03
London	0.19	0.10	3.47	1	0.06	1.21
South East	-0.03	0.09	0.16	1	0.69	0.97
South West	0.19	0.10	3.83	1	0.05	1.21
Wales	0.18	0.12	2.55	1	0.11	1.20
Scotland	(baseline)					
Barriers to address			28.98	1	0.00	
No barriers	0.47	0.09	28.98	1	0.00	1.60
One or more	(baseline)					
Relative condition of the address			49.28	2	0.00	
Better	0.80	0.11	48.51	1	0.00	2.22
About the same	0.38	0.09	18.77	1	0.00	1.46
Worse	(baseline)					
Dwelling type			18.17	5	0.00	
Semi-detached house	-0.13	0.06	5.38	1	0.02	0.88
Terraced house	-0.22	0.06	14.79	1	0.00	0.80
Flat – purpose built	-0.02	0.09	0.05	1	0.82	0.98
Flat – conversion	-0.09	0.14	0.39	1	0.53	0.92
Other	-0.35	0.21	2.67	1	0.10	0.70
Detached house	(baseline)					
Population density of the postcode sector	-0.003	0.001	13.35	1	0.00	0.997
Constant	-0.31	0.15	4.39	1	0.04	0.73

Notes:
The response is 1 = individual responding to the survey, 0 = non-response
Only variables that are significant at the 0.05 level are included in the model
The model R^2 is 0.02 (Cox and Snell)
B is the estimate coefficient with standard error **S.E.**
The **Wald**-test measures the impact of the categorical variable on the model with the appropriate number of degrees of freedom **df**. If the test is significant (**sig.** < 0.05), then the categorical variable is considered to be 'significantly associated' with the response variable and therefore included in the model

The non-response weight is calculated as the inverse of the predicted response probabilities saved from the logistic regression model. The non-response weight was then combined with the selection weights to create the final non-response weight. The top one per cent of the weight were trimmed before the weight was scaled to the achieved sample size (resulting in the weight being standardised around an average of one).

Calibration weighting

The final stage of weighting was to adjust the final non-response weight so that the weighted sample matched the population in terms of age, sex and region.

Table A.2 Weighted and unweighted sample distribution, by GOR, age and sex

	Population	Unweighted respondents	Respondents weighted by selection weight only	Respondents weighted by un-calibrated non-response weight	Respondents weighted by final weight
Govt Office Region	%	%	%	%	%
North East	4.4	5.6	4.1	5.0	4.4
North West	11.5	12.1	6.3	11.0	11.5
Yorks. and Humber	8.7	8.2	8.3	8.9	8.7
East Midlands	7.5	7.8	9.2	7.2	7.5
West Midlands	9.0	9.4	4.6	9.4	9.0
East of England	9.6	10.2	4.0	10.5	9.6
London	12.7	10.3	9.2	11.4	12.7
South East	14.0	12.7	4.9	13.9	14.0
South West	8.9	9.0	8.7	8.5	8.9
Wales	5.0	5.5	11.0	4.9	5.0
Scotland	8.8	9.2	10.5	9.3	8.8
Age & sex	%	%	%	%	%
M 18–24	6.2	2.8	4.1	4.1	6.2
M 25–34	8.2	5.9	6.3	6.5	8.2
M 35–44	9.4	8.4	8.3	8.5	9.4
M 45–54	8.3	8.6	9.2	9.2	8.3
M 55–59	3.7	4.4	4.6	4.6	3.7
M 60–64	3.7	3.8	4.0	3.8	3.7
M 65+	9.0	9.6	9.2	9.0	9.0
F 18–24	5.9	4.0	4.9	5.0	5.9
F 25–34	8.1	9.2	8.7	8.9	8.1
F 35–44	9.6	11.5	11.0	11.0	9.6
F 45–54	8.6	9.5	10.5	10.4	8.6
F 55–59	3.8	4.0	4.2	4.2	3.8
F 60–64	3.9	4.8	4.5	4.5	3.9
F 65+	11.7	13.6	10.5	10.4	11.7
Base	*46,920,219*	*3421*	*3421*	*3421*	*3421*

Only adults aged 18 and over are eligible to take part in the survey; therefore the data have been weighted to the British population aged 18+ based on the 2008 mid-year population estimates from the Office for National Statistics/General Register Office for Scotland.

The survey data were weighted to the marginal age/sex and GOR distributions using raking-ratio (or rim) weighting. As a result, the weighted data should exactly match the population across these three dimensions. This is shown in Table A.2.

The calibration weight is the final non-response weight to be used in the analysis of the 2009 survey; this weight has been scaled to the responding sample size. The range of the weights is given in Table A.3.

Table A.3 Range of weights

	N	Minimum	Mean	Maximum
DU and person selection weight	3421	0.55	1.00	2.22
Un-calibrated non-response weight	3421	0.42	1.00	2.38
Final calibrated non-response weight	3421	0.33	1.00	3.78

Effective sample size

The effect of the sample design on the precision of survey estimates is indicated by the effective sample size (neff). The effective sample size measures the size of an (unweighted) simple random sample that would achieve the same precision (standard error) as the design being implemented. If the effective sample size is close to the actual sample size, then we have an efficient design with a good level of precision. The lower the effective sample size is, the lower the level of precision. The efficiency of a sample is given by the ratio of the effective sample size to the actual sample size. Samples that select one person per household tend to have lower efficiency than samples that select all household members. The final calibrated non-response weights have an effective sample size (neff) of 2,766 and efficiency of 81 per cent.

All the percentages presented in this report are based on weighted data.

Questionnaire versions

Each address in each sector (sampling point) was allocated to either the A, B or C portion of the sample. If one serial number was version A, the next was version B and the third version C. Thus, each interviewer was allocated ten cases from each of versions A, B and C. There were 2,260 issued addresses for each version.

Fieldwork

Interviewing was mainly carried out between June and September 2009, with a small number of interviews taking place in October and November.

Fieldwork was conducted by interviewers drawn from the *National Centre for Social Research*'s regular panel and conducted using face-to-face computer-assisted interviewing.[3] Interviewers attended a one-day briefing conference to familiarise them with the selection procedures and questionnaires.

The mean interview length was 75 minutes for version A of the questionnaire, 70 minutes for version B and 66 minutes for version C.[4] Interviewers achieved an overall response rate of between 54.8 and 55.9 per cent. Details are shown in Table A.4.

Table A.4 Response rate[1] on *British Social Attitudes*, 2009

	Number	Lower limit of response (%)	Upper limit of response (%)
Addresses issued	6780		
Out of scope	591		
Upper limit of eligible cases	6189	100.0	
Uncertain eligibility	76	1.2	
Lower limit of eligible cases	6113		100.0
Interview achieved	3421	55.3	56.0
With self-completion	2942	47.5	48.1
Interview not achieved	2692	43.5	44.0
Refused[2]	2109	34.1	34.5
Non-contacted[3]	266	4.3	4.4
Other non-response	317	5.1	5.2

1 Response is calculated as a range from a lower limit where all unknown eligibility cases (for example, address inaccessible, or unknown whether address is residential) are assumed to be eligible and therefore included in the unproductive outcomes, to an upper limit where all these cases are assumed to be ineligible (and are therefore excluded from the response calculation)

2 'Refused' comprises refusals before selection of an individual at the address, refusals to the office, refusal by the selected person, 'proxy' refusals (on behalf of the selected respondent) and broken appointments after which the selected person could not be recontacted

3 'Non-contacted' comprises households where no one was contacted and those where the selected person could not be contacted

As in earlier rounds of the series, the respondent was asked to fill in a self-completion questionnaire which, whenever possible, was collected by the interviewer. Otherwise, the respondent was asked to post it to the *National Centre for Social Research*. If necessary, up to three postal reminders were sent to obtain the self-completion supplement.

A total of 479 respondents (14 per cent of those interviewed) did not return their self-completion questionnaire. Versions A and B of the self-completion questionnaire were returned by 85 per cent of respondents to the face-to-face interview and version C by 89 per cent. As in previous rounds, we judged that it was not necessary to apply additional weights to correct for non-response to the self-completion questionnaire.

Advance letter

Interviewers were supplied with letters describing the purpose of the survey and the coverage of the questionnaire, which they posted to sampled addresses before making any calls.[5]

Analysis variables

A number of standard analyses have been used in the tables that appear in this report. The analysis groups requiring further definition are set out below. For further details see Stafford and Thomson (2006). Where there are references to specific question numbers, the full question text, including frequencies, can be found at www.natcen.ac.uk/bsaquestionnaires

Region

The dataset is classified by the 12 Government Office Regions.

Standard Occupational Classification

Respondents are classified according to their own occupation, not that of the 'head of household'. Each respondent was asked about their current or last job, so that all respondents except those who had never worked were coded. Additionally, all job details were collected for all spouses and partners in work.

With the 2001 survey, we began coding occupation to the new Standard Occupational Classification 2000 (SOC 2000) instead of the Standard Occupational Classification 1990 (SOC 90). The main socio-economic grouping based on SOC 2000 is the National Statistics Socio-Economic Classification (NS-SEC). However, to maintain time-series, some analysis has continued to use the older schemes based on SOC 90 – Registrar General's Social Class and Socio-Economic Group, though these are now derived from SOC 2000. The deriviation of the Goldthorpe schema had become unreliable and so has been discontinued on British Social Attitudes from 2009.

National Statistics Socio-Economic Classification (NS-SEC)

The combination of SOC 2000 and employment status for current or last job generates the following NS-SEC analytic classes:

- Employers in large organisations, higher managerial and professional
- Lower professional and managerial; higher technical and supervisory
- Intermediate occupations
- Small employers and own account workers
- Lower supervisory and technical occupations
- Semi-routine occupations
- Routine occupations

The remaining respondents are grouped as "never had a job" or "not classifiable". For some analyses, it may be more appropriate to classify respondents according to their current socio-economic status, which takes into account only their present economic position. In this case, in addition to the seven classes listed above, the remaining respondents not currently in paid work fall into one of the following categories: "not classifiable", "retired", "looking after the home", "unemployed" or "others not in paid occupations".

Registrar General's Social Class

As with NS-SEC, each respondent's social class is based on his or her current or last occupation. The combination of SOC 90 with employment status for current or last job generates the following six social classes:

I	Professional etc. occupations	
II	Managerial and technical occupations	'Non-manual'
III (Non-manual)	Skilled occupations	
III (Manual)	Skilled occupations	
IV	Partly skilled occupations	'Manual'
V	Unskilled occupations	

They are usually collapsed into four groups: I & II, III Non-manual, III Manual, and IV & V.

Socio-Economic Group

As with NS-SEC, each respondent's Socio-Economic Group (SEG) is based on his or her current or last occupation. SEG aims to bring together people with jobs of similar social and economic status, and is derived from a combination of employment status and occupation. The full SEG classification identifies 18 categories, but these are usually condensed into six groups:

- Professionals, employers and managers
- Intermediate non-manual workers
- Junior non-manual workers
- Skilled manual workers
- Semi-skilled manual workers
- Unskilled manual workers

As with NS-SEC, the remaining respondents are grouped as "never had a job" or "not classifiable".

Industry

All respondents whose occupation could be coded were allocated a Standard Industrial Classification 2007 (SIC 07). Two-digit class codes are used. As with social class, SIC may be generated on the basis of the respondent's current occupation only, or on his or her most recently classifiable occupation.

Party identification

Respondents can be classified as identifying with a particular political party on one of three counts: if they consider themselves supporters of that party, as closer to it than to others, or as more likely to support it in the event of a general election. The three groups are generally described respectively as *partisans*, *sympathisers* and *residual identifiers*. In combination, the three groups are referred to as 'identifiers'. Responses are derived from the following questions:

> *Generally speaking, do you think of yourself as a supporter of any one political party? [Yes/No]*

> *[If "No"/"Don't know"]*

Do you think of yourself as a little closer to one political party than to the others? [Yes/No]

[If "Yes" at either question or "No"/"Don't know" at 2nd question]
[Which one?/If there were a general election tomorrow, which political party do you think you would be most likely to support?]

[Conservative; Labour; Liberal Democrat; Scottish National Party; Plaid Cymru; Green Party; UK Independence Party (UKIP)/Veritas; British National Party (BNP)/National Front; RESPECT/Scottish Socialist Party (SSP)/Socialist Party; Other party; Other answer; None; Refused to say]

Income

Two variables classify the respondent's earnings (REarn) and household income (HHInc) on the questionnaire (see www.natcen.ac.uk/bsaquestionnaires). Two new derived variables were added to the *British Social Attitudes* 2008 dataset giving quartiles of these variables. They are [REarnQ] and [HHIncQ] and are calculated based on quartiles of all valid responses to the questions.

Attitude scales

Since 1986, the *British Social Attitudes* surveys have included two attitude scales which aim to measure where respondents stand on certain underlying value dimensions – left–right and libertarian–authoritarian.[6] Since 1987 (except 1990), a similar scale on 'welfarism' has been asked. Some of the items in the welfarism scale were changed in 2000–2001. The current version of the scale is listed below.

A useful way of summarising the information from a number of questions of this sort is to construct an additive index (Spector, 1992; DeVellis, 2003). This approach rests on the assumption that there is an underlying – 'latent' – attitudinal dimension which characterises the answers to all the questions within each scale. If so, scores on the index are likely to be a more reliable indication of the underlying attitude than the answers to any one question.

Each of these scales consists of a number of statements to which the respondent is invited to "agree strongly", "agree", "neither agree nor disagree", "disagree" or "disagree strongly".

The items are:

Left–right scale

Government should redistribute income from the better off to those who are less well off. *[Redistrb]*

Big business benefits owners at the expense of workers. *[BigBusnN]*

Ordinary working people do not get their fair share of the nation's wealth. *[Wealth]*[7]

There is one law for the rich and one for the poor. *[RichLaw]*

Management will always try to get the better of employees if it gets the chance. *[Indust4]*

Libertarian–authoritarian scale

Young people today don't have enough respect for traditional British values. *[TradVals]*

People who break the law should be given stiffer sentences. *[StifSent]*

For some crimes, the death penalty is the most appropriate sentence. *[DeathApp]*

Schools should teach children to obey authority. *[Obey]*

The law should always be obeyed, even if a particular law is wrong. *[WrongLaw]*

Censorship of films and magazines is necessary to uphold moral standards. *[Censor]*

Welfarism scale

The welfare state encourages people to stop helping each other. *[WelfHelp]*

The government should spend more money on welfare benefits for the poor, even if it leads to higher taxes. *[MoreWelf]*

Around here, most unemployed people could find a job if they really wanted one. *[UnempJob]*

Many people who get social security don't really deserve any help. *[SocHelp]*

Most people on the dole are fiddling in one way or another. *[DoleFidl]*

If welfare benefits weren't so generous, people would learn to stand on their own two feet. *[WelfFeet]*

Cutting welfare benefits would damage too many people's lives. *[DamLives]*

The creation of the welfare state is one of Britain's proudest achievements. *[ProudWlf]*

The indices for the three scales are formed by scoring the leftmost, most libertarian or most pro-welfare position, as 1 and the rightmost, most authoritarian or most anti-welfarist position, as 5. The "neither agree nor disagree" option is scored as 3. The scores to all the questions in each scale are added and then divided by the number of items in the scale, giving indices ranging from 1 (leftmost, most libertarian, most pro-welfare) to 5 (rightmost, most authoritarian, most anti-welfare). The scores on the three indices have been placed on the dataset.[8]

The scales have been tested for reliability (as measured by Cronbach's alpha). The Cronbach's alpha (unstandardised items) for the scales in 2009 are 0.81 for the left–right scale, 0.82 for the welfarism scale and 0.75 for the libertarian–authoritarian scale. This level of reliability can be considered "good" for the left–right and welfarism scales and "respectable" for the libertarian–authoritarian scale (DeVellis, 2003: 95–96).

Other analysis variables

These are taken directly from the questionnaire and to that extent are self-explanatory (see www.natcen.ac.uk/bsaquestionnaires). The principal ones are:

Sex (Q. 356)
Age (Q. 357)
Household income (Q. 1374)
Economic position (Q. 1014)
Religion (Q. 1139)
Highest educational qualification obtained (Qs. 1261–1262)
Marital status (Qs. 451–457)
Benefits received (Qs. 1329–1367)

Sampling errors

No sample precisely reflects the characteristics of the population it represents, because of both sampling and non-sampling errors. If a sample were designed as a random sample (if every adult had an equal and independent chance of inclusion in the sample), then we could calculate the sampling error of any percentage, *p*, using the formula:

$$s.e. \; (p) = \sqrt{\frac{p(100 - p)}{n}}$$

where n is the number of respondents on which the percentage is based. Once the sampling error had been calculated, it would be a straightforward exercise to calculate a confidence interval for the true population percentage. For example, a 95 per cent confidence interval would be given by the formula:

$$p \pm 1.96 \text{ x s.e. } (p)$$

Clearly, for a simple random sample (srs), the sampling error depends only on the values of p and n. However, simple random sampling is almost never used in practice, because of its inefficiency in terms of time and cost.

As noted above, the *British Social Attitudes* sample, like that drawn for most large-scale surveys, was clustered according to a stratified multi-stage design into 226 postcode sectors (or combinations of sectors). With a complex design like this, the sampling error of a percentage giving a particular response is not simply a function of the number of respondents in the sample and the size of the percentage; it also depends on how that percentage response is spread within and between sample points.

The complex design may be assessed relative to simple random sampling by calculating a range of design factors (DEFTs) associated with it, where:

$$\text{DEFT} = \sqrt{\frac{\text{Variance of estimator with complex design, sample size n}}{\text{Variance of estimator with srs design, sample size n}}}$$

and represents the multiplying factor to be applied to the simple random sampling error to produce its complex equivalent. A design factor of one means that the complex sample has achieved the same precision as a simple random sample of the same size. A design factor greater than one means the complex sample is less precise than its simple random sample equivalent. If the DEFT for a particular characteristic is known, a 95 per cent confidence interval for a percentage may be calculated using the formula:

$$p \pm 1.96 \text{ x complex sampling error } (p)$$

$$= p \pm 1.96 \text{ x DEFT x } \sqrt{\frac{p(100 - p)}{n}}$$

Calculations of sampling errors and design effects were made using the statistical analysis package STATA.

Table A.5 gives examples of the confidence intervals and DEFTs calculated for a range of different questions. Most background variables were fielded on the whole sample, whereas many attitudinal variables were asked only of a half or quarter of the sample; some were asked on the interview questionnaire and some on the self-completion supplement.

Table A.5 Complex standard errors and confidence intervals of selected variables

	% (p)	Complex standard error of p	95% confidence interval	DEFT	Base
Classification variables					
Q. 563 Party identification (full sample)					
Conservative	28.0	1.0	26.1–30.0	1.29	*3421*
Labour	26.1	1.0	24.0–28.2	1.39	*3421*
Liberal Democrat	9.7	0.6	8.5–11.0	1.29	*3421*
Q. 1124 Housing tenure (full sample)					
Owns	70.0.	1.2	67.6–72.3	1.50	*3421*
Rents from local authority	9.8	0.9	8.1–11.9	1.84	*3421*
Rents privately/HA	18.6	1.0	16.7–20.7	1.49	*3421*
Q. 1132 Religion (full sample)					
No religion	50.7	1.0	48.7–52.8	1.22	*3421*
Church of England	20.0	0.8	18.4–21.6	1.17	*3421*
Roman Catholic	8.6	0.5	7.6–9.7	1.15	*3421*
Q.1193 Age of completing continuous full-time education (full sample)					
16 or under	52.0	1.1	49.8–54.1	1.28	*3421*
17 or 18	22.2	0.8	20.5–23.9	1.18	*3421*
19 or over	22.0	1.1	20.0–24.2	1.50	*3421*
Q. 551 Home internet access (full sample)					
Yes	78.0	0.8	76.3–79.5	1.15	*3421*
No	22.0	0.8	20.5–23.7	1.15	*3421*
Q. 1128 Urban or rural residence (full sample)					
A big city	9.5	1.1	7.6–11.9	2.10	*3421*
The suburbs or outskirts of a big city	23.4	2.0	19.8–27.5	2.70	*3421*
A small city/town	49.3	2.5	44.5–54.2	2.88	*3421*
Country village	14.6	1.8	11.4–18.5	2.94	*3421*
Farm/home in the country	2.4	0.4	1.7–3.4	1.57	*3421*
Attitudinal variables (face-to-face interview)					
Q. 572 Benefits for the unemployed are … (1/3 sample)					
… too low	29.4	1.6	26.4–32.5	1.16	*1139*
… too high	50.8	1.7	47.4–54.2	1.17	*1139*
Q. 873 Do you put yourself first or think about others? (2/3 sample)					
Put self first and leave others to do the same	3.5	0.4	2.8–4.4	1.07	*2267*
Put self first but also consider other people's needs	31.9	1.2	29.6–34.4	1.22	*2267*
Consider everyone's needs equally, including your own	53.0	1.3	50.5–55.5	1.17	*2267*
Put other people's needs and interests above your own	11.2	0.7	10.0–12.6	1.00	*2267*

Table continued on next page

	% (p)	Complex standard error of p	95% confidence interval	DEFT	Base
Q. 848 How serious a problem is traffic congestion in towns, cities (full sample)					
A very serious problem	13.6	0.8	12.2–15.2	1.30	*3421*
A serious problem	36.4	1.0	34.4–38.4	1.23	*3421*
Not a very serious problem	36.3	1.0	34.4–38.2	1.19	*3421*
Not a problem at all	13.5	0.9	11.8–15.4	1.57	*3421*
Q. 929 Do you think Britain spends too much money, too little money, or about the right amount on improving the living conditions of immigrants from non-western countries? (1/3 sample)					
Too little	10.7	1.4	8.3–13.7	1.48	*1128*
About right	32.1	1.5	29.2–35.2	1.09	*1128*
Too much	50.4	1.8	46.9–54.0	1.20	*1128*

Attitudinal variables (self-completion)

	% (p)	Complex standard error of p	95% confidence interval	DEFT	Base
A65a B43a Government should redistribute income from the better off to those who C35a are less well off (full sample)					
Agree strongly	7.5	0.4	6.6–8.4	0.91	*2942*
Agree	29.0	1.0	27.1–31.0	1.18	*2942*
Neither agree nor disagree	26.9	1.0	25.0–28.8	1.18	*2942*
Disagree	28.9	1.0	27.0–30.9	1.16	*2942*
Disagree strongly	5.5	0.6	4.5–6.7	1.34	*2942*
B30a Do you personally tend to think of disabled people as getting in the way? C18a (2/3 sample)					
Most of the time	0.5	0.1	0.3–0.9	0.85	*1984*
Some of the time	6.3	0.7	5.0–7.9	1.30	*1984*
Hardly ever	23.7	1.0	21.7–25.7	1.07	*1984*
Never	64.6	1.1	62.4–66.7	1.00	*1984*
A49 Generally speaking, would you say that people can be trusted or that you can't be too careful in dealing with people? (1/3 sample)					
Most people can be trusted	36.9	1.8	33.4–40.5	1.14	*958*
Can't be too careful	55.5	2.0	51.5–59.4	1.24	*958*

The table shows that most of the questions asked of all sample members have a confidence interval of around plus or minus two to three per cent of the survey percentage. This means that we can be 95 per cent certain that the true population percentage is within two to three per cent (in either direction) of the percentage we report.

Variables with much larger variation are, as might be expected, those closely related to the geographic location of the respondent (for example, whether they live in a big city, a small town or a village). Here, the variation may be as large as six or seven per cent either way around the percentage found on the survey. Consequently, the design effects calculated for these variables in a clustered sample will be greater than the design effects calculated for variables less strongly associated with area. Also, sampling errors for percentages based only on respondents to just one of the versions of the questionnaire, or on subgroups within the sample, are larger than they would have been had the questions been asked of everyone.

Analysis techniques

Regression

Regression analysis aims to summarise the relationship between a 'dependent' variable and one or more 'independent' variables. It shows how well we can estimate a respondent's score on the dependent variable from knowledge of their scores on the independent variables. It is often undertaken to support a claim that the phenomena measured by the independent variables *cause* the phenomenon measured by the dependent variable. However, the causal ordering, if any, between the variables cannot be verified or falsified by the technique. Causality can only be inferred through special experimental designs or through assumptions made by the analyst.

All regression analysis assumes that the relationship between the dependent and each of the independent variables takes a particular form. In *linear regression*, it is assumed that the relationship can be adequately summarised by a straight line. This means that a one percentage point increase in the value of an independent variable is assumed to have the same impact on the value of the dependent variable on average, irrespective of the previous values of those variables.

Strictly speaking the technique assumes that both the dependent and the independent variables are measured on an interval-level scale, although it may sometimes still be applied even where this is not the case. For example, one can use an ordinal variable (e.g. a Likert scale) as a *dependent* variable if one is willing to assume that there is an underlying interval-level scale and the difference between the observed ordinal scale and the underlying interval scale is due to random measurement error. Often the answers to a number of Likert-type questions are averaged to give a dependent variable that is more like a continuous variable. Categorical or nominal data can be used as *independent* variables by converting them into dummy or binary variables; these are variables where the only valid scores are 0 and 1, with 1 signifying membership of a particular category and 0 otherwise.

The assumptions of linear regression cause particular difficulties where the *dependent* variable is binary. The assumption that the relationship between the dependent and the independent variables is a straight line means that it can produce estimated values for the dependent variable of less than 0 or greater than 1. In this case it may be more appropriate to assume that the relationship between the dependent and the independent variables takes the form of an S-curve, where the impact on the dependent variable of a one-point increase in an independent variable becomes progressively less the closer the value of the dependent variable approaches 0 or 1. *Logistic regression* is an alternative form of regression which fits such an S-curve rather than a straight line. The technique can also be adapted to analyse multinomial non-interval-level dependent variables, that is, variables which classify respondents into more than two categories.

The two statistical scores most commonly reported from the results of regression analyses are:

A measure of variance explained: This summarises how well all the independent variables combined can account for the variation in respondents' scores in the dependent variable. The higher the measure, the more accurately we are able in general to estimate the correct value of each respondent's score on the dependent variable from knowledge of their scores on the independent variables.

A parameter estimate: This shows how much the dependent variable will change on average, given a one-unit change in the independent variable (while holding all other independent variables in the model constant). The parameter estimate has a positive sign if an increase in the value of the independent variable results in an increase in the value of the dependent variable. It has a negative sign if an increase in the value of the independent variable results in a decrease in the value of the dependent variable. If the parameter estimates are standardised, it is possible to compare the relative impact of different independent variables; those variables with the largest standardised estimates can be said to have the biggest impact on the value of the dependent variable.

Regression also tests for the statistical significance of parameter estimates. A parameter estimate is said to be significant at the five per cent level if the range of the values encompassed by its 95 per cent confidence interval (see also section on sampling errors) are either all positive or all negative. This means that there is less than a five per cent chance that the association we have found between the dependent variable and the independent variable is simply the result of sampling error and does not reflect a relationship that actually exists in the general population.

Factor analysis

Factor analysis is a statistical technique which aims to identify whether there are one or more apparent sources of commonality to the answers given by respondents to a set of questions. It ascertains the smallest number of *factors* (or dimensions) which can most economically summarise all of the variation found in the set of questions being analysed. Factors are established where respondents who give a particular answer to one question in the set, tend to give the same answer as each other to one or more of the other questions in the set. The technique is most useful when a relatively small number of factors are able to account for a relatively large proportion of the variance in all of the questions in the set.

The technique produces a *factor loading* for each question (or variable) on each factor. Where questions have a high loading on the same factor, then it will be the case that respondents who give a particular answer to one of these questions tend to give a similar answer to the other questions. The technique is most commonly used in attitudinal research to try to identify the underlying ideological dimensions which apparently structure attitudes towards the subject in question.

International Social Survey Programme

The *International Social Survey Programme* (ISSP) is run by a group of research organisations, each of which undertakes to field annually an agreed module of questions on a chosen topic area. Since 1985, an *International Social Survey Programme* module has been included in one of the *British Social Attitudes* self-completion questionnaires. Each module is chosen for repetition at intervals to allow comparisons both between countries (membership is currently standing at over 40) and over time. In 2009, the chosen subject was Inequality, and the module was carried on the A version of the self-completion questionnaire (Qs. 1.1–1.24).[9]

Notes

1. Until 1991 all *British Social Attitudes* samples were drawn from the Electoral Register (ER). However, following concern that this sampling frame might be deficient in its coverage of certain population subgroups, a 'splicing' experiment was conducted in 1991. We are grateful to the Market Research Development Fund for contributing towards the costs of this experiment. Its purpose was to investigate whether a switch to PAF would disrupt the time-series – for instance, by lowering response rates or affecting the distribution of responses to particular questions. In the event, it was concluded that the change from ER to PAF was unlikely to affect time trends in any noticeable ways, and that no adjustment factors were necessary. Since significant differences in efficiency exist between PAF and ER, and because we considered it untenable to continue to use a frame that is known to be biased, we decided to adopt PAF as the sampling frame for future *British Social Attitudes* surveys. For details of the PAF/ER 'splicing' experiment, see Lynn and Taylor (1995).
2. This includes households not containing any adults aged 18 and over, vacant dwelling units, derelict dwelling units, non-resident addresses and other deadwood.
3. In 1993 it was decided to mount a split-sample experiment designed to test the applicability of Computer-Assisted Personal Interviewing (CAPI) to the *British Social Attitudes* survey series. CAPI has been used increasingly over the past decade as an alternative to traditional interviewing techniques. As the name implies, CAPI involves the use of lap-top computers during the interview, with interviewers entering responses directly into the computer. One of the advantages of CAPI is that it significantly reduces both the amount of time spent on data processing and the number of coding and editing errors. There was, however, concern that a different interviewing technique might alter the distribution of responses and so affect the year-on-year consistency of *British Social Attitudes* data.

Following the experiment, it was decided to change over to CAPI completely in 1994 (the self-completion questionnaire still being administered in the conventional way). The results of the experiment are discussed in *The 11ᵗʰ Report* (Lynn and Purdon, 1994).

4. Interview times recorded as less than 20 minutes were excluded, as these timings were likely to be errors.

5. An experiment was conducted on the 1991 *British Social Attitudes* survey (Jowell *et al.*, 1992) which showed that sending advance letters to sampled addresses before fieldwork begins has very little impact on response rates. However, interviewers do find that an advance letter helps them to introduce the survey on the doorstep, and a majority of respondents have said that they preferred some advance notice. For these reasons, advance letters have been used on the *British Social Attitudes* surveys since 1991.

6. Because of methodological experiments on scale development, the exact items detailed in this section have not been asked on all versions of the questionnaire each year.

7. In 1994 only, this item was replaced by: Ordinary people get their fair share of the nation's wealth. *[Wealth1]*

8. In constructing the scale, a decision had to be taken on how to treat missing values ("Don't knows", "Refused" and "Not answered"). Respondents who had more than two missing values on the left–right scale and more than three missing values on the libertarian–authoritarian and welfarism scales were excluded from that scale. For respondents with just a few missing values, 'Don't knows' were recoded to the midpoint of the scale and "Refused" or "Not answered" were recoded to the scale mean for that respondent on their valid items.

9. See www.natcen.ac.uk/bsaquestionnaires

References

DeVellis, R.F. (2003), *Scale Development: Theory and Applications*, 2ⁿᵈ edition, Applied Social Research Methods Series, 26, Thousand Oaks, Calif.: Sage

Jowell, R., Brook, L., Prior, G. and Taylor, B. (1992), *British Social Attitudes: the 9ᵗʰ Report*, Aldershot: Dartmouth

Lynn, P. and Purdon, S. (1994), 'Time-series and lap-tops: the change to computer-assisted interviewing', in Jowell, R., Curtice, J., Brook, L. and Ahrendt, D. (eds.), *British Social Attitudes: the 11ᵗʰ Report*, Aldershot: Dartmouth

Lynn, P. and Taylor, B. (1995), 'On the bias and variance of samples of individuals: a comparison of the Electoral Registers and Postcode Address File as sampling frames', *The Statistician*, **44**: 173–194

Spector, P.E. (1992), *Summated Rating Scale Construction: An Introduction*, Quantitative Applications in the Social Sciences, 82, Newbury Park, Calif.: Sage

Stafford, R. and Thomson, K. (2006), *British Social Attitudes and Young People's Social Attitudes surveys 2003:*, Technical Report, London: National Centre for Social Research

Subject index